GOVERNANCE IN THE
EUROPEAN UNION

D0293969

GOVERNANCE IN THE EUROPEAN UNION

Gary Marks, Fritz W. Scharpf,
Philippe C. Schmitter and Wolfgang Streeck

SAGE Publications
London • Thousand Oaks • New Delhi

First published 1996

 SAGE Publications Ltd
6 Bonhill Street
London EC2A 4PU

SAGE Publications Inc
2455 Teller Road
Thousand Oaks, California 91320

SAGE Publications India Pvt Ltd
32, M-Block Market
Greater Kailash – I
New Delhi 110 048

British Library Cataloguing in Publication data

A catalogue record for this book is
available from the British Library

ISBN 0 7619 5134 2
ISBN 0 7619 5135 0 (pbk)

Library of Congress catalog record available

Typeset by Mayhew Typesetting, Rhayader, Powys
Printed in Great Britain by The Cromwell Press Ltd,
Broughton Gifford, Melksham, Wiltshire

Contents

Preface

This book is part of a broad stream of theorizing about the dynamics and consequences of institutional creation in the European Union. The topic, taken in the round, is a massive one for it touches on virtually every aspect of politics in the member states, and it would have been self-defeating for us to try to cover but a fraction of it. What we have sought to do, however, is to illuminate certain critical dynamics of European integration. Fritz Scharpf analyses the asymmetry between deregulation based in supranational EU law and re-regulation which must work its way through the EU's political process; Doug McAdam, Gary Marks and his collaborators examine the responses of domestic political actors to supranational political opportunities; Wolfgang Streeck analyses the stresses between national social policy regimes and European-wide markets and competition; and Philippe Schmitter conceptualizes alternative scenarios for the emerging Euro-polity.

The European Union is a moving target in two senses: first, because of the sheer extent of institutional reconfiguration over the past decade; second, because change in the EU is iterative (i.e. events at t_0 feed into the sources of change at t_1). The result is an extraordinarily dynamic polity in which innovations agreed by national governments in the major treaties create webs of constraints and inducements that lead to new conflicts and pressures on governments for further institutional negotiation. As this book makes clear, it would be naive to view the process through a teleological lens as leading inexorably to political integration. The terms used in this book to describe governance in the Euro-polity – variable geometry, multi-level, *à la carte*, *condominio*, *consortio* – have in common the assumption that central state executives and supranational institutions, distinctive national systems of economic governance and international markets coexist and will continue to coexist.

Each of the chapters of this book deals with the tensions that arise in a multi-level polity: among national governments regarding the allocation of resources and decision-making competencies; between national executives and supranational actors; between subnational and national governments. The logical consequence of tying actors at different levels into a single polity is that sources of contention about resources and decision-making increase exponentially. Disputes that were formerly handled by national governments in interstate negotiation are domesticated within a polity driven by a mix of national, supranational and subnational actors. Few, if any, observers claim that a single type of actor monopolizes decision-making. The task we have set ourselves is to generalize the dynamics of such interactions across a variety of policy areas.

The intellectual journeys the authors have taken over the past several years have crossed at many points. Philippe Schmitter, Wolfgang Streeck and Gary Marks collaborated in a larger group with David Cameron, Geoffrey Garrett, Peter Lange, Alberta Sbragia and David Soskice concerned with institutional change in the European Community. The group started out as a joint venture of scholars based at Duke University, the University of North Carolina-Chapel Hill, Stanford University and the University of Wisconsin-Madison. It received generous support from the Social Science Research Council in New York. Some group members had the opportunity to spend all or part of the 1992/3 academic year at the Center for Advanced Study in the Behavioral Sciences at Stanford. The Center provides a most congenial forum for bringing together scholars from diverse fields, and the Marks/McAdam chapter originated in a series of sunlit conversations that took place there.

Acknowledgements

Chapters 1 and 6 were originally written while the author was a fellow of the Center for Advanced Study in the Behavioral Sciences where he benefited inestimably from the informal exchange of ideas that characterizes this privileged site. Both chapters have been repeatedly discussed with colleagues in Europe and the United States and cannibalized for presentation at numerous conferences. Bits-and-pieces of them (along with new material) have been published as: 'Representation and the Future Euro-polity', *Staatswissenschaften und Staatspraxis*, III, 3 (1992), pp. 379–405; 'Quelques alternatives pour le futur système politique européen et leurs implications pour les politiques puliques europeennes' in Yves Mény, Pierre Muller et Jean-Louis Quermonne (eds), *Politiques Publiques en Europe* (Paris: L'Harmattan, 1995), pp. 27–47; 'The Future Euro-Polity and Its Impact upon Private Interest Governance within Member States', *Droit et Société*, No. 28 (1994), pp. 659–676.

Work on Chapter 2 was in part supported by the Robert Schuman Centre at the European University Institute, Florence. For helpful comments the author is indebted to Colin Crouch, Dieter Freiburghaus, Philipp Genschel and Yves Mény.

The authors of Chapter 3 are indebted to Richard Haesley and Ivan Llamazares for ideas and research assistance. They would like to thank Liesbet Hooghe, David Lowery, participants in the Comparative Politics Discussion Group at the Department of Political Science, UNC-CH, and the anonymous referees for comments and advice. This research was made possible in part by grants from the Institute for Research in the Social Sciences at the University of North Carolina (to Marks), the University Research Council at the University of North Carolina (to Nielsen) and from the Josiah Trent Memorial Foundation at Duke University (to Salk). Gary Marks's co-authors are listed in alphabetical order. Part of this chapter was printed in *Comparative Political Studies*.

Chapter 4 was written while the author was a Fellow at the Wissenschaftskolleg Berlin. A preliminary version was presented at a conference at the European University Institute in Florence in May 1994. Part of the chapter was printed in *European Law Journal*, Vol. 1, No. 1, pp. 31–59.

Work on Chapter 5 began while both authors were Fellows at the Center for Advanced Study in the Behavioral Sciences. They are thus indebted to the Center and its staff for the role they played in facilitating this collaboration. In addition the authors would like to thank the following people for their useful comments on various versions of the manuscript: Elisabeth Clemens, Myra Marx Ferree, Neil Fligstein, Christian Joppke, Alfonso Morales, Tony Oberschall, Charles Perrow, Woody Powell, Jeremy Richardson, Sidney Tarrow, Charles Tilly and Cyrus Ernesto Zirakzadeh. The order of authorship for this chapter was determined alphabetically. Part of the chapter was printed in *West European Politics*.

1

Examining the Present Euro-Polity with the Help of Past Theories

Philippe C. Schmitter

Europe's self-imposed deadline of 31 December 1992 for the completion of its internal market has passed. Thanks to the Single European Act (SEA), the process of European integration was given a new momentum and the European Community (EC) began to acquire a new institutional configuration. Most of the 282 directives anticipated by the SEA were subsequently drafted by the Commission and approved by the Council of Ministers. Only fifty or so did not make it through the process on schedule and, admittedly, some of these dealt with quite controversial matters. At the level of transposition, or the conversion of EC directives into national law, progress was much less rapid and more uneven, but no one can say that the '1992 Process' did not advance very far – perhaps it went further than its signatories in 1985 intended or believed possible.

The subsequent agreement reached at Maastricht in December 1991 represents a potentially more significant extension of EC activity and even authority in two broad domains: monetary union and political cooperation. More than the SEA, the Maastricht Treaty (MAT) helps to clarify the rules of the game and the institutional *compétences* of the emergent Euro-polity. It also gave the outcome a new name: the European Union (EU), although only time will tell if this label sticks.

The unprecedented difficulties faced in ratifying MAT, especially the narrow victories for it in the Danish and French national referenda, the severe division in the parliamentary Conservative Party in the United Kingdom and the constitutional challenge in Germany – along with considerable evidence of growing disaffection in public opinion throughout member states – have led some to question whether its more ambitious commitments will ever be met. The least one can say, in the words of the out-going President of its Commission, Jacques Delors, is that the EC/EU is still *un objet politique non-identifié*.

As we near-sighted outsiders peer at this complex process of polity formation, what we see coming over the horizon depends very much on the theories we have used to grind our lenses. Since the inception of the European integration process in the mid-1950s, scholars have politely but insistently disagreed about its likely outcome – and forty some years of activity do not seem to have appreciably diminished that fundamental disagreement. The extremes are fairly clear:

1 The EC/EU will remain an *intergovernmental organization* limited to the collective pursuit of those tasks which protect and enhance the sovereign autonomy of its member states.
2 The EC/EU will become a *supranational state* and inherit all those tasks currently performed by its member states, which will have transferred their sovereignty to this new set of authoritative institutions.

Needless to say, between these two outcomes would seem to lie a wide range of potential intermediate outcomes, but these have proven difficult to imagine and label. For one thing, our political vocabulary lacks the proper terminology. We are familiar with the properties of states and intergovernmental organizations – even if we recognize that they come in various shapes and sizes – but we would have to go far back in European history to recapture a more diverse language about political units.[1] And, even if we could recover these ancient labels or invent new ones to describe other political forms, we might still find it difficult to accept them as stable solutions to the problem of political order. There is an almost inevitable temptation to assume that such things as confederacies, covenants, compacts, leagues, co-principalities, confraternities, commonwealths, *Bündnisse*, *Ämter*, *Eidgenossenschaften*, *Stammesherzogtümer*, *Städtebünde*, *Reich*, *consortii*, *communae*, *regnae*, *conjuratii*, *parléments*, *confrèries*, *leghe*, *repubbliche*, etc., are only passing phenomena, destined eventually to be moulded into more coherent states, even nation-states.

Moreover, it is abundantly clear that the contemporary promoters of the integration process do not themselves have a consistent 'model' of where they are headed politically – least of all, one that has an obvious historical referent. The closest approximation used to be the notion of the 'United States of Europe', but virtually no one today seems to believe that the United States of America offers an attractive *Vorbild* to Europeans. *Federation* is probably the concept that best expresses where many of them think they are headed, but even that is subject to diverse interpretation, not to say, 'essential contestation'.[2]

European integration has always 'really' been about supranational *political* integration – protestations by national actors to the contrary notwithstanding. This does not, however, resolve the issues of what will be the form and content of its politics and how different are they going to be from the form and content of politics practised by existing nation-states. Another way of putting it is that the EC/EU may have no strategic design, but will emerge in an improvised fashion from tactical responses to much more concrete and immediate problems. But this is to get ahead of our argument since expectations of this sort are very contingent upon the theory one uses to approach the issue.

Presently, there seem to be three sets of lenses 'pre-ground' for observing the process of European integration: (1) the *neo-realist*, (2) the *neo-functional* and (3) the *neo-rational*.[3] My personal suspicion is that each leads to different expectations about its eventual outcome. All, however, are primarily theories about process and do not begin from explicit assumptions about end-states. Since it is my (self-assigned) objective in this chapter to explore the 'far-sightedness' of only one set of lenses – the neo-functional – I will largely refrain from speculating about what the other two are likely to see coming over the horizon. Not only is 'tri-focalism' very difficult to accomplish, but practitioners of the other theories are notoriously reluctant to be told by a non-believer what it is that they are supposed to be seeing in the future!

It does seem incumbent upon me to suggest very briefly, however, what I consider to be the hallmarks of the other theories before explicating the features of my more modest perspective. All three theories/perspectives, however, have the following two (often implicit) assumptions in common:

1   The process of European integration will be consensual in that no actor – national, sub- or supranational – is likely to use physical force or organized violence to bring about the rules, institutions or policies it prefers. Old-fashioned realists may wince at this, but the EC/EU does constitute a 'pluralistic security community', in the sense of Karl Deutsch et al. (1957) and Richard Van Wagenen (1952), within which this strategic alternative is not contemplated by any of its member states, and probably could not be threatened or applied. The same constraint, needless to say, does not necessarily hold for Eastern Europe or for integration processes elsewhere.

2   The actors in the process of European integration will, for the foreseeable future, remain independent in the formation of their preferences and disregarding of the welfare of each other. In other words, the basic problem is how to make 'Europe without Europeans'. If one could presume that its states, peoples or individuals cared sufficiently about each other's welfare that they would not distinguish it from their own, none of these three approaches would hold.

Scanning neo-realism

Neo-realism is a relatively well-known commodity, especially among students of international relations, where it still seems to dominate the field. Its key actors are sovereign national or nation-states with distinctive interests and capabilities for unitary action. Despite the 'anarchy' of the environment in which they live and the intrinsic hostility with which they regard each other, states can engage in cooperative activities through the formation of 'regimes', but only to enhance or protect their respective power in the interstate system. Any action which either diminishes that capability deliberately or assigns it irrevocably to another polity is (theoretically) incomprehensible. According to this theory, the putative outcome of the EC/EU would, therefore, be an intergovernmental organization which did not displace or transcend the authority of its member states.

Scanning neo-rationalism

Neo-rationalism is also a well-known theoretical commodity, having been imported into political science from liberal economics. It has, however, largely been confined to explaining micro-behaviour within national polities rather than the macro-dynamics of negotiation and change between them.[4] Its key actors are individuals (or units that can be treated as if they were individuals) who have well-established, self-regarding preferences and who calculate the costs and benefits of different courses of action, choosing the one that minimizes the former and maximizes the latter. Needless to say, they do this under constraints which in the interstate system might include such things as the relative power of their adversaries, the transaction costs of reaching an agreement, the level of available information and the extent to which they discount future benefits. To the extent that neo-rationalists postulate that states are equivalent to individuals, i.e. have well-entrenched, unitary national interests, their conclusions about probable outcomes would not seem to diverge from those of neo-realists. If they admit that member states might not be irreducible units but composed of individuals or groups with distinct preferences and strong incentives for behaving opportunistically, then my hunch is they are likely to be led quickly to the conclusion that only the imposition of a system of hierarchical enforcement, i.e. a supranational state, can resolve the emergent temptations for free-riding or defection and ensure the steady production of needed public goods.

Applying neo-functionalism

While it would be misleading – for reasons to be discussed below – to interpret the signing of the Single European Act itself as a successful example of spill-over and, hence, a belated confirmation of the validity of neo-functionalism, several analysts have observed that in the aftermath of the SEA this approach to explaining the dynamics of integration has regained credibility.[5] Once the log-jam that piled up from the mid-1960s to the 1970s had been broken by shifting away from the presumption of harmonization, regulation and unanimity towards the new techniques of mutual recognition, deregulation and qualified-majority voting, it now seemed possible that its views on the complex interdependence between policy arenas, the mobilization of infranational interests and the active intervention of supranational actors would finally be vindicated. At last, so it seemed, the shackles of realistic 'intergovernmentalism' had been cast aside and the Twelve could proceed, if not automatically, at least predictably, toward the political unity that had heretofore escaped them!

Before turning to an evaluation of the past demerits and possible future merits of neo-functionalism, let us look briefly at a few of its most distinctive features. There is no need to provide a full exposition, since this has already been done and is readily available in the introductory chapters of Ernst B. Haas's *Beyond the Nation-State* (1964). The following maxims are not necessarily unique to its way of looking at integration processes. No doubt, some of them have been 'borrowed' and inserted into other, more ambitious and abstract, theories. Taken as a whole, however, they represent a quite considerable critique of the dominant modes of thinking about international relations, in particular, and about political power, influence and bargaining, in general.

1   *States are not the exclusive and may no longer be the predominant actors in the regional/international system.* The fact that they do still possess nominal sovereignty and, therefore, must be the formal co-signatories of the treaties that typically constitute and punctuate the integration process is potentially illusory in that:

(a)   their commitment to treaty terms rests on an imagined predominance of national interest that most likely reflects only a temporary equilibrium among the conflicting interests of classes, sectors, professions, parties, social movements, ethnic groups, etc.;
(b)   their presumed capacity for unitary and authoritative action masks the possibility that important subnational groups can act independently to either reinforce, undermine or circumvent the policies of national states.

2   *Interests, rather than shared ideals or common identity, are the driving force behind the integration process,* but this does *not* mean that:

(a)   their definition will remain constant once the integration process has begun and is distributing its (usually uneven) benefits. Actors can learn from their experiences in cooperative decision-making, modify their preferences, and even develop new ideals and identities;
(b)   their expression will be confined to the national level once new opportunities for exercising influence have opened up within institutions at the supranational level.

3   *Decisions about integration are normally taken with very imperfect knowledge of their consequences and frequently under the pressure of deadlines or impending crises.* Given the absence of clear historical precedents, actors are likely to miscalculate

(a)   not only their capability to satisfy initial mutually agreed-upon goals;
(b)   but also the impact of these efforts upon other, less consensual goals.

4   *Functions or issue arenas provide the usual foci for the integration process (at least, in Western Europe), beginning with those that are initially considered the least controversial and, hence, easiest to deal with.* Given the intrinsic (if uneven) interdependence of these arenas – *l'engrenage* is the jargon term – in modern societies:

(a)   advancement toward the solution of concrete problems or production of collective goods in one arena is bound to affect performance and interests in other arenas, and may even lead to demands for their explicit inclusion in the process;[6]

(b) even where one issue arena can be separated from others, advancement toward the fulfilment of initially consensual tasks may generate increased controversy, thereby widening the range of actors potentially involved.

5   *Actors in the integration process are plural and diverse in nature and cannot be confined to existing national states or their subnational interest groups.* They include supranational persons, secretariats and associations whose careers and resources become increasingly dependent upon the further expansion of integrative tasks. Even where their nomination is formally controlled or monitored by national actors, they may:

(a) develop an increasingly independent *ésprit de corps* and interject ideas and programmes into the process that cannot be reduced to the preferences of national or subnational groups;

(b) acquire, often as the unintended by-product of problem-solving in discrete issue arenas, increased resources and even authoritative capacities to act in ways that countermand or circumvent the intentions of national authorities.

6   *Strategies with regard to integration are convergent, not identical.* Actors agree upon rules and policies not because they have the same objective, but because their different preferences overlap. This implies that:

(a) when divergences in benefits and external effects emerge from the process, actors will respond with different demands for changes in rules and policies;

(b) from these inevitable conflicts, new convergences based on new combinations of actors can emerge which will redefine the level and scope of common obligations in ways not originally anticipated.

7   *Outcomes of international integration are neither fixed in advance by the founding treaty, nor are they likely to be expressed exclusively through subsequent formal agreements.* They should be recognized as the transient results of an ongoing process, rather than the definitive product of a stable equilibrium. Which is not to say that all attempts at integration among initially consenting states are equally likely to be successful or to expand functionally, since:

(a) all of the above – the mix of actors, the diversity of their interests, the extent of convergence in their strategies, the interdependence of issue arenas, the degree of knowledge and, hence, potential for miscalculation, the inequalities in benefits and unanticipated consequences – will differ systematically from one experience to another;

(b) these differences will be associated with differences in initial endowment and subsequent performance and will lead, in turn, to differences in outcome, ranging from encapsulated intergovernmental organizations to emergent supra-states. Between these extremes lie a wide variety of intermediary forms of regional/international organization which may be no less stable and may even be more likely to emerge.

From these assumptions, neo-functionalists have derived most of their concepts and hypotheses. As we shall see, not all of these have proven equally useful or been equally verified by the experience with European integration since its institutional origin in the European Coal and Steel Community (ECSC) in 1952. There is evidence to suggest that its perspective overlooked some key variables and focused too much attention on others.

Responding to critics

It is important to note, however, that several of the critiques of neo-functionalism that emerged in the 1970s misrepresented its claims and distorted its arguments. For example, this perspective never argued that its central process, spill-over, would be either automatic or free of conflict. Quite the contrary, emphasis was placed on the likelihood of increasing controversy and difficulty in reaching agreement, as the process expanded to affect more actors and adjacent issue arenas. This was called politicization in the neo-functionalist jargon. Nor did it necessarily predict transcendence – the unlimited and irreversible accumulation of tasks by the regional centre at the expense of national member states. Such a supra-state based on a complete transfer of sovereignty was only one possible outcome – and not the most likely by any means. A good deal of neo-functionalist effort was spent exploring the probability of entropy and encapsulation setting in, rather than momentum and expansion inexorably taking over.[7] Finally, the sheer fact that the EC had not spilled over into several new issue arenas during the first thirty years of its existence and had appeared for some time (roughly from the mid-1960s to the early 1980s) not to be extending the authority of its central institutions did not, in itself, disconfirm the perspective since none of its proponents dared to place a specific timeframe around their suppositions. This embarrassing lack of temporal specificity is shared with many other theories of political change.

Which is not to say that neo-functionalism emerges blameless from a confrontation with several generations of experience with European integration. Although few, if any, of the close academic observers of the EC were using it when the SEA was signed in December 1985 – intergovernmentalism, a variety of neo-realism, dominated their thinking – I doubt if its concepts, maxims and hypotheses would have been of much help. The decision to move toward the so-called 'completion of the internal market' by 31 December 1992 could not have been anticipated using its lenses (although I am not convinced that neo-realist or neo-rationalist lenses would have been much better for seeing what was coming).

Some after-the-fact reflections

Reflecting *ex post*, I would stress the following features about the event – none of which have attracted much prior attention on the part of neo-functionalists and all of which are likely to continue to be salient in determining the future course of integration:

(a)   the crucial role of heads of government/state, meeting in the European Council, in actually putting the 1992 package together;

(b)   the impact of economic trends and cycles originating *outside* Europe and threatening the region as a whole with declining competitiveness and low growth rates;

(c)   the quiet accumulation of decisions by the European Court of Justice that established the supremacy of Community over national law and set precedents, such as mutual recognition, proportionality, direct effect and implied powers, that could be used to resolve other disputes;

(d)   the indirect effect of Community enlargement, first to nine and later to twelve members, upon internal decision-making processes;

(e)   the importance, not of well-entrenched European-level interest associations, but of *ad hoc* and even *ad personam*, informal groups such as the European Business Roundtable;

(f)   the relatively low level of mass public attention and, hence, of politicization of issues which 'should have' attracted greater controversy;

(g)   the 'catalytic role' played by the European Parliament when it shifted to a more overtly political or 'federalist' strategy by introducing the Draft Treaty Establishing European Union in early 1984;[8]

(h)   the indirect, but steady, impact of an ideological shift at the national political level from a predominance of social-democratic to a growing hegemony of neo-liberal values.

Analyses of the process leading to the SEA recognize the above features (to varying degrees and in differing mixes) and they tend to interpret them as lending credence either to a neo-realist (Sandholtz and Zysman 1989; Moravcsik 1991) or to a neo-rational interpretation (Garrett 1992; Garrett and Weingast 1992). In my view, if one contemplates the entire list, it contains items which both substantiate and disconfirm the expectations of these theories. Picking and choosing from among them *after* the decision was made can be quite misleading – not to say, deceptive – and is far removed from the capacity to anticipate such a major shift.

What cannot be questioned is that the putting into effect of the SEA has unleashed a veritable avalanche of interdependencies between issue arenas, Eurocratic initiatives, shifts in interest association activity, redefinitions of Community authority, mobilization of subnational actors, and further expansions of the functional agenda – culminating in the Maastricht Agreements of December 1991. It may not have been produced as a neat spill-over motivated by the externalities of closely linked policies and unevenly distributed benefits and promoted by a joint conspiracy of

European civil servants and interest groups that outwitted the entrenched interests of national governments and state bureaucracies, but it has demonstrated *ex post* that, as Ernst Haas (1976) put it, neo-functionalism may have been obsolescent but it was not obsolete.

Evaluating past performance

The optimistic expectations of early neo-functionalists that European integration would exploit the latent interdependencies of complex, welfare-oriented societies and spill over inexorably (but not immediately or uncontroversially) from one issue arena to another were rather quickly frustrated. The whole approach was rooted in a serious 'dual paradox' which, if not overcome, threatened to confine it to political impotence and academic obscurity.

On the one hand, for the process to begin, existing states had to converge upon some relatively non-controversial, apparently separable and easily targeted issue arena where tangible gains from cooperation were sufficient to warrant giving up some portion of their respective autonomy to a common institution. But if this arena really were so non-controversial and separable, then there was little reason to expect any further expansion. The new regional organization would merely perform its task unobtrusively and, in so doing, reinforce the status and capabilities of the states that composed and continued to control it. The present international system – global and regional – is virtually saturated with such stagnant functional organizations, none of which seem to be contributing much to transforming its basic, i.e. statist, structure.

On the other hand, if the proponents of integration did manage to select an issue arena with greater potential for *l'engrenage*, i.e. linkage to other, initially unattended arenas and for eventual politicization, i.e. capacity to attract the efforts of a wider set of actors, then, they ran the risk that neo-functionalism would become self-disconfirming. Statesmen (or women) had only to catch on to the strategy (or read the academic analyses) to realize that whatever the immediate benefits they might reap from such international cooperation, these would eventually be overwhelmed by the rising costs in terms of diminished sovereignty and irreversible entanglements. To the extent that they could internalize the implications of such long-term effects and discount the short-term pay-offs, they would rationally choose to refuse to enter such arrangements or, as seems to have been the case with de Gaulle, pull the plug before the process had advanced too far.

This is not the time or place to analyse how the founders of the ECSC managed to pick an arena with considerable potential for spill-over and to steer it past national politicians in the early 1950s.[9] Nor to go over again the relatively well-known story of how its successor, the European Economic Community (EEC), was more or less stopped in its tracks in the mid-1960s by a combination of increased awareness of its emerging impact upon national sovereignty and the capability of national states to pursue their own macro-economic policies. Although it is risky to rely on just a few variables to explain why the neo-functionalist strategy-cum-perspective again became relevant, I am convinced that the turnaround in the late 1970s and, especially, mid-1980s can be attributed *grosso modo* to two changes in the European policy environment:

(a)   a vague, but widespread, *subjective* notion that Europe as a whole was destined to decline in its competitiveness (and, ultimately, in its relative standard of living) vis-à-vis other developed world regions, specifically Japan, the Pacific Basin and North America;

(b)   a specific, but generalizable, *objective* demonstration by the Socialist government of François Mitterrand (1981–3) that measures taken independently by national policy-makers were incapable of attaining desired macro-economic outcomes and could even lead to perverse outcomes in terms of growth and monetary stability.

Only the second of these changes can be said to have any intrinsic connection with neo-functionalism via underlying and increasingly irreversible functional interdependencies and policy entanglements. The first is a parametric and exogenous shift that was not – and could not – be identified by such an approach. At best, its relevance might be spotted *ex ante* by an alert neo-realist trained to be sensitive to perceptions of relative power and dependence.

Establishing a trajectory

Before trying to peer at the horizon with our newly polished neo-functionalist telescope – and it is a telescope not a wide-angle lens – we should turn around briefly and glance back at where the EEC/EC has come from. There is no assurance that the Euro-polity, especially after its accelerated transformation since 1985, will continue to pursue the same trajectory, but it cannot hurt to try to capture the logic of its past dynamic (or lack thereof).

   In this regard, we are fortunate in having a uniquely systematic assessment of the EEC's progress as of 1968: Leon Lindberg and Stuart Scheingold's *Europe's Would-be Polity* (1970). Its authors surveyed the full scope of national governmental functions and attempted to measure the extent to which the EEC since its inception in 1958 had altered the locus of decision-making. They argued that some very important 'upward' shifts had occurred in specific arenas of economic policy-making and external relations, but the overall pattern was disappointing. Their prediction was that, while the integration process had succeeded in its narrow objectives and managed to gain a 'permissive consensus' in mass and élite publics, it was headed for protracted 'equilibrium'. Alone, 'functional spill-over cannot be viewed in and of itself as a dynamic force making for integration' due to discontinuities and lags between issue arenas (Lindberg and Scheingold

1970: 301). Contrary to the assumptions of the perspective, the pressures stemming from issue interdependencies were either not so compelling as or the counter-pressures from state and national interests were more compelling than anticipated. They had to be supplemented by other factors extraneous to it. Lindberg and Scheingold did not preclude an eventual assertion of functional linkages once the customs union had been in operation for some time, and they wisely left room for possible external shocks and induced crises, but the general message was clear – and surprisingly accurate for fifteen years or so: the EEC would not even succeed in establishing a genuine economic union, much less develop into a political one.

In Figure 1.1, I have taken their categories of governmental functions (changing them somewhat in light of subsequent policy developments and relabelling them 'issue arenas') and cross-tabulated them with a selected set of contextual and processual variables.[10] Its basic objective is to discern *whether* more spill-overs have occurred in the years following Lindberg and Scheingold's pessimistic assessment, and, if so, *where*. From its distributions, it does seem possible to draw a few general conclusions about the past strengths and weaknesses of the neo-functional perspective.

1   *There were, indeed, underlying interdependencies that may have taken some time to mature, but did serve to compel actors into reaching agreements that were not initially intended.* The volume of intra-Community transactions continued to rise relative to the exchanges of its member economies with other countries and this triggered a spill-over into capital markets and monetary affairs at the very core of an increasingly regionalized economic system. Not only was the customs union eventually converted into a more genuine common market, but virtually the entire scope of government functions previously performed exclusively at the national level came within at least the purview of the EC. It is less clear, however, that the role assigned to Eurocrats and specifically to Euro-associations in this process was so significant.[11]

2   *This impressive expansion in the number and variety of EC activities has meant a vast increase in the frequency with which national representatives meet*, e.g. the Council of Ministers in its various guises meets over one hundred times a year and the quantity of national expert reunions runs well into the thousands. *And this seems to have induced important learning effects in the ranks of these representatives and even to have resulted in shifts in conceptions of national interest which may have been more important than the upward shift to regional interest politics predicted by neo-functionalists.*

3   *Moreover, the policy expansion – when coupled with the persistent increase in commercial, financial and personal transactions between individuals, firms and subnational groups – has made it not only easier but even imperative to reach complex 'log-rolls' and 'package-deals' sufficient to extend further Community* compétences *and buy out even the most recalcitrant of opponents.* The process may even have crossed 'the threshold of irreversibility' beyond which the threat by any individual member state to

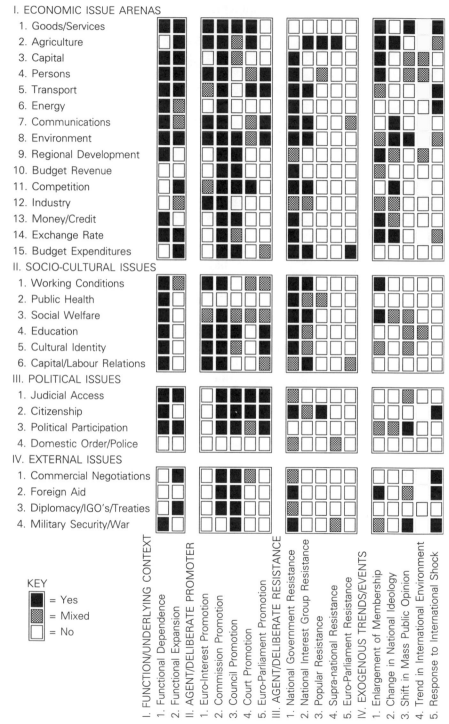

Figure 1.1   *Issue arenas and explanatory variables: 1950–92*

defect is no longer credible, just as the previous attainment of the status of a security community had already removed the credibility of using force to impose one's preferred outcome.

4   Which is not to say that the neo-functionalist momentum that Lindberg and Scheingold failed to find in the late 1960s has necessarily emerged. *Much of what has happened since the mid-1970s can better be attributed to external trends and shocks than to purely internal processes and functional* engrenages. It was correct to emphasize the declining capacity of national states in Europe to control macro-economic outcomes within their borders, i.e. to couple the loss of external sovereignty with the decline in internal sovereignty, but it is doubtful that this would have had such an impact were it not for the generalized perception that Europe as a whole was declining relative to other competing regions of the world. For example, neo-functionalists were right to stress the underlying interdependence of energy policy with those conditions determining the relative competitiveness of producers within a single market, but very little happened in the energy sector until actors were made aware of the overriding importance of the dependency of the region as a whole upon foreign suppliers by the successive oil shocks of the 1970s. A similar case could be made for European monetary policy in the aftermath of Nixon's 'shocking' decision to take the US dollar off the gold standard in 1971.[12]

5   In their singular concentration on interdependencies rooted in production and exchange and, hence, the roles played by representatives of classes and sectors, *the neo-functionalists tended to overlook very significant extensions of the scope and, especially, the level of Community authority that were going on right under their noses, namely as a result of the deliberations and decisions of the European Court of Justice.* Its assertion of the primacy of Community law – in effect, converting the Treaty of Rome into a proto-constitution for Europe – and its imaginative interpretations of specific (if vague) clauses were crucial for supranationalism.[13] The effective implementation of these new rules, however, depended upon a quite different form of interdependency: that embodied in a common legal profession, doctrine of jurisprudence and respect for the rule of law which extended across intra-European borders into the very entrails of the national state.[14]

6   Finally, *neo-functionalists failed to recognize (or, at least, to 'problematize') the significance of the enlargement of the EEC/EC to include new members.* Neither it nor any other theory of integration can explain why the Community began with six – rather than seven or nine – subsequently expanded to twelve, and may even reach twenty-five or thirty before exhausting itself somewhere on the Asian steppes. And yet, it is impossible to deny that increasing the number of participants has had a marked effect on decision-making rules within Community institutions or that increasing the heterogeneity of member interests has had a significant impact upon the functional scope of Community policies. With the EC/EU now facing this issue as never before – there are already six states in the queue, another five

in various stages of application, and a tentative list of seven or eight more in the wings – the absence of any clear guidelines is particularly striking. All the discussion about 'widening vs deepening' is taking place in a theoretical vacuum.[15]

Conclusion

For better or worse, with varying degrees of enthusiasm or foreboding, no one doubts that the EC/EU will continue to be the dominant supranational political institution in Europe for the foreseeable future. With virtually every European country – except for Norway and Switzerland – trying to become a member and no alternative arrangement to it in sight, this political object may still be 'unidentified', but the EC/EU is not likely to disappear or quietly recede over the horizon.

Which does not tell us what 'it' will become. How closely will it resemble the forms of political domination that we are used to dealing with, i.e. the national state and the intergovernmental organization? Or will it become something significantly different, something that will rely on an unprecedented format of stable governance and legitimate authority?

The principle underlying assumption of this chapter is that the formation of the Euro-polity will *not* be a 'rerun' of the processes and policies that earlier made the national state the predominant political institution of Europe – and, subsequently, the world. Nor can it be confined to the status of a mere 'confederation' or 'regional organization', even one of unprecedented scope and powers. The EC/EU is well on its way to becoming something new – and that will have major implications for the actors, the processes and the outcomes of policy-making at all levels in Europe: supranational, national and subnational.

2

Negative and Positive Integration in the Political Economy of European Welfare States

Fritz W. Scharpf

The process of European integration is characterized by a fundamental asymmetry which Joseph Weiler (1981) accurately described as a dualism between supranational European law and intergovernmental European policy-making. Weiler is also right in criticizing political scientists for having focused for too long only on aspects of intergovernmental negotiations while ignoring (or, at least, not taking seriously enough) the establishment, by judge-made law, of a European legal order that takes precedence over national law (Weiler 1994). This omission is all the more critical since it also kept us from recognizing the politically highly significant parallel between Weiler's dualism and the more familiar contrast between 'negative' and 'positive integration' (Tinbergen 1965; Rehbinder and Stewart 1984), i.e. between measures increasing market integration by eliminating national restraints on trade and distortions of competition, on the one hand, and common European policies to shape the conditions under which markets operate, on the other hand.

The main beneficiary of supranational European law has been negative integration. Its basic rules were already contained in the 'primary law' of the Treaties of Rome. From this foundation, liberalization could be extended. without much political attention, through interventions of the Europea Commission against infringements of Treaty obligations, and through the decisions and preliminary rulings of the European Court of Justice. By contrast, positive integration depends upon the agreement of national governments in the Council of Ministers; it is thus subject to all of the impediments facing European intergovernmental policy-making. This fundamental institutional difference is sufficient to explain the frequently deplored asymmetry between negative and positive integration in EC policy-making (Kapteyn 1991; Merkel 1993). The most likely result is a competency gap, in which national policy is severely restrained in its problem-solving capacity, while European policy is constrained by the lack of intergovernmental agreement. To the extent that this is true, the political economy of capitalist democracies, which had developed in Western Europe during the postwar decades, is being changed in a fundamental way.

Negative integration: the loss of boundary control

In the history of capitalism, the decades following the Second World War were unusual in the degree to which the boundaries of the territorial state had become coextensive with the boundaries of markets for capital, services, goods and labour.[16] These boundaries were by no means impermeable, but transactions across them were nevertheless under the effective control of national governments. As a consequence, capital owners were generally restricted to investment opportunities within the national economy, and firms were mainly challenged by domestic competitors. International trade grew slowly, and since governments controlled imports and exchange rates, international competitiveness was not much of a problem. While these conditions lasted, government interest rate policy controlled the rate of return on financial investments. If interest rates were lowered, job-creating real investments would become relatively more attractive, and vice versa. Thus, Keynesian macro-economic management could smooth the business cycle and prevent demand-deficient unemployment, while union wage policy, where it could be employed for macro-economic purposes, was able to control the rate of inflation. At the same time, government regulation and union collective bargaining controlled the conditions of production. But since all effective competitors could be, and were, required to produce under the same regimes, the costs of regulation could be passed on to consumers. Hence the rate of return on investment was not necessarily affected by high levels of regulation and union power;[17] capitalist accumulation was as feasible in the union-dominated Swedish welfare state as it was in the American free enterprise system.

During this period, therefore, the industrial nations of Western Europe had the chance to develop specifically national versions of the capitalist welfare state – and their choices were in fact remarkably different (Esping-Andersen 1990). In spite of the considerable differences between the 'social-democratic', 'corporatist' or 'liberal' versions of the welfare state, however, all were remarkably successful in maintaining and promoting a vigorous capitalist economy, while also controlling, in different ways and to different degrees, the destructive tendencies of unfettered capitalism in the interest of specific social, cultural and/or ecological values (Scharpf 1991a; Merkel 1993). It was not fully realized at the time, however, how much the success of market-correcting policies did in fact depend on the capacity of the territorial state to control its economic boundaries. Once this capacity was lost, through the globalization of capital markets and the transnational integration of markets for goods and services, the 'golden years' of the capitalist welfare state came to an end.

Now the minimal rate of return that investors can expect is determined by global financial markets, rather than by national monetary policy, and real interest rates are generally about twice as high as they used to be in the 1960s. So if a government should now try to reduce interest rates below the international level, the result would no longer be an increase of job-creating real investment in the national economy, but an outflow of capital, devaluation and a rising rate of inflation.[18] Similarly, once the territorial state has lost, or given up, the capacity to control the boundaries of markets for goods and services, it can no longer make sure that all competing suppliers will be subject to the same regulatory regime. Thus, if now the costs of regulation or of collective-bargaining are increased nationally, they can no longer be passed on to consumers. Instead, imports will increase, exports decrease, profits will fall, investment decline and firms will go bankrupt or move production to more benign locations.[19]

Thus, when boundary control declines, the capacity of the state and the unions to shape the conditions under which capitalist economies must operate is also diminished. Instead, countries are forced into a competition for locational advantage which has all the characteristics of a Prisoner's Dilemma game (Sinn 1994). The paradigmatic example of this form of 'regulatory competition' was provided, during the first third of this century, by the inability of 'progressive' states in the United States to regulate the employment of children in industry. Under the 'negative commerce clause' decisions of the Supreme Court, they were not allowed to prohibit or tax the import of goods produced by child labour in neighbouring states. Hence locational competition in the integrated American market prevented all states from enacting regulations that would affect only enterprises within their own state (Graebner 1977). In the same way, the increasing transnational integration of capital and product markets, and especially the completion of the European internal market, reduces the freedom of national governments and unions to raise the regulatory and wage costs of national firms above the level prevailing in competing locations. Moreover, and if nothing else changes, the 'competition of regulatory systems' that is generally welcomed by neo-liberal economists (Streit and Mussler 1995) and politicians may well turn into a downward spiral of competitive deregulation in which all competing countries will find themselves reduced to a level of protection that is in fact lower than preferred by any of them.

If nothing else changes – but what might change is, again, illustrated by the child-labour example. In the United States it was ultimately possible – after the 'constitutional revolution' of 1937 – to solve the problem through legislation at the federal level. Similarly, in Europe there is a hope, at least among unions and the political parties close to them, that what is lost in national regulatory capacity might be regained through social regulation at the European level. Against these hopes, however, stands the institutional asymmetry of negative and positive integration, which was mentioned in the introduction.

In the abstract, the desirability of negative integration, or liberalization, is not seriously challenged in the member states of the Union. The basic commitment to create a 'common market' was certainly shared by the governments that were parties to the Treaties and by the national parliaments that ratified these agreements. It found its legal expression in the 'primary law' of Treaty provisions requiring the elimination of tariff and non-tariff barriers to trade and the establishment of a system of undistorted competition. What may not have been clearly envisaged in the very beginning were the doctrines of the direct effect and supremacy of European law that were early on established through decisions of the European Court of Justice. Why national governments should have acquiesced in these decisions has become an interesting test case for competing approaches to integration theory.[20] In the present context, however, the explanation is less interesting than the effect of their acquiescence. Once the direct effect and supremacy of European law was accepted, the Commission and the Court of Justice had the opportunity to continuously expand the scope of negative integration without involving the Council of Ministers.[21] At the same time, under the Luxemburg Compromise of 1966, measures of positive integration could be blocked in the Council by the veto of a single member government.

The political-economic significance of this institutional asymmetry becomes clear when it is compared to the situation under national constitutions. Even in the Federal Republic of Germany, where neo-liberal theory has gained the greatest influence on the constitutional discourse, the neo-liberal concept of a 'social market economy' does not imply the single-minded perfection of a competitive order, but has been defined, by its original promoter, as the combination of the 'principle of market freedom with that of social compensation' (Müller-Armack 1956: 243). Moreover, the German Constitutional Court has consistently refused to grant constitutional status to any economic doctrine, neo-liberal or otherwise, insisting instead on the 'neutrality of the Basic Law in matters of economic policy'. Thus, economic freedom is protected against state intervention only within the general framework of human and civil rights, and the goals of competition policy have no higher constitutional status than all other legitimate ends of public policy. Accordingly, market-creating and market-correcting measures are equally legitimate in principle, and – witness the uneven history of cartel legislation and practice – both have to cope with the same difficulties of finding political support, in a highly pluralistic political system. This is also true in other member states of the European Community, where, generally speaking, public policy is even less constrained by doctrines of the 'economic constitution' type.

It does not follow from the text of the Treaties of Rome or from their genesis that the Community was meant to abolish this constitutional parity between the protection of economic freedom and market-correcting intervention (VerLoren van Themaat 1987; Joerges 1991, 1994a; Groeben 1992). Nevertheless, through the supremacy of European law, the four economic freedoms and the injunctions against distortions of competition have in fact gained constitutional force vis-à-vis the member states (Mestmäcker 1994: 270) while the corresponding options for social and economic intervention (which at the national level would have competed on an equal footing) are impeded by the high level of intergovernmental consensus required for positive integration at the European level.[22]

Positive integration: the limits of intergovernmentalism

While negative integration was advanced, as it were, behind the back of political processes by the Commission and the Court, measures of positive integration require explicit political legitimation. As long as the Luxemburg Compromise was still applied, indirect democratic legitimacy could be derived from the necessary agreement of all national governments in the Council of Ministers. The price of unanimity was, of course, an extremely cumbersome decision process. The Single European Act of 1986 was supposed to change this by returning, for harmonization decisions 'which have as their object the establishment and functioning of the internal market' (Art. 100A), to the rule of qualified-majority voting in the Council. As a consequence, the decision process has in fact been accelerated, since it is now no longer necessary to bargain for every last vote (Dehousse and Weiler 1990). However, voting strengths and voting rules in the Council are adjusted in such a way that groups of countries united by common interests can rarely be outvoted. In any case, the veto remains available as a last resort even to individual countries, and the unanimity rule still continues to apply to a wide range of Council decisions. Thus, the need for consensus remains very high for measures of positive integration.

Nevertheless, the Community is actively harmonizing national regulations in such areas as health and industrial safety, environmental risks and consumer protection (Majone 1993; Joerges 1994b), and it had in fact begun to do so long before the Single European Act (Rehbinder and Stewart 1984). It is also reported that these regulations are indeed defining high levels of protection in many areas (Eichener 1993; Voelzkow 1993; Héritier et al. 1994). How can these findings be reconciled with my claim that positive integration is impeded by the high consensus requirements in the Council of Ministers?

In order to resolve this apparent puzzle, it is necessary to examine the underlying constellation of interests among governments represented in the Council of Ministers.[23] Unanimous or qualified-majority voting rules institutionalize veto positions – and it is analytically true that – *ceteris paribus* – the existence of multiple veto positions reduces the capacity for political action (Tsebelis 1995). But whether this will in fact result in blockages depends on the actual constellations of interests among the participants. If these are harmonious ('pure coordination games') or at least partly overlapping ('mixed-motive games'), unanimous agreement is possible in principle, and effective solutions can be reached in spite of high consensus requirements. Blockages are only to be expected in constellations of conflicting interests – and even then, agreement may be achieved if the losers can be compensated through side payments or package-deals (Scharpf 1992b). Thus, if positive integration in Europe should run into insurmountable barriers, the likely explanation will be conflicts of interests among member states that are too intense to be settled within the institutional framework of the European Union.

Such conflicts do in fact exist, but they are not everywhere, and there is no reason to think that they are always virulent in areas that substantively and procedurally would be defined as positive integration. In order to show this, I will concentrate on the regulative policies of the Community (thus neglecting the fields of foreign policy and security policy, justice and home affairs, common agricultural policy, technology and industrial policy or the social funds). Disregarding for the moment ideological differences, one may generally assume that rationally self-interested national governments will consider three criteria in evaluating proposed regulations at the European level: (a) the extent to which the mode of regulation agrees with, or departs from, established administrative routines in their own country; (b) the likely impact on the competitiveness of national industries and on employment in the national economy; and – where these are politically activated – (c) specific demands and apprehensions of their national electorates.

The exceptional importance of the expected costs of administrative and procedural adjustment in countries that are committed to active regulation, has been identified in studies by Adrienne Héritier and her collaborators (1994). It explains conflicts even between countries that have a common interest in high levels of regulatory protection. However, if agreement is reached at all, it is unlikely to reduce existing levels of protection.[24] In the following analysis, I will therefore concentrate on conflicts over economic and political interests.[25]

There, the boundary separating consensual and conflict-prone constellations can be roughly equated with the conventional distinction between product-related and process-related regulations (Rehbinder and Stewart 1984: 10). In the case of product-related regulations, the continuation of different national quality and safety requirements would perpetuate the very fragmentation of European markets which the Treaties of Rome and the Single European Act were designed to overcome. Since all countries agreed to the creation of the single market, it can also be assumed that the common economic interest in unified European standards outweighs divergent interests. Thus, while countries might differ in their substantive and procedural preferences, agreement on common standards is in the end likely to be reached. That is not true for process-related environmental and safety regulations,[26] and it is even less true for social regulations of the processes of production (Lange 1992; Leibfried and Pierson 1992). Since they increase the cost of production, national regulation is rendered increasingly difficult under the dictates of international competition. So it is here that 'social-democratic' aspirations for re-regulation at the European level would seem to be most pertinent. But it is also here that economic conflicts of interest among member states must be most acute. In order to justify this proposition, a somewhat more precise analysis of interest constellations seems useful.

In the case of product-related regulations, the interest constellation is shaped by the institutional framework. Under Art. 30 of the Treaty, 'quantitative restrictions on imports and all measures having equivalent

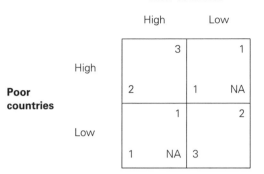

Figure 2.1   *Preference for high or low European-wide standards in product-related regulations. In case of non-agreement (NA), no common standard is adopted*

effect' are prohibited between member states. Under Art. 36, however, such measures are nevertheless allowed if they are 'justified on grounds of public morality, public policy or public security; the protection of health and life of humans, animals or plants'. In other words, if national regulations should in fact serve one of the purposes specified in Art. 36, the default outcome in the absence of a common European regime would result in the continuation of fragmented European markets. Assuming that this is a prospect which all countries will want to avoid, they will still differ with regard to the aspiration level of common European regulations. Rich countries will generally prefer higher levels of consumer and environmental protection than poor countries would like to impose on their own consumers. Thus, the resulting constellation of interests is likely to resemble the 'Battle of the Sexes' game (Figure 2.1) – a game in which negotiated agreement is generally difficult, but not impossible to achieve.[27]

Moreover, even when European regulations have been harmonized, Art. 100A (4) gives countries with a preference for high levels of protection a chance to introduce national regulations applying even more stringent standards. This changes the default outcome in favour of high-regulation countries and increases their bargaining power in negotiations about the common standard. Thus it is indeed plausible that, by and large, the harmonization of product-related regulations should in fact have achieved the 'high level of protection' envisaged for 'health, safety, environmental protection and consumer protection' in Art. 100A (3) (Eichener 1993).

For process-oriented regulations, however, the institutional framework and the interest constellations are very different. Such regulations do not affect the useability, the safety or quality of products so produced. Steel from furnaces with high sulphur dioxide emissions is indistinguishable from steel produced with the most expensive emission controls – and the same is true for automobiles produced by workers with or without paid sick leave in firms with or without codetermination. As a consequence, there is no way in which Art. 36, or any of the other escape clauses contained in the Treaties, could justify excluding, or taxing, or in other ways discriminating against, products produced under conditions differing from those prevailing in the importing state.

Just as in the American child-labour example, the obvious implication is that, in the absence of common European regulation, all member states would find themselves in a Prisoner's Dilemma constellation, in which all would be tempted to reduce process-related regulations, and to cut back on the welfare state, in order to improve their competitive position. By itself, of course, that would facilitate, rather than impede, the adoption of common European standards. The Prisoner's Dilemma loses its pernicious character if binding agreements are possible, and since this is assured in the European Community, European re-regulation at the level desired by member states should be entirely possible. Yet it is here that the difficulties begin.

There are, first, the differences among national styles of regulation that Adrienne Héritier and her collaborators (1994) discovered in the field of air-quality regulations. As was suggested above, this would constitute a Battle of the Sexes game superimposed on the Prisoner's Dilemma,[28] which, by itself, would not rule out agreement. Greater difficulties arise from manifest ideological differences. Some governments may not share 'social-democratic' or 'green' preferences for high levels of regulation, and may actually welcome external competitive pressures to achieve deregulation which they could not otherwise push through at home. But since these difficulties may change from one election to the next, they will not be further investigated here. What is unlikely to change from one election to another are conflicts of interest arising from different levels of economic development.[29]

After its Southern expansion, the European Community now includes member states with some of the most efficient economies in the world alongside others that have barely risen above the level of threshold economies. This contrast manifests itself in large differences in (average)[30] factor productivity. Thus, if the economically less developed countries are to remain competitive in the European internal market, their factor costs – in particular their wage costs, non-wage labour costs and environmental costs – have to be correspondingly lower as well. And in fact, industrial labour costs in Portugal and Greece are, respectively, one sixth and one quarter of those in Germany,[31] and differences in the levels of social-security systems (Ganslandt 1993; Sieber 1993) and in environmental costs (Fröhlich 1992) are of the same magnitude.

Now, if these costs were raised to the level of the most productive countries, by harmonizing social-welfare and environmental regulations, the international competitiveness of the economies with lower productivity would be destroyed. If exchange rates were allowed to fall accordingly, the result would be higher domestic prices and, hence, impoverished consumers.

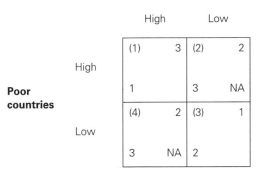

Figure 2.2 *Preference for high or low European-wide standards in process-related regulations. In case of non-agreement (NA), no common standard is adopted*

If exchange rates were maintained (e.g. in a monetary union), the result would be deindustrialization and massive job losses – just as they occurred in East Germany when the relatively backward GDR economy was subjected to the full range of West German regulations under a single currency. The more enterprises are subject to international price competition,[32] the less democratically accountable politicians in the economically less developed countries could agree to cost-increasing harmonization initiatives.[33] And this is even more true since – in contrast to the relation between East and West Germany – the rich EC countries would certainly not be willing (or even able) to compensate the victims of the industrial catastrophe through massive transfer payments.

Nor would agreement be easier if the costs of social or environmental regulations were not imposed on enterprises, but financed through higher income or consumption taxes. As long as average incomes in the poorest EC countries amount to less than one fifth of average incomes in the rich countries, the less developed EC countries must defend themselves against the European harmonization of environmental and welfare regulations at levels of protection which may perhaps reflect the aspirations and the willingness to pay of citizens in the rich member states, but which are beyond the means of economically less developed countries. Moreover, unlike East Germany in the process of German unification, these countries are fully aware of their own best interests, and the constitution of the European Union provides them with an effective veto. The resulting interest constellation is represented as a game matrix in Figure 2.2.

As an illustration, take the case of air-pollution control applied to industrial emissions. Highly industrialized and highly polluted rich countries are likely to have a clear preference for European-wide standards at high levels of protection (Figure 2.2, cell 1), which would also protect their own industries against 'ecological dumping', and they would least like to have

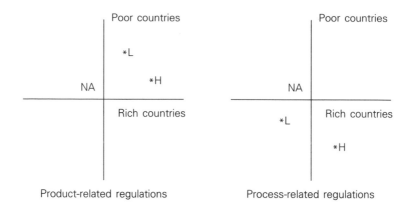

Figure 2.3 *Negotiated agreement on high (H) and low (L) European standards as compared to non-agreement (NA) in the case of product-related and process-related regulations*

common (and binding) standards at low levels of protection (cell 3). For the poor countries, by contrast, high standards (cell 1) would amount to the destruction of less productive branches of industry. But even common rules imposing uniformly low standards (cell 3) would be unattractive, since the less productive, indigenous enterprises would then be exposed to the sharper competition of deregulated competitors from countries with high productivity. So, for them, the best outcome would be non-agreement (cells 2 and 4), which would also be the second-best outcome for the rich countries. As a consequence, the status quo is likely to continue.[34]

The differences between negotiations over product- and process-related regulations may become even clearer if the options are represented in the form of two-dimensional negotiation diagrams in which the horizontal and vertical dimensions represent utilities associated with particular outcomes for rich and poor countries, respectively (Figure 2.3). Points H and L represent the location of binding agreements on high standards and low standards, respectively. However, since the origin (NA) is chosen to represent the best outcome that each country could achieve if no agreement on European standards is reached (so that national standards will continue to apply), the negotiation space is effectively limited to the 'north-eastern' quadrant above and to the right of the origin.

In the case of product-related regulations, rich countries would prefer agreement on high standards (H), while poor countries would prefer agreement on low standards (L). But both groups of countries would prefer either solution to the outcome associated with non-agreement (NA). Hence both solutions are located within the negotiation space, and agreement on one of them, or on a compromise rule located between H and L, ought to be possible in principle. Of course, under the unanimity rule, bargaining over relative advantage might still drag on, and under unfavourable conditions, negotiations might even fail. Thus it appears completely rational that governments, in the Single European Act, finally agreed to move toward qualified-majority voting specifically for the harmonization of product-related regulations (Art. 100A). It permits them to avoid deadlocks and speed up negotiations in constellations where they generally prefer agreement to disagreement.

The situation is different in the case of process-related regulations. Here there is no solution in the upper-right-hand quadrant that would be preferred to the status quo by both rich and poor countries. From the point of view of the poor countries, even the adoption of common European standards at a low level of protection would be worse than the status quo. The rich countries, on the other hand, would prefer to improve their situation by introducing European-wide high-level standards, but this solution could not be imposed against the resistance of poor countries.[35]

To summarize, positive integration at the European level has achieved remarkable progress in the harmonization of product-related regulations, but the harmonization of process-related environmental and welfare regulations is proving much more difficult, while negative integration is effectively restricting national capacities for dealing with the problems generated by the integration of markets for capital, goods and services. If that state of affairs is considered unsatisfactory, one may logically seek for solutions in two directions – either by increasing the capacity for problem-solving at the European level, or by protecting national capacities for effective action even under the conditions of transnationally integrated markets.

Solutions I: increasing European problem-solving capacity?

In the face of pervasive conflict of interest, problem-solving on the European level might be facilitated either through institutional reforms that would increase the capacity for conflict resolution, or through the search for substantive or procedural strategies that are able to reduce conflict to more manageable levels.

Majoritarian solutions?

Obviously, the capacity for conflict resolution would be most directly strengthened if the Union would continue the move toward majority voting in the Council of Ministers that began with the Single European Act, and gained more ground in the Maastricht Treaty. If decisions generally could be reached by simple majority, the high-productivity countries could, at least for the time being and provided that they are able to agree among themselves, impose high standards on the rest of the Community. But, of course, constitutional changes in the European Union continue to depend on unanimous agreement, and the fact that the Northern enlargement of the Union nearly foundered on the voting issue shows that the presumptive losers are unlikely to agree to a regime in which they might be consistently outvoted. In this regard, the 'joint decision trap' (Scharpf 1988) is still in good repair.

Moreover, if it were possible to move further toward majority voting in the Council of Ministers, the debate about the 'democratic deficit' in the European Union would resume with a vengeance. As long as the democratic legitimacy of European governance must rest primarily on the agreement of democratically accountable national governments, the citizens of countries whose governments are outvoted have no reason to consider such decisions as having democratic legitimation.[36] In fact, even the cautious expansions of qualified-majority voting in the Single European Act and in the Maastricht Treaty have triggered judicial responses and public debates in the member states which are so critical of the legitimacy of majority decisions in the Council that any further progress will need to be based on more solid foundations of legitimation (Groeben 1992; Weidenfeld 1995).[37]

Many of the critics still assume that the most appropriate solution was defined by the Spinelli draft constitution, which would have transformed the European Community into a federal state with a bicameral legislature, consisting of the directly elected European Parliament as the first chamber with full legislative and budgetary powers, and the Council as a second chamber representing member state interests in the fashion of the German *Bundesrat*. The Commission would then take the place of a European government, elected by and accountable to the European Parliament (Williams 1991; Featherstone 1994). What stands in the way is, of course, the institutional egotism of member state governments that are unwilling to relinquish their own control over European policy-making. But that is not all. Proposals of this type also rest on weak foundations in democratic theory.

Democratic legitimacy is, after all, not merely a question of the formal competencies of a parliament. Representation and majority rule will assure legitimacy only in the context of (a) the pre-existing collective identity of a body politic, which may justify the imposition of sacrifices on some members of the community in the interest of the whole; (b) the possibility[38] of public discourse over which sacrifices are in fact to be imposed for which purposes and on whom; and (c) the political accountability of leaders who are visible to the public and are able to exercise effective power.

In the history of democratic governance, these preconditions have so far not yet been satisfied anywhere above the level of the nation-state (Calhoun 1993; Dahl 1994). They are not now satisfied in the European Union, and it is certainly not clear that they could be created in the foreseeable future (Grimm 1992; Kielmansegg 1992; Scharpf 1992a, 1993). As of now, in any case, the political–cultural identity of the European Union is still very weak (Wilson and Smith 1993); the lack of a common language is a major obstacle to the emergence of a European-wide public discourse (Gerhards 1993); and, as a consequence, we have no European-wide media, no European-wide political parties and no political leaders with European-wide visibility and accountability. These conditions are not easily changed by constitutional reforms,[39] and as long as they prevail, majority votes in the European Parliament will not do much for the acceptance of decisions in countries or groups whose interests are being sacrificed.

For the time being, at any rate, it is, then, unlikely that institutional reforms could greatly increase the capacity for conflict resolution on the European level. Thus Weiler's (1981) diagnosis, cited at the beginning of this chapter, will continue to hold: in contrast to the legal processes defining and enforcing the supranational law of negative integration, the political processes required for positive integration will retain their inter-governmental character and will be easily blocked when national interests diverge. If that is so, however, it seems worthwhile also to explore the possibility that conflict-minimizing European strategies might nevertheless be able to deal effectively with problems that can no longer be handled at the national level.

Conflict-avoiding solutions?

There are in fact a whole range of such strategies (Scharpf 1994). One has already been mentioned above. In the harmonization of product-related standards, agreement is facilitated by restricting Council involvement to the formulation of 'principles', and by leaving details to be worked out in corporatist standardization bodies. Moreover, in process-related environmental regulations, Art. 130T now generally allows any member state to maintain or introduce more stringent protective measures, provided that they 'must be compatible with this Treaty' (i.e. with negative integration). Thus, one way to overcome the blockage described above would be to agree on minimum levels of protection that are just barely acceptable to the poor member states, while the economically more advanced countries remain free to maintain the higher standards which they consider necessary.

But how could this be considered an effective solution? For countries that had very low standards to begin with, it is true, the common standard might well require substantial improvements. But high-standard countries would still find themselves in the Prisoner's-Dilemma-like 'competition among regulatory systems' that had prevented the American states during the first third of this century from adopting child-labour regulations.

For this problem, a partial solution was provided by the Commission's switch from German-type emissions standards to the air-quality standards favoured by the British government (Héritier et al. 1994). Since, on the whole (except for metropolises like Athens), air pollution is more of a problem in the highly industrialized regions of the Community, the seemingly uniform standard will generally require the economically more advanced countries to adopt more stringent anti-pollution measures than are needed in the less developed countries. Thus, the differential impact of air-quality regulation will not only facilitate the agreement of poor countries to higher standards, but it will also protect high-regulation countries against the temptations of competitive deregulation.

But, of course, the lucky accident by which the intensity of the pollution problem varies directly with the ability and willingness of countries to pay for solutions cannot always be relied upon. It would not have worked, for instance, in the paradigmatic case of child-labour regulations. Nevertheless, there may be a generally useful lesson to be learned from air-quality regulations: it is not necessarily true that European harmonization, in order to be useful, must have the same impact on all member states or regions of the community.

Regulation at two levels?

More specifically, I am suggesting that the obstacles to agreement on process-related regulations might be considerably reduced by a variant of the idea of a 'Europe with variable geometry', which, as far as I know, is not being considered in present discussions of institutional reform of the Community.[40] This suggestion is based on the assumption that the Prisoner's Dilemma game that European countries are forced to play against each other, in the presence of negative integration and in the absence of European-wide harmonization, is not played with equal intensity among all member states. The competition among regulatory systems is likely to be most acute between countries that are in direct economic competition because they produce the same type of goods at similar levels of productivity and of production costs. By contrast, countries producing at very different levels of productivity and production costs are generally not directly competing against each other in the same markets. If this is true, the failure of adopting a single European-wide standard would imply that at least two separate Prisoner's Dilemma games are being played, one among the economically most efficient countries that are able to compete on productivity, and the other one among the less efficient economies that must compete on factor costs.

On this analysis, the solution seems obvious: in order to stop the pressure toward competitive deregulation,[41] there is clearly a need for the harmonization of process-related regulations at the European level – but there is no need for a single, uniform standard. Instead, what would be needed is an explicit agreement on two standards offering different levels of protection at different levels of cost. The rich countries could then commit themselves to the high-standard regulations that are in keeping with their own levels of environmental and social aspirations, while the less developed countries could establish common standards at a lower level that would still protect them against the dangers of ruinous competition among themselves. In the course of their economic development, the lower standard could of course be raised, step by step, and brought into line with the higher one.

Compared to the difficulties of reaching agreement between rich and poor countries on European-wide uniform standards, negotiations on double standards should be much easier (Figure 2.4). Moreover, in contrast to other proposals for a two-speed Europe, the club of high-regulation countries

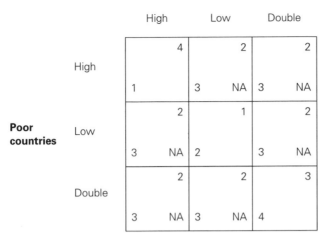

Figure 2.4 *Process-related regulations with the option of a double standard*
NA = outcome in the case of non-agreement

would have no interest at all in excluding applicants who think that their country is able to conform to the more demanding standards. The most difficult choice would have to be faced by countries 'in the middle', like Britain or Italy, who would need to decide whether they dare to compete on productivity or must compete on cost.

But what if institutions matter?

So far we have looked only at the negotiations between rich and poor countries, and we have assumed that within each of these groups agreement should be relatively unproblematic – provided that national differences in the styles of regulation are not of very high salience. But what has been said applies fully only to the harmonization of process-related environmental regulations. In the case of industrial-relations and social-welfare regulations, by contrast, even harmonization at two levels would run into enormous difficulties because of the much greater salience of qualitative and institutional differences. Thus, while it may be assumed that all countries would prefer a less polluted environment if they could afford it, that assumption of common aspirations cannot be made in the industrial-relations and welfare fields (Esping-Andersen 1990).

Sweden and Switzerland, for example, are economically among the most highly developed countries in the world, and yet they differ greatly in the share of GDP which they devote to publicly provided welfare transfers and services. And while Germany and Britain have similar levels of union density, they have different structures of union organization and radically different collective bargaining systems. Even more important is the fact

Governance in the European Union

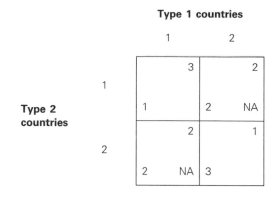

Figure 2.5   *Harmonization of welfare and industrial-relations regulations among countries of a similar level of economic development, but with different types of institutions NA = non-agreement*

that German industrial relations are embedded in highly developed, and judicially enforced, systems of labour law, collective-bargaining law and codetermination law, while British labour relations have, from the beginning of this century, developed under the maxim of 'free collective bargaining' and on the understanding that the law of the state should not interfere with the interactions between capital and labour. Thus, it may be true that, quite apart from any cost considerations or possible side-payments, any kind of legal regulation of industrial relations at the European level would be unacceptable not only to employers but also to unions in Britain. By contrast, unions in Germany, or in Austria and France for that matter, have come to rely precisely on the legal effectiveness and judicial enforceability of state regulations (Crouch 1993). And, of course, these institutional differences are defended by politically powerful organized interests which no government could lightly disregard.

In the fields of social welfare and industrial relations, therefore, the constellation of interests even among countries at high levels of economic development cannot be interpreted as the relatively benign Battle of the Sexes game which we postulated in the field of environmental regulations. Instead, if we assume that the high-regulation group of countries includes two qualitatively different types of institutional arrangements, we would have a game constellation in which both sides might prefer non-agreement over agreeing to a harmonized system of different characteristics (Figure 2.5).

Potentially quite similar constellations of interest are likely to exist in all areas where institutional differences between member states are of high political salience – either because powerful interest groups will defend the institutional status quo, or because the traditional institutional structure has become an element of social and political identities. This is most obviously true of political and administrative institutions themselves, but it is also true of the institutional structures in a great many other sectors which, in all countries, have been protected, in one form or another, against the operation of market forces by the territorial state. Traditionally, at least in Western Europe, these 'sectors close to the state' (Mayntz and Scharpf 1995) would have included education and basic research, health care, radio and television, telecommunications, transportation, energy and water supply, waste disposal, financial services, agriculture, and several others.

This is a heterogeneous set, in which the justifications for state involvement vary as widely as the modalities – from the direct provision of services and infrastructure facilities by tax-financed state agencies through customer-financed public or highly regulated private monopolies, and state-supported forms of professional self-regulation, all the way to the state-subsidized private provision of marketable goods and services. What is common to all of them is some form of insulation against unlimited market competition. And what matters here is that the attenuation of market pressures combined with the variety of possible forms of state intervention have generally facilitated the evolution of remarkably different institutional arrangements governing the provision of identical goods and services in the member states of the European Union (see, e.g., Alber and Bernardi-Schenkluhn 1992).

From the point of view of the European Community, practically all these institutional arrangements could be considered as non-wage barriers and, certainly, as distortions of competition. So the logic of negative integration implies that they should be removed – as is currently happening in telecommunications, in air transportation and in financial services. On the other hand, not all of these restrictive and protective institutional arrangements may be without valid justification, so that – under the logic of Arts 36 and 100A, or of Art. 76 for that matter, the European harmonization of these sectoral regimes might seem a more appropriate response.

But, then, how could the Council reach agreement on a common European system of financing and delivering health care that would replace the British, Italian and Swedish varieties of national health service systems as well as the French, German and Austrian varieties of systems combining compulsory health insurance and private health care provision with corporatist negotiations between insurance systems and organized providers? Here the obstacles to harmonization would be at least as great as they are in the field of old-age pensions, where the move from the German pay-as-you-go insurance system to a (perhaps more desirable) common system based on the British two-tier model combining tax-financed basic pensions and (voluntary or compulsory) supplementary private insurance is practically impossible, since the now active generation would be required to pay twice – once for the present generation of pensioners under the old system, and once for their own life insurance under the new system.

A particularly instructive example is provided by the comparison of the telecommunications and energy sectors, which appear rather similar in most economic respects (Schmidt 1995). In both sectors, monopolistic structures had prevailed unchallenged until the mid-1980s, and in both the Commission has been working toward liberalization since then. But while in telecommunications the combination of European liberalization, national deregulation and privatization, and cautious re-regulation at the European level, did succeed with remarkable speed (Sauter 1995), the Commission's repeated attempts to liberalize the European electricity market have so far failed in the Council. As Susanne Schmidt (1995) has shown in her comparative study, one of the two important factors explaining the different trajectories of liberalization is institutional differences.[42] Whereas in telecommunications, institutional structures in all Western European countries had, by the 1970s, converged on a single model of public PTT monopolies which were the owners of the physical networks as well as the suppliers of all services and terminal equipment (Schneider 1995), the electricity sector is characterized by considerable institutional heterogeneity. While there are network monopolies everywhere, these may be nationwide, regional or local; they may be owned by the state, or by private investors; they may be restricted to the generation and distribution of electricity, or they may also distribute gas and other forms of energy. Moreover, there are also considerable differences in the regulatory regimes under which these monopolies operate, and in the basic logic of their pricing structures; and there are, of course, also fundamental differences in the way in which the conflict over nuclear energy is handled in each of the member states. As a consequence, liberalization would affect suppliers in different countries in rather different ways, while the call for 'harmonization before liberalization' would confront national governments with the even more unpalatable task of challenging vested institutional interests head on.

The short of it is that there are in fact important sectors for which the European-wide harmonization of national regulatory and institutional systems may not be a feasible option. The question there is whether negative integration should nevertheless be allowed to run its course in all sectors in which existing institutional structures can be interpreted as restraints on trade or distortions of competition. If so, existing balances of values and interests incorporated in specific national institutions will be upset. In some sectors, these costs have been considered politically acceptable – but there is no reason to assume that this will be the case everywhere.[43] Where it is not, negative integration will either be forcefully resisted or its consequence may well be social disintegration and political delegitimation of the kind that was caused in East Germany by the destruction of indigenous institutions.

Solutions II: restoring national boundary control?

It seems useful, therefore, also to think about ways in which limits can be set to the unreflected and quasi-automatic advance of negative integration, motivated purely by considerations of economic efficiency, in the European

Community. That is, of course, not much of a problem in areas where liberalization must in fact be achieved through decisions of the Council of Ministers. Governments that are seriously concerned about maintaining existing institutional structures are still quite capable of blocking Commission initiatives – as was demonstrated again in 1995 in the failure of attempts to liberalize the European markets for electricity. Governments have no formal power, however, to prevent the Commission from proceeding against nationally privileged 'undertakings' by way of directives under Art. 90 (3) of the Treaty,[44] and they have even less control over the Commission's use of its power to issue 'decisions' against individual governments under the same article, or to initiate infringement procedures before the Court under Art. 169.[45] Moreover, given the direct effect of primary European law, any individual or corporation could challenge existing national institutional arrangements before a national court, which could then obtain a preliminary ruling from the European Court of Justice under Art. 177.

Thus, political controls will not generally work – or, more precisely, they work in a highly asymmetrical fashion. As long as the Council must proceed through qualified-majority or even unanimous decisions, a small minority will be able to block positive action, but very large majorities would have to be mobilized to correct any extension of negative integration through decisions of the Commission[46] or of the Court of Justice.[47] The question, then, is whether it may be possible to use legal instruments to limit the capacity of the Commission and the Court to extend negative integration beyond the limits of what the Council would also find politically acceptable.

In Maastricht, it is true, governments took care to exclude the Court from the areas of 'a common foreign policy and security policy' and of 'cooperation in the fields of justice and home affairs' (Art. L). This is, surely, an indication that the Court's power to convert Treaty obligations into supranational law, and to interpret their meaning beyond the original intent of the contracting parties, has finally become a matter of concern to member states. It is also possible that similar concerns about the Court's role may have contributed to the inclusion of a 'subsidiarity clause' in Art. 3B (2) of the EC Treaty. If they did, however, that purpose is unlikely to be achieved through the clause itself (as distinguished from the change in the political climate which it symbolizes).

By restricting subsidiarity to 'areas which do not fall within [the Community's] exclusive competence', negative integration – which, if it is to be practised at all, must of course be an exclusive European competency – is left untouched – and, as I have argued, it is negative integration where Commission and Court are able to exercise their greatest, and for national autonomy most damaging, power. Moreover, even with regard to positive integration the subsidiarity clause is unlikely to have much legal effect (Dehousse 1993). Given the heterogeneity of conditions and capacities among the member states, it is hardly conceivable that a court could strike down any European measure that was in fact supported by a qualified

majority in the Council of Ministers by denying that 'the objectives of the
proposed action cannot be sufficiently achieved by the Member States'.
Thus, it is probably more realistic to see the clause primarily as a political
appeal for self-restraint directed at the Council of Ministers itself.[48]

What might make a legal difference, for negative as well as for positive
integration, is indicated by the very decision which advanced negative
integration by a giant step. In *Cassis de Dijon* (120/78 ECR, 1979, 649), the
Court did not hold, as is sometimes assumed, that the 'mutual recognition'
of products licensed by other member states was an unconditional obligation of member states. Before Germany was ordered to admit the French
liqueur, the Court had examined the claim that the German requirement of
a higher alcohol content was justified as a health regulation, and found it
totally spurious (Alter and Meunier-Aitsahalia 1994: 538–539). If that had
not been so, the import restriction would have been upheld under Art. 36
of the Treaty, which as was noted above, permits quantitative restrictions
'justified on grounds of public morality, public policy or public security; the
protection of health and life of humans, animals or plants', provided that
such measures 'do not constitute a means of arbitrary discrimination or a
disguised restriction on trade between Member States'.

Thus, the Treaty itself recognizes certain national policy goals that are
able to override the dictates of market integration. Admittedly, the Commission, and the European Court of Justice even more so, have done their
best to ensure the priority of negative integration by applying extremely
tough tests before finding that a national regulation is neither discrimina-
tory nor a disguised restriction on trade. In fact, the Commission has
followed a consistent line, according to which product-related national
regulations either will be struck down, under *Cassis*, because they serve no
valid purpose, or must be replaced by harmonized European regulations
under Art. 100A (Alter and Meunier-Aitsahalia 1994). What matters here,
however, is the reverse implication: national regulations restricting imports
that serve one of the valid purposes listed in Art. 36 must be allowed to
stand unless, and until, European harmonization is achieved.

For product-related regulations, therefore, negative integration does not
take precedence over positive integration, and the competency gap mentioned in the introduction is in fact avoided. However, that is not true of
process-related regulations, which, since they do not affect the quality or
safety of the products themselves, would never justify exclusion under Art.
36. Moreover, such regulations must also not violate the rules of European
competition law (Arts. 85ff), they must not insulate public service agencies
against competition (Art. 90), and they must not amount to competition-
distorting state aid (Art. 92).

What is important here is that these prohibitions apply regardless of
whether prior policy harmonization at the European level has been
achieved or not. One example is provided by European transport policy,
which, along with agriculture, was one of the two fields in which the
original Treaty had envisaged a fully Europeanized policy regime (Arts

74ff). Since, in the face of massive conflicts of interest among the member states, the Council had failed to act for more than twenty-five years, it was ordered by the Court (in a proceeding initiated by the European Parliament under Art. 175) to establish at least the conditions of negative integration according to Art. 75 (1) lit. (a) and (b). Moreover, the Commission and the Court have intervened against national regulations (such as the German levy on road haulage) that could be interpreted as a discrimination of non-national carriers (Art. 76). Against the original intent of the contracting parties, therefore, the European transport market is now being actively liberalized, even though agreement on a common European regulatory regime is still not in sight.

If this state of affairs is considered unsatisfactory, one may need to go further in the direction indicated by provisions like those contained in Arts 36, 48 (3), 56 (1), 66 and 100A (4) which allow restraints on the free movement of goods, persons and services if these restraints serve one of the 'police-power' purposes of public morality, public policy, public security, public health, etc. In practice, however, none of these exceptions is still of great importance, since the Commission, and even more so the Court, have interpreted them in extremely restrictive fashion – and the same has been true of other provisions, serving similar purposes, such as the partial exemption of infrastructural or revenue-producing national undertakings from the competition rules in Art. 90 (2) or the reservation regarding national systems of property ownership in Art. 222. In all these instances, the *de facto* priority of negative integration over national policy preferences and institutional traditions has been re-established through judicial interpretation.

It remains to be seen whether the same fate is also waiting for some of the even more explicit reservation clauses introduced by the Maastricht Treaty, as for instance in Art. 126 (1), which permits the Community only a very limited entry into the education field, 'while fully respecting the responsibility of the Member States for the content of teaching and the organization of education systems and their cultural and linguistic diversity'. By its language at least, the clause will only set limits to the narrowly circumscribed educational competencies of the Community, but would not otherwise offer immunity against charges that national education systems might represent restraints on trade and distortions of competition in the market for educational services.

If national policy preferences and institutional traditions should have a chance to survive, it seems that more powerful legal constraints are needed to stop the imperialism of negative integration. A radical solution would be to abolish the constitutional status of European competition law by taking it out of the Treaty altogether, leaving the determination of its scope to the political processes of 'secondary' legislation by Council and Parliament. This would, at the European level, create a constitutional balance among competing policy purposes as it exists in all national policy systems. In addition, it might be explicitly stated that national legislation will remain in force unless, and until, it is shown to be in concrete conflict with a specific provision of European legislation. This is the law as it has stood in the United States since the demise of the 'negative commerce clause doctrine' in 1937 (Schwartz 1957; Rehbinder and Stewart 1984), and this is the *de facto* state of European law with regard to product-related regulations in the market for goods. It could and should be extended to the markets for services, and in particular to transportation and financial services.

These would be changes which, unlike the subsidiarity clause, would really make a difference, and the Intergovernmental Conference in preparation for 'Maastricht II' would have an opportunity to promote them. In addition, it might be worthwhile specifically to enumerate, in the Treaty itself, policy areas for which member states will retain primary responsibility. The most plausible candidates would be the areas discussed above – namely education, culture, the media, social welfare, health care and industrial relations – and, of course, political and administrative organization.

As I have argued elsewhere, this would give the constitution of the Community a bi-polar character, similar to the 'dual federalism' which the American Supreme Court had read into the US Constitution before 1937, or to the case law of the German Constitutional Court protecting the *'Kulturhoheit'* of the *Länder* in the fields of education and the media (Scharpf 1991b, 1994; Weidenfeld 1995). There is, of course, no hope that a clear demarcation line between European and national areas of policy responsibility could be defined. But the explicit dualism would force the Court and the Commission to balance the claims for the economic perfection of market integration against equally legitimate claims for the maintenance of national institutional autonomy and problem-solving capacity in the light of the concrete circumstances of the specific case. Instead of deciding against national regulations whenever the slightest distortion of competition can be identified, the Court would then have to weigh the degree of restriction of competition or mobility, on the one hand, against the importance of the measure for the realization of legitimate member state goals, on the other. What is required, in other words, is the 'management of interdependence' (Dehousse 1993; Joerges 1994a) in ways which should deal, in the 'vertical' relationship between national and European competencies, with exactly the same tensions between economic and non-economic purposes which, in the nation-state, are accommodated in the 'horizontal' dimension, through interdepartmental conflicts that must be settled in the Cabinet or in Parliament.

But what difference would it make if such constitutional changes could be adopted, and, if adopted, if they would have the desired impact on the judicial interpretation of negative integration? The European Community, after all, must remain committed to the creation of a common market, and so it also must retain legal instruments to defend the free access to national markets against the economic protectionism of its member states. Thus, prohibitions against quantitative restrictions on trade and against the discrimination of foreign suppliers would certainly need to remain in place.

What could change is the degree of perfectionism with which they are being defined and their, as it were, 'lexicographic' precedence over all competing considerations. Even more important: constitutional changes of the type discussed here would protect, or re-establish, the power of national governments to take certain sectors out of the market altogether, or to organize them in ways that restrict the operation of market forces. If that should imply a loss of economic efficiency, it should not be the business of the Community to prevent member states from paying this price.

Social regulation in one country?

But even if the legal straitjacket of negative integration should be loosened, and if some sectors should be allowed to remain under the more intense control of the territorial state, that would not generally reverse the fundamental changes in the political economy of capitalist welfare states that have occurred since the end of the postwar period. The larger part of the national economy is exposed to transnational competition, capital has become globally mobile and enterprises are able to relocate production throughout Western Europe without risking their access to national markets. And as the mobility of economic factors has increased, so the national capacity to reduce the rate of return on capital investments below the international level, either by lowering interest rates or by imposing additional costs on firms, has been irrevocably lost (Sinn 1993). In that sense, there is certainly no path that would lead back to the postwar 'golden age' of capitalist welfare states.

From the point of view of political democracy, it would be dangerous to deny the existence of these economic constraints; but it would be equally dangerous to exaggerate their significance. It is true that the capacity for Keynesian macro-economic management is no longer available at the national level, and not yet available supranationally. It is also true that the rate of return from productive investment, which capital owners can exact, has increased considerably. Any attempt, by governments or unions, to reverse these losses by redistributive programmes pursued in a national context would be bound to fail.

Beyond that, however, the basic character of the relationship between capitalist economies and democratic states is still the same. As I pointed out above, even in the postwar period, social regulation of the capitalist economy was successful only because costs of regulation that were, in the first round, imposed on firms could, in the second round, be passed on to consumers. As a consequence, returns on investment remained positive, and capitalism remained equally viable in the Swedish welfare state, in the German social market economy or in the American free enterprise system. In other words, the postwar symbiosis of capitalism and democracy could only be successful because ultimately the costs of the welfare state were borne by workers and consumers, rather than by capital owners.

If this 'impossibility theorem of redistribution' is accepted, the loss of national regulatory capacity reduces itself to the relatively technical question of where the costs of (new)[49] regulation should be placed in the first round. If they are placed on firms that are exposed to international competition, and if all other conditions remain the same, there will now be a loss of international competitiveness, and a concomitant fall in profits, investment and employment. But, of course, other conditions need not remain the same. The rise in the costs of regulation could be compensated through wage concessions, through a rise in productivity or, as long as European Monetary Union does not yet exist, through devaluation. In effect, these compensatory measures would, again, shift the costs on to workers and domestic consumers.

However, the same result could be achieved more directly and with much greater certainty if, even in the first round, costs were not imposed on firms at all. If new social regulations, such as the German disability-care insurance, were financed through taxes on incomes and consumption, rather than through payroll taxes, enterprises would stay competitive and investments profitable. One example is provided by Denmark, where 85 per cent of social costs are financed from general tax revenues. Since the international competitiveness of Danish enterprises is not affected, the (very costly) welfare state apparently does not play any role in current discussions about the international competitiveness of the Danish economy (Münster 1993).[50] Of course, consumable incomes will be reduced, but this is as it would, and should, be in any case.

I do not wish to claim, however, that all objectives of social regulation in the postwar decades could also be obtained in the future without endangering international competitiveness. Even less would I suggest that the growing tax resistance of voters would be easy to overcome.[51] Compared to the postwar decades, the range of choices available to democratic political processes at the national level has certainly become more narrow. But it is not as narrow as the economic determinism of many contributions to the current debate would seem to suggest. Moreover, it can be widened to the extent that countries and regions succeed in developing the comparative advantages of their given institutional and industrial structures in order to exploit their own niches in increasingly specialized world markets. The precondition, of course, is a high degree of policy flexibility, and a capacity to respond to specific locational conditions and changing market opportunities, at all levels of policy-making, European, national and subnational – as well as in management and industrial relations.

Thus, the European economy may indeed need the larger market, and hence common rules, in order to be able to keep up with American and Japanese competitors in branches of production in which economies of scale make a significant difference. But Europe will certainly fall behind if negative integration paralyses national and subnational problem-solving, while on the European level only unsatisfactory compromises can be reached after long and difficult negotiations.

To succeed in the global economy, Europe depends on more effective European policy-making with better democratic legitimation. But it depends equally on the autonomous problem-solving capacities of national and subnational polities. While the debate about subsidiarity may help to limit the perfectionism and the rigidities of positive integration, we also need a debate about the need to limit the perfectionism of negative integration. Only if we succeed in both will we be able to combine the economic efficiency of the larger market with the problem-solving capacities of political action on the European level and of democratic politics on the national and subnational levels.

3

Competencies, Cracks and Conflicts: Regional Mobilization in the European Union

Gary Marks, François Nielsen, Leonard Ray and Jane Salk

The 1990s have seen the growth of a new and unheralded form of regional mobilization in the European Union.[52] At the time of writing, fifty-four regional and local governments representing roughly three-sevenths of the population of the European Union have established offices in Brussels. Although they have no legal or formal place in the Union, the largest and best funded of these offices combine several functions. They provide the Commission and Parliament with regional viewpoints on all issues that concern them; they survey the European scene for upcoming issues to be brought to the attention of policy-makers in their home governments; they participate in dense networks with other regional offices and EU organizations of every type; and they lobby for a greater voice in EU decision-making. These offices exist in the shadows of the EU, sometimes in ignorance of the existence of similar efforts on the part of other regions from their own country. But their numbers and their staff and resources have grown rapidly. The first regional offices, from Saarland and Hamburg, were set up in 1985. By 1988 there were fifteen such offices. Five years later their number had more than tripled. On average the regional offices that are currently established in Brussels are barely five years old (Hooghe and Marks forthcoming; Salk et al. 1995).[53]

The growth in regional representation in Brussels is already grist to the mill of a debate between those who theorize an emergent European polity characterized by strong regional organizations, regional identities and regional governments within a multi-level polity and those who argue that member states will succeed in projecting their domination of the process of institutional creation into the future (Anderson 1991; Marks 1992, 1993; Caporaso and Keeler 1993; Moravcsik 1993; Constantelos 1994; Hooghe and Keating 1994; Keating and Jones 1995; Pierson 1995; Hooghe 1996). Here we are concerned with some basic empirical questions that feed into this debate. Why have subnational governments been drawn to Brussels? Which subnational governments are represented and which not? How can we explain the emerging pattern of regional representation? These are obvious questions, yet we have had little systematic information to bring to bear on them, largely because the phenomenon is so new and dynamic. Our aim is to provide answers to these questions using information from a census and survey of regional offices undertaken by the authors.

What do theories of the European Union have to say?

The mobilization of subnational governments in Brussels is a phenomenon that, by most accounts, should not be taking place. For the past two decades the state-centric approach has informed our understanding of the European Union.[54] State centrists view the European Union as a set of institutions to facilitate collective action among national states, and have little to say about the emergence of regional representation at the European level.[55] According to the state-centric perspective, states remain the commanding political actors on account of their control of the European Council, an intergovernmental meeting of heads of state which sets general priorities, and the Council of Ministers, the most powerful body responsible for policy in the EU. Supranational institutions such as the European Commission, the European Court of Justice or the European Parliament are either agents of states or have only a symbolic role. When state centrists model the activities of domestic interests, they do so in the context of a two-level game (Garrett 1992; Moravcsik 1993). At the European level, member state executives bargain with each other about institutions and policy in the EU; within each member state domestic interests try to influence what happens in the EU indirectly by lobbying their respective government. If domestic interests wish to influence EU policy they must operate in their respective national arenas to pressure their respective member states to bargain their interests in intergovernmental negotiation at the European level.

A number of scholars have begun to formulate an alternative approach to the EU in response to the inability of the state-centric approach to recognize or explain the independent influence of supranational institutions and the mobilization of domestic actors directly in the European arena (Marks 1993; Christiansen 1994; Leibfried and Pierson 1995; Marks et al. forthcoming; Pierson 1995; Hooghe 1996). Instead of a bifurcated model of politics across two autonomous levels, these theorists conceptualize the EU as a single, multi-level polity.

The point of departure for this multi-level governance (MLG) approach is the existence of overlapping competencies among multiple levels of governments and the interaction of political actors across those levels. Member state executives, while powerful, are only one set among a variety of actors in the European polity. States are not an exclusive link between domestic politics and intergovernmental bargaining in the EU. Instead of the two level game assumptions adopted by state centrists, MLG theorists posit a set of overarching, multi-level policy networks. The structure of political control is variable, not constant, across policy areas. In some cases, as in the EU's structural policy, political influence over outcomes is dispersed among contending subnational, national and supranational actors (Marks 1996). MLG theorists argue that in a growing number of cases no one of these actors has exclusive competence over a particular policy. The presumption of multi-level governance is that these actors participate in diverse policy networks and this may involve subnational actors – interest groups and subnational governments – dealing directly with supranational actors.

However, MLG theorists have not framed clear expectations about the dynamics of this polity. If, as these theorists claim, competencies have slipped away from central states both up to the supranational level and down to the subnational level, then, *ceteris paribus*, one would expect greater interaction among actors at these levels. But the details remain murky, and, apart from a generalized presumption of increasing mobilization across levels, they provide no systematic set of expectations about which actors should mobilize and why.

Framing hypotheses

Here we conceptualize the sources of regional representation in Brussels along two theoretical tracks. The first focuses upon the resources that may lure subnational governments to Brussels or reduce the costs of setting up an office. This line of theorizing builds on the commonsensical notion that the decision to gain representation in a particular political arena is likely to reflect the relative economic costs and benefits of doing so. From this perspective, the likelihood of representation is a positive function of the amount of money that is potentially available in the targeted arena and a negative function of the costs of representation relative to subnational government income. A slightly more sophisticated version of a resource theory of subnational representation takes into account cultural as well as economic resources as a spur to representation. Representation may result from learning as well as instantaneous calculation, and actors with more associational experience may better recognize the benefits of representation in new arenas because they have access to better information or because they are more entrepreneurial.

A second line of theorizing focuses on the political relationships forged under multi-level governance to explain patterns of subnational representation in Brussels. To the extent that competencies are spun off from central states up to supranational institutions and down to subnational governments, so both sides may have common concerns that draw them into direct communication. Multi-level governance also involves conflicts among governments as well as shared competencies, and subnational governments may mobilize in Brussels in response to differences in interest or identity that may exist between the regions they represent and the states of which they are a part. As we explain below, such conflicts may generate demands for an autonomous voice at the European level and intensify the determination of distinctive subnational governments to exploit the multiplicity of cracks for potential influence in a fragmented multi-level polity.

In what follows we elaborate these two lines of theorizing into five discrete hypotheses and test them against the evidence of regional representation in Brussels based on a census carried out by the authors in November 1993. While little systematic attention has been devoted to subnational representation in Europe, the topic is an established one in the United States, and we draw extensively on this literature in framing our hypotheses.

Our first hypothesis is a *resource pull* hypothesis derived from public choice accounts of the interaction of government and interest groups (Mueller and Murrell 1986; Mitchell and Munger 1991; Lowery and Gray 1995). Government grows because distributional groups seek rents from the public. Conversely, groups are attracted to government because of its potential to redistribute wealth. According to this view, the decision to gain representation in a particular arena reflects the present value for a group of its efforts to gain some share of the wealth allocated there. A fully specified *resource pull* hypothesis would conceive the likelihood of representation as a function of the probability (p_r) that an actor will be able to influence the allocation of some pool of resources (r). However, we may assume that the unmeasurable component of this function, p_r, is roughly the same for all regional governments, so that *resource pull* will vary with EU spending available for subnational governments. The money available for subnational governments varies across well-defined subsets. The EU's structural policy, amounting to around ECU60 billion in the 1989 to 1993 period, was exclusively at the poorer regions of the EU. Hence, one would expect that governments representing these regions would have the greatest inducement to mobilize in Brussels.

A second hypothesis also stresses resources, but centres on a subnational government's capacity to undertake representation. Building on the central tenet of the resource mobilization perspective that availability of resources facilitates social movement activity (McCarthy and Zald 1977), we formulate a *resource push* hypothesis. The relevant resources in this case are the financial resources available to subnational governments, but the logic is the same: 'the aggregation of resources (money and labor) is crucial. . . . Because resources are necessary for engagement in social conflict, they must be aggregated for collective purposes' (McCarthy and Zald 1977: 1216). Here we hypothesize that the greater the financial resources of a subnational government, the greater the likelihood that it will be represented in Brussels.

Our third hypothesis is that regions having a stronger *associational culture* will be more likely to be represented at the European level. Scholars from Alexis de Tocqueville to Robert Putnam have argued that the character of political institutions is deeply influenced by the density of associational life in a society, and they locate the sources of this in the level of social trust, education, organized religion and a variety of other socio-cultural factors that lead individuals into closer social relations with their neighbours (Tocqueville, 1954; Putnam 1993, 1995). Regional representation in Brussels is the result of institutional decision-making rather than association of like-minded individuals, but it is not far-fetched to believe that where the art of association is strong, representation of public bodies within the polity will be enhanced. In a region with a strong associational culture, those in government may be more adept at finding and exploiting diverse opportunities for political influence. The skills and habits developed within a strong associational culture may spill over into public life, so that governments in such regions may be more willing and more able to create and sustain networks of public interaction, including an office in Brussels.

The hypotheses we have discussed above focus on the resources, both material and cultural, that can pull or push subnational governments into the European arena. However, the decision to open and maintain an office in Brussels is not simply a decision to extend representation to an additional arena, but a decision to do so independently of the central state. Regional representation in Brussels has, therefore, an expressly political logic having to do with the interaction, friction or even conflict that may arise between regional governments and central governments in a multi-level polity.

Our fourth hypothesis links the representation of a subnational government to the scope of its competencies. Our point of departure is the observation that, unlike collective associations of individuals, public institutions do not have to overcome the free-rider problem, i.e. the presence of actors who receive the benefits of collective effort without paying the costs. A subnational office in Brussels is, therefore, not a collective good provided to a constituency, but a way for a subnational government to extend its reach. Here we hypothesize that subnational governments that have significant political autonomy within their respective polities are more likely to mobilize in the EU because they are more affected by decisions that are made there. The general principle here is summarized by Robert Salisbury in a discussion of the sources of public interest representation in the United States: 'the very size and complexity of an institution renders it vulnerable to a much broader array of specific policy impacts, positive and negative, present and prospective' (1984: 69). Logically, it is the degree of overlap between the competencies exercised at the subnational and supranational levels that is decisive, but only the subnational part of this equation varies across our cases. We hypothesize that the larger the scope of political autonomy of a subnational government, the more it will seek information concerning policy developments in the European pipeline and the more it will wish to express its interests there. According to this logic, subnational governments are drawn to Brussels by a variable demand for *informational exchange*.

Our final hypothesis theorizes the implications of *regional distinctiveness* as a source of friction between regional and national governments and, hence, of subnational mobilization. Subnational and national governments are not simply differentiated layers of decision-making, but institutions of interest aggregation based on different constituencies with potentially conflicting interests and identities. One potential source of friction lies in the existence of multiple territorial identities, cultures and languages within a state, a condition that is the norm rather than the exception in the member states of the EU. Another source of friction lies in durable differences in party-political colouration across territory, which is also a common enough phenomenon across Europe.

The force of both sources of conflict between subnational and national governments is exacerbated by the power of central state executives in the Council of Ministers and in the treaty-making process. The legitimacy of state executive influence in the EU is based on the claim that state executives are the democratic expression of distinct territorial interests rooted in national identities (Taylor 1991). To the extent that regions are differentiated from the countries of which they are a part by strongly rooted identities or durable partisan preferences, we hypothesize that subnational governments will be spurred to create channels of communication and influence that are independent of the central state.

To the extent that a subnational government is in conflict with its respective central executive, so one might expect it to try to exploit other points of political access. The European system of multi-level governance, like the American, provides ample opportunities for what Morton Grodzins (1967) called 'the multiple crack', the strategic exploitation of multiple points of access. Grodzins used the term 'multiple crack' in two senses, both of which are appropriate to the EU. First, it refers to the existence of numerous points of access at different levels of government that result from the extraordinarily fragmented character of decision-making. State executives play a major role in the EU, and much lobbying is channelled through them, but the Commission and the European Parliament (and on occasion the European Court of Justice) are also worthy targets for subnational governments. Second, the term 'means a wallop, a smack at government in an attempt to influence policy' (Grodzins 1967: 134), and in such a fragmented polity interest groups could be expected to disperse their efforts according to rough criteria of efficiency and hit several points of access simultaneously.

Data

Units of analysis

Table 3.1 lists the subnational governments that had offices in Brussels by country and level of representation as of November 1993.[56] The data are compiled on the basis of lists of regional offices maintained by the Association of European Regions and the Council of the Brussels Region and a census conducted by the authors.

Table 3.1 *Regional offices in Brussels, November 1993*

| | Level of representation | | | |
	NUTS 1	NUTS 2	NUTS 3	Other
Belgium	Vlaams Gewest[1] Région Wallonne			
Germany	Baden-Württemberg Bayern Berlin Brandenburg Bremen Hessen Mecklenburg-Vorpommern Niedersachsen Nordrhein-Westfalen Rheinland-Pfalz Saarland Sachsen Sachsen-Anhalt Thüringen			Hanse[2]
Spain		Andalucia Cataluña Galicia Madrid[3] Extremadura Pais Vasco Comunidad Valenciana		

continued overleaf

France

Murcia
Canarias[4]

Nord Pas-De-Calais[5]
Alsace
Bretagne[6]
Côte d'Azur
Martinique
Pays de la Loire[6]
Picardie[7]
Rhône-Alpes

Bouches-du-Rhône
Manche Expansion[8]

Centre Atlantique[9]
Grand Est[10]
Grand Sud[11]

Italy

Lazio[12]

Mezzogiorno[13]

UK

North of England
Northern Ireland
Scotland
Wales
Yorkshire and Humberside

Cornwall and Devon
East Midlands
Essex[7]
Highlands and Islands

Table 3.1 (*Continued*)

	Level of representation			
	NUTS 1	NUTS 2	NUTS 3	Other
UK (*cont.*)		Kent Lancashire	Strathclyde Surrey	East of Scotland

1. At the time of writing Flanders has not selected a representative for this office.
2. The Hanse office represents Hamburg and Schleswig-Holstein.
3. Madrid is also a NUTS 1 and NUTS 3 region.
4. The Canary Islands is also a NUTS 1 region.
5. Nord Pas-De-Calais is also a NUTS 1 region.
6. Brittany and Pays de la Loire share an office.
7. Picardie and Essex share an office.
8. The Manche Expansion office represents Manche.
9. The Centre Atlantique office represents Poitou-Charente, Centre and Castille-Leon.
10. The Grand Est office represents Champagne-Ardenne, Bourgogne, Lorraine, Alsace and Franche-Comte.
11. The Grand Sud office represents Acquitaine, Mid-Pyrenees, Languedoc-Roussillon, Provence-Alpes-Côtes d'Azur and Corse.
12. The Lazio office is funded by private firms rather than the regional government of Lazio.
13. The Mezzogiorno office is funded by the Italian state, not regional governments.

With few exceptions, representation in Brussels is dominated by the upper level of subnational governance in a country, and we use this principle to determine units of analysis in countries which have no subnational representation. In Germany it is the *Länder* that monopolize representation in Brussels; in Spain it is the *comunidad autónomas*; and in Belgium the *régions*. In France, almost all offices represent *régions*, individually or in territorially contiguous groups. Group offices are funded by constituent régions. The United Kingdom has the widest mix of representation. Wales, Scotland and Northern Ireland are represented alongside less encompassing groups of counties in England. We follow the pattern of country representation outside England, and use what are termed Standard Regions within England in determining our units of analysis.[57] We extend the principle of highest administrative unit to units of analysis in countries where there is no subnational representation. For Greece this is the development region; for Ireland the Planning Region; for Italy the *regioni*; for the Netherlands the *landsdelen*; and for Portugal the *commissaoes de coordenacao regional* and *regioes autónomas* (the Canary Islands and Madeira).

Resource pull

Ideally, to indicate the economic lure of the EU for subnational governments we would have data on the overall distribution of potential EU spending for each region. Such data are unavailable, for the Commission does not disaggregate all EU spending to the regional level. However, we do have detailed data on the regional distribution of structural funding, and this accounts for a significant share of EU spending in the regions, and indeed for around one quarter of total spending (ECU14 billion per annum) in the early 1990s. Structural spending is by far the most salient allocation of resources for subnational governments. The data limitations that face the researcher also face subnational decision-makers, and their own perception of the resource pool available at the European level is likely to be strongly oriented to structural funding.

There are important differences in the political process of allocating the money across countries and across regions which we should take into account.[58] Countries that qualify in their entirety for structural funding, i.e. the very poorest countries eligible for objective 1 funding, are covered by nation-wide Community Support Frameworks (CSFs) which include both regional and sectoral programmes, whereas countries that qualify for objective 2 funding have regional CSFs. When it comes to the sectoral CSFs, it is difficult for subnational governments in the poorer regions to present the case for regional priorities against central government assertion of national priorities. Hence, only a portion of the budget for structural policy can be considered a realistic incentive for regional lobbying. Commission documents divide spending between a regional category that is broken down by region and a sectoral category that is not, and we use this regional category in our data analysis.

Resource push

Our measure of resource push is total subnational spending prorated by regional population and converted to common European Currency Units (ECUs) (International Monetary Fund 1993: 301–303). In the absence of comparative data for government spending at the level of individual subnational governments, we have adopted a second-best solution derived from data on government spending at the subnational level, and we prorate this across regions based on their population.

Associational culture

There are no comparative data that directly measure the strength of associational culture across our cases. The nearest available indicator is share of the workforce in the industrial sector, a variable that is closely related to associational culture ($r = .84$) as measured by Robert Putnam (1993: 153) in his study of the topic in Italy. Our confidence in this parameter is reinforced because its significance and size is robust in the face of controls for subnational revenues and regional GDP per capita.

Informational exchange

No single indicator appears to provide a valid measure of subnational political autonomy, so we have designed a composite index, represented in Table 3.2, which sums scores for general constititutional provisions, special provisions for particular regions and competencies exercised by regions that go beyond the formal constitution. The first element is based on the constitutional character of the state, indicated here on a scale ranging from a unitary state (0) to a fully federal political system (4), which we set out in column 1. However, the political functions of some regions, including some in Portugal, the United Kingdom and France, are not represented in formal constitutional provisions for the state as a whole, but are established as extraordinary provisions for particular regions, and we account for these in column 2. Regional governments play an active role in framing central government policies, as in Belgium and Germany. This dimension of regional power is indexed in the third column of Table 3.2.

Regional distinctiveness

Regional identification We use data provided by *Euro-Barometer* 36 (October–November 1991) to measure the strength of regional identity vis-à-vis national identity across regions. Of the available data on regional identification, these are the closest to the time period for this analysis. We calculate relative regional identification by subtracting attachment to the nation from attachment to the region. The resulting score is aggregated to our regional units of analysis.[59]

Table 3.2 *Regional autonomy index*

	Federalism (0–4)	Special territorial autonomy (0–2)	Role of regions in central government (0–2)	Summary score (0–8)
Belgium	3	1	2	6
Denmark	0	0	0	0
France	1	0	0	1
Overseas territories	1	1	0	2
Germany	4	0	2	6
Greece	0	0	0	0
Ireland	0	0	0	0
Italy	1	0	0	1
Luxemburg	0	0	0	0
Netherlands	0	0	0	0
Portugal	0	0	0	0
Madeira, Azores	0	2	0	2
Spain				
Régimen extraordinare	3	2	0	5
Régimen ordinario	3	1	0	4
UK				
England	0	0	0	0
Scotland, Wales and N. Ireland	0	1	0	1

Notes: This table is an updated, revised and expanded version of the institutional autonomy index designed by Jan-Erik Lane and Svante Ersson (1991: Chap. 6). The major differences between our index and the Lane–Ersson index are as follows: Lane and Ersson score federalism 0 to 2, with only Germany (2) and Belgium (1) having positive scores. We adopt a wider range and, in addition to Germany and Belgium, we have a high positive score for Spain and low scores for France and Italy to distinguish them from truly unitary states such as Portugal and Greece. Likewise, we have a wider spread of scores for special territorial autonomy (with three intervals instead of two) to enable us to distinguish between the broad-gauged special autonomy of Catalonia, the Basque Country and other Spanish regions under the exceptional constitutional provisions, on the one hand, and the smaller degree of autonomy accorded to the French overseas territories, Northern Ireland and Spanish regions under the ordinary constitutional provisions, on the other. Spanish regions and French overseas territories are not scored positively by Lane and Ersson. Following Richard Nathan (1991), we adopt an index of the involvement of regional governments in the machinery of central government. This component variable allows us to do justice to Belgian regions which have not found it necessary to claim a greater share of spending and taxation because they are so entrenched within their state executive. Finally, we dispense with what Lane and Ersson describe as functional autonomy, an index of the autonomy of interest groups and other domestic associations, including the church, vis-à-vis the state.

The resulting index encompasses the dimensions of federalism conceptualized by Richard Nathan with the exception of his cultural dimension, which we deal with as a separate variable.

Federalism: This refers to the constitutional scope for regional governance in the state. Given that most regional offices have been created since 1990, we have scored federalism for each country *c*. 1989.

0 – highly unitary state which does not have a regional level of governance or only a weakly institutionalized regional level of governance.
1 – unitary state in which regions have restricted and specialized competencies.

continued overleaf

Table 3.2 (*Continued*)

2 – regionalist state in which regions have extensive and diversified competencies, but with less autonomy than category 3.
3 – federal state in which regions are defined by a high level of political, administrative and financial autonomy.
4 – federally dominated state in which regions significantly influence the policies of the central government.

Special territorial autonomy: This modifies the federalism index by scoring regions within states to the extent they have special arrangement for home rule. Regions having narrowly defined special arrangements are scored 1; regions having wide-ranging special arrangements are scored 2.

Role of regions in central government: Regions having a very strong role in central government decision-making are scored 2; regions having a strong role are scored 1; others are scored 0.

Political divergence   The indicator of political divergence is constructed to capture both the magnitude of political divergence between a region and the country as a whole and its duration. We first establish the party composition of the national government in April of 1986, 1987, 1988 and 1989. Data from the corresponding *Euro-Barometer* surveys (nos 25, 27, 29 and 31) are used to determine the proportion of voters in each region who support opposition parties for each of the four years. The yearly values are then averaged to provide a measure of cumulative political divergence before 1989, the mean date for the establishment of regional offices in Brussels.

Examining the evidence

Resource pull

The resource pull hypothesis predicts that subnational governments having potential access to more resources at the European level are more likely to open an office in Brussels. This hypothesis finds little or no confirmation on the basis of EU spending for structural policy. The coefficient for structural funding in the simple regression is small and insignificant (Model 1). When we control for regional expenditure, industrial share of the labour force, political divergence and regional attachment, the structural funding variable is significant at the .1 level (Models 7, 8 and 9), but it is weak and insignificant in our fully specified model (Model 10).

It is possible that these results suffer from measurement error. But we have created an index of resource pull that is narrowly focused on spending available for regional governments. Instead of measuring overall structural spending, we count only spending available directly for regional governments. The effect of this is to increase the relative share of funding for declining industrial regions in the United Kingdom, France, Belgium and Germany, which have high rates of regional representation, while decreasing the relative share of funding for poorer countries, including Ireland, Greece and Portugal, which emphasize sectoral policies and which lack

Table 3.3   *Correlation matrix*

	Regional representation	Structural funding	Regional expenditure	Industrial labour force	Political autonomy	Political divergence
Regional representation	1.000					
Structural funding	−.0816 (.3328)	1.000				
Regional expenditure	.1748 (.0458)	.0753 (.3945)	1.000			
Industrial labour force	.2867 (.0006)	−.1005 (.2390)	.2553 (.0038)	1.000		
Political autonomy	.4880 (.0001)	.1895 (.0234)	.3457 (.0001)	.2351 (.0050)	1.000	
Political divergence	.3887 (.0001)	−.0963 (.2719)	.0025 (.9779)	.0024 (.9784)	−.0445 (.6110)	1.000
Regional attachment	.2827 (.0010)	.0683 (.4382)	.0711 (.4386)	.2015 (.0200)	.4327 (.0001)	.0639 (.4667)

Pearson correlation (*p* value)

Table 3.4 *Univariate logistic regression results*

	Model					
	1	2	3	4	5	6
Structural funding	.0914 (.3436)					
Regional expenditure		.2374 (.0770)				
Industrial labour force			.3572 (.0010)			
Political autonomy				.6337 (.0001)		
Political divergence					.5574 (.0001)	
Regional attachment						.3596 (.0023)
% predicted	52.1	58.6	66.7	64.5	72.3	68.4
Number of observations	143	131	141	150	133	133

Standardized coefficients reported.
p values in parentheses.

Table 3.5 *Multivariate logistic regression results*

	Model			
	7	8	9	10
Structural funding	.2151 (.0613)	.2373 (.0612)	.2662 (.0371)	.1129 (.4097)
Regional expenditure		.2964 (.0936)	.2516 (.1841)	.0076 (.9747)
Industrial labour force	.4092 (.0025)		.2657 (.0533)	.2698 (.0921)
Political autonomy				.7887 (.0002)
Political divergence	.6789 (.0001)	.7250 (.0001)	.7460 (.0001)	.9608 (.0001)
Regional attachment	.3174 (.0154)	.3302 (.0111)	.2984 (.0272)	.0749 (.6235)
% predicted	81.5	80.8	81.9	87.6
Number of observations	131	120	120	120

Standardized coefficients reported.
p values in parentheses.

regional representation. In other words, we have bent over backwards to devise a measure that could pick up resource pull, if it existed.

When we return to structural funding in the aggregate, it is striking that the overwhelming proportion of the regions that receive the bulk of funding are not represented. Not a single subnational government from Portugal, Greece, Ireland or Southern Italy has an office in Brussels. Hence, the association between aggregate structural spending and representation is always negative, irrespective of our controls.

Does this indicate that subnational governments are not motivated to increase EU spending in their regions? To make such a claim we would need to know the extent to which having an office enables a subnational government to influence the allocation of spending at the European level, which is the p_r term described above. The most plausible explanation for the feebleness of the resource pull hypothesis is that regional offices are simply not effective channels for subnational governments to influence EU spending, a line of argument that accords with analyses of structural funding (Pollack 1995; Marks 1996). Member state executives and, to a lesser extent, the European Commission determine the budget for structural funding and its spatial allocation, not regional governments. EU regional spending is, no doubt, of intense concern to subnational governments, but they realize that opening an office in Brussels will not do much to help them get more.

There are two main problems with applying a resource pull hypothesis to interest mobilization in the EU. First, the resources at stake tend to be meagre. The EU spends little more than 1 per cent of European GDP, and this covers administration as well as programmes. However, the force of this argument is less for subnational governments than for most other domestic interests because a sizeable share of total EU resources is channelled into structural policy. So the weight of explanation for the inability of resource pull to explain regional mobilization falls onto a second feature of the Euro-polity – the inability of subnational governments to influence spending at the European level. The allocation of moneys in the EU is determined largely through hard bargaining among member state executives. When it comes to finances, the EU is a state-centric polity, and a regional government that is oriented to money will operate through national rather than European channels.

If the EU were mainly concerned with taxing and spending, then subnational governments would have little to gain by operating directly in Brussels. The fact that the EU concentrates a significant bulk of its spending in cohesion policy directed at regions is a false clue in our effort to understand regional representation.

Resource push

We find little support for the hypothesis that subnational governments having greater access to financial resources will be more likely to be represented in Brussels. Our measure of subnational revenue is significantly associated with representation in univariate analysis (Model 2), but the association does not survive the multivariate controls we exert. While the parameter estimates for subnational revenue always have the correct sign, the closest they come to significance is .0936 in Model 8, which excludes political autonomy and industrial share of the labour force.

The capacity of subnational governments to extract resources is weakly related, if at all, to the likelihood that they will be independently represented in Brussels. This stands to reason given the range in the size of regional offices in Brussels. At one extreme are the Catalan and some of the German *Länder* offices, which employ as many as twenty-two full-time officials and operate as unofficial embassies from impressive buildings. At the other extreme are single-room offices employing just one or two part-time staff. The costs of maintaining an office in Brussels vary widely with the financial commitment of a subnational government, and can be relatively small even for poor government. The contrast between well-funded and poorly funded regions lies in the *size* rather than the *existence* of a regional office. Relatively wealthy subnational governments in Denmark, the Netherlands and France (most notably the Paris region) are absent; relatively poor ones, such as Cornwall and Devon or Lancashire in England and Murcia or Extremadura in Spain, are present.

To summarize our findings so far, subnational governments are mobilized in Europe neither in response to spending at the European level, nor on account of their relative capacity to fund representation. We find little or no evidence supporting economic push/pull hypotheses. Money does not drive the establishment of subnational offices. We must, therefore, turn to cultural and political factors to provide a plausible explanation for the pattern of regional representation.

Associational culture

Our results concerning industrial share of the labour force provide indirect evidence supporting the hypothesis that subnational governments in associationally rich regions are more likely to seek representation in Brussels. Industrial share of the labour force is strongly and significantly associated with regional representation in univariate regression (Model 3), and retains significance at the .1 level or better when we add controls (Models 7, 9 and 10).

However, we are not measuring associational culture directly, and we cannot discount the possibility that the association we find has other sources. One possible interpretation which we are able to test and reject is that industrial share of the labour force taps the effect of per capita income in a region. When we add a variable measuring regional per capita income to our models the effect of industrial share of the labour force remains strong and significant and in none of our models does the variable of regional per capita income attain significance. Regional per capita income is significantly correlated with industrial share of the labour force, but it is even more strongly correlated with subnational government expenditure. Adding a per capita income variable to our models does not change our results.

To the extent that material resources matter for regional representation, one would expect them to matter at the level of governments rather than mass publics. But no matter how we test this, we find that financial resources are not as important as cultural resources. The evidence we uncover is, at the very least, congruent with the hypothesis that stronger associational cultures increase the willingness of governments to extend their own organization into transnational political arenas. But this effect is not particularly strong. The weight of our explanation lies in political factors that have to do with the dynamics of multi-level governance.

Informational exchange

The informational exchange hypothesis views subnational governments as suppliers and consumers of information concerning policy. Subnational governments with the most extensive political role in their respective domestic political systems are both the most hungry for and the best supplied with information and the most likely to open an office in Brussels. The variable which we have designed to measure this, regional political autonomy, is very strongly and significantly associated with regional representation in simple regression (Model 4), and the effect is no less significant under the controls we exert in our fully specified model (Model 10).

This finding accords with more impressionistic evidence concerning the functions of regional offices based on open-ended interviews conducted by the authors. The staff of most regional offices are keenly aware that they do not exert palpable political power in the European arena. Most view their role as that of interlocutor between administrators and representatives in their home region and European political actors, particularly in the Commission. For administrators in regional governments that have broad-ranging competencies, this function is critical, because they are affected by European regulations on so many fronts, including structural policy, environmental policy, educational policy, transport and communications, alongside several other policy areas (Mazey and Mitchell 1993). Maintaining a regional office is part of an effort to gain early warning of policy initiatives that are entering the pipeline. Given the labyrinthine character of the policy process in the EU (Mazey and Richardson 1993), one can well imagine why those running subnational governments would find it useful to have a physical presence near key decision-making institutions. An office in Brussels is a form of insurance against the hazards of a notoriously unpredictable policy environment.

Regional office administrators tend to be formidable information-gatherers. Closed-ended questions in our survey give us a detailed picture of who they communicate with, how they communicate and how often. The average regional office is in weekly contact with seven Directorate Generals. But they do not only tap the Commission for information. Of regional offices surveyed, 44 per cent were in contact with a member of the European Parliament in the previous week.

Information is not a one-way street. Regional offices have information that key actors at the European level lack, and in gathering information they are intent on conveying the particular concerns of their regional governments. Regional office administrators rarely make explicit demands on supranational actors, but, in a spirit of informational exchange, endeavour to explain the costs and benefits of alternative policies from the standpoint of the region. Translated into the terms of interest group politics, regional offices 'lobby' those in power, though administrators of regional offices usually describe their activities in more bureaucratically acceptable language. While they do not carry heavy sticks to force their will into policy, the information conveyed by regional offices usually falls upon eager ears, for the Commission is a small organization with very large responsibilities, and it continually strives to diversify the sources of its information beyond member state executives.

One of the insights of the policy network approach is that information and power are intimately connected, and this is nowhere more true than in the EU (Bache et al. 1996). The emphasis on consensus rather than majoritarian decision-making and on detailed, technocratic regulation in a setting of extreme territorial diversity place a premium on information concerning the preferences of multiple state and non-state actors (Majone 1994d). Politics in the EU is usually about regulation in a complex and fragmented environment, and a Brussels office serves a vital function as a subnational government's ears and voice.

The association between regional political autonomy and representation in Brussels is clear for several countries. Regions having the most political autonomy and broadest functions within their respective states, i.e. those in Germany and Belgium, are all present in Brussels. In contrast, the unitary states of Portugal, Ireland and Greece, where regional governments are weak, have no offices. In these cases the pattern of regional representation is essentially a country pattern, and subnational political autonomy, which varies little within countries and greatly across them, is precisely pitched to the dependent variable. But not all of the variation on the dependent variable is country-based, and here subnational autonomy is a less powerful predictor. The outlying cases are eight highly autonomous Spanish regions which lack offices and seven English offices representing weak regions. To explain these one must turn to variables that are more sensitive to within-country variation.

Regional distinctiveness

The regional distinctiveness hypothesis explains subnational representation in terms of the tension between a region and the country of which it is a part, and predicts that regions that are politically and culturally different from their respective national societies are more likely to mobilize in the EU.

We find that regional identity is correlated with regional representation in the expected way ($r = .28$) and that its coefficient is highly significant in a single variable logistic regression, predicting 68.4 per cent of the cases correctly (Model 6). This effect withstands controls for any set of variables except regional political autonomy, as in Models 7, 8 and 9. But whenever we control for regional political autonomy, the parameter for regional identity loses its significance (Model 10) chiefly because this variable is strongly associated with regional political autonomy ($r = .43$).

Inspecting the pattern of regional representation in Table 3.1, we can see that almost all regions that have a strong regional identity, i.e. ethnically, culturally and/or linguistically distinct regions, are represented in Brussels. This variable is particularly strong for the two countries which have the greatest internal variation in regional representation, the United Kingdom and Spain. Scotland, Wales, Northern Ireland and Cornwall, the most culturally distinctive areas of the United Kingdom, are all present, while just two regions in the South of England are represented. In Spain, the Basque Country and Catalonia are present, as are Galicia, Valencia and the Canary Islands. With the exception of Navarre, the small distinctive region east of the Basque Country, the unrepresented regions in Spain are generally less distinct.

Our results for regional identity are not difficult to fathom. The effect of regional identity is swallowed by regional political autonomy because the two are closely associated. The causal nexus between these variables probably runs in both directions. Strong regional identity intensifies demands for regional governance; strongly entrenched regional governments intensify regional identity.

Our measure of political divergence is strongly and significantly associated with subnational representation. In the simple regression represented in Model 5 this variable correctly predicts 72.3 per cent of cases. Under any set of controls this variable is highly significant and has the strongest impact (Models 7 to 10).

Our results provide strong confirmation of the regional distinctiveness hypothesis. Regional governments are induced to organize in Brussels because they represent territories that are distinct from the country as a whole. Rather than rely on their respective central state executives for information, regional governments have sought an independent channel. Our analysis suggests that the demand for an independent channel is greatest where those representing a region believe that it has special circumstances that differentiate it from the country as a whole. The logic of the argument applies whether the sense of distinctiveness is party-political or cultural; in either case regional governments are driven to Brussels to secure independent representation.

It is worth stressing we are not arguing that governments from distinctive regions are drawn to Brussels to displace central states and so create a Europe of the Regions. The notion of a Europe of the Regions is sometimes used as a straw man to dismiss regional empowerment by linking it to the chimera of a non-state order run by independent regions. One may explain regional representation in Brussels without referring at all to the notion of a Europe of the Regions. A more suggestive term is that suggested by Liesbet Hooghe (1996): 'a Europe *with* the Regions', which refers to the demand on the part of regional governments for influence alongside, rather than in place of, state executives, and this does play a role in the decision to create regional offices. Administrators in offices representing the most distinctive and strongly entrenched regions in Europe, such as Catalonia, the Basque Country and Bavaria, stress that their goal is to empower regional governments and restructure decision-making in the EU, and that maintaining a regional office is a step in that direction.

Conclusion

The sources of variation in the representation of subnational governments in the EU are to be found in a political logic of multi-level governance rather than in the resource logic focusing on the money available to subnational governments.

The greater the overlap between the competencies of subnational and supranational government, the more likely that a subnational government will be represented in Brussels. Hence, it is the most entrenched subnational governments with the broadest range of competencies that have regional offices, including every *Land* in Germany and every région in Belgium. Given their scope, such governments have an intense need for information concerning upcoming legislation and regulation. At the same time, they are a valuable source of information for the European Commission, which is a resource-poor organization that often finds itself uncomfortably dependent on information provided by member state executives. This is a story of informational exchange, though it is worth stressing that information and power are intimately connected in the decision-making networks of the EU. There is no clear line, for example, between explaining the objective problems of a region and making the political case that some policies are feasible and others infeasible.

The logic of regional representation has also a harder political edge which results from conflicting regional and national interests in a multi-level polity with multiple 'cracks' or points of access. Regional governments may mobilize in Europe because they have political demands which conflict with those of their national governments, either because those in the region have a strong sense of separate identity, reinforced perhaps by a distinct language and/or culture, or because they have a durable party-political orientation that is not represented in the national government. One finds such distinctiveness in the North of England, with its cultural and political friction with Conservative-dominated governments drawing their support from the South. Regional/national conflict of interest underlies the representation of many regions in Europe, including Galicia, the Canary Islands, Brittany, Northern Ireland, Wales, Scotland, Catalonia and the Basque Country. The Directors of the Catalan and Basque offices say that they do not represent regions in Europe, but distinct countries, a claim symbolized by the Basques with an extra yellow star on their European Union flag.[60]

Subnational governments representing distinctive regions are reluctant to channel their interests exclusively within central states if they wish to influence decisions at the European level. In its national political arena a subnational government is likely to find itself pitched against a national majority, whereas in the European arena it represents one among a far larger number of national groups, none of which is dominant. Such considerations amplify the political ambitions of distinctive regional governments to gain institutional access at the European level, ambitions that contributed to the decision under the Maastricht Treaty to create a Committee of the Regions, but which remain largely unfulfilled from the standpoint of real political power. From this perspective, maintaining a well-staffed permanent office in Brussels is a step in the direction of authentic autonomy within Europe.

If the decisions that mattered to subnational governments were made exclusively by state executives in the Council of Ministers or in other state-dominated fora, then there would be little incentive to open an office in Brussels. Subnational governments would in that case do what state centrists theorize they should do, that is focus their activity exclusively on lobbying their respective state executives, which would then represent their views in intergovernmental negotiation. But the European polity has some of the characteristics of 'the multiple crack' (Grodzins 1967), diverse points of access which allow subnational governments and a wide variety of interest groups multiple opportunities to influence outcomes. We find that the broader the competencies of a subnational government and the more intense its conflicts of interest or identity with the national state, the more likely it will mobilize in Brussels.

This argument has little to do with resources, whether controlled by subnational governments or offered to them by the EU. Subnational governments are not lured into creating offices in Brussels by the possibility of getting more money from the EU. EU spending is relatively small, and is insignificant in relation to its regulatory impact. Like other poor government agencies, the EU's influence lies in telling others what they can and cannot do rather than in paying them to do it. And the money that *is* spent is determined largely in intergovernmental fashion by bargaining among member state executives.

We also find that differences in the spending power of subnational governments do not have any significant effect once one controls for the political factors discussed here. The annual budgets of regional offices in

Brussels vary from several million ECU to the less than two hundred thousand ECU for a small office with one or two part-time staff. Small regional governments with meagre resources have the option of setting up equivalently small regional offices.

The only resource we find evidence for is that of associational culture, which presumably is linked to the entrepreneurialism of subnational decision-makers in pursuing opportunities for political communication and influence beyond their own region. Our evidence here is based on the share of the regional workforce employed in industry, which we offer as an indirect measure of the strength of a region's associational culture. Our confidence in this reading of the evidence is strengthened because we are able to test and reject the alternative interpretation that the industrial share of the workforce is significant because it picks up the effect of per capita income.

We explain regional mobilization in Brussels as an outcome of over-lapping competencies, tensions and conflicts in a system of multi-level governance, but one should note that this does not lead us to discount the importance of intergovernmental bargaining in the EU. Intergovernmental bargaining is an important feature of decision-making in the EU, but it is not a constant or immovable feature that floats above politics. Over the past two decades state executives have shifted a range of competencies to supranational institutions and in the process they have created intense demands for direct informational exchange among actors in different political arenas. With the Single European Act of 1986 and the process of supranational regulation that followed it, state executives decisively altered the structure of political opportunities in Europe. This has given rise to an unprecedented (and, from the standpoint of most state executives, un-intended) mobilization of subnational actors at the European level.

But there are stark variations in the engagement of subnational actors at the European level. Regional mobilization does not empower regional governments in general, but only a select subset of them. The picture of regional mobilization we present here is one of wide divergence among regional governments, rather than convergence. There is little evidence of a Europe of the Regions here. Rather we have seen the emergence of a Europe *with* the Regions, or, more accurately, a Europe with *some* regions. Because multi-level governance in the EU encompasses territories with sharply contrasting democratic polities, we find that territory itself is a potent source of political variation in the activities of groups at the Euro-pean level.[61] The EU brings together actors from different countries and regions, and thus exacerbates rather than diminishes the role of territorial factors in politics. This chapter is an initial attempt to shed some light on how it does so.

4

Neo-Voluntarism: A New European Social Policy Regime?

Wolfgang Streeck

Maastricht and its aftermath should have finally made clear what could have been recognized long ago:[62] that the integrated Europe of the European Union will never be a supranational state on the model of European nation-states. Instead what is developing in Western Europe today is a polity of a new kind: an international order, controlled by intergovernmental relations between sovereign nation-states, that serves as a domestic order for a transnational economy. The politics of this unique arrangement is not easily understood and will take a long time to explore, in practice just as in theory. But what should be obvious is that it is *not* driven by a logic of 'spill-over' from international market integration to supranational state formation, or from joint market-making to common political and social citizenship – and that in particular there is no functionalist dynamic inherent in the emerging system that would provide for a supranational replication of the national state as we have come to know it in the twentieth century.

Social policy in integrated Europe, this implies, can be understood only if one dissociates oneself radically from the received image of a slowly but steadily evolving European federal welfare state. That image is responsible for the weaknesses of most previous analyses of the subject, which tended to interpret the results and non-results of Community, or, now, Union, social policy in terms of steps taken, or not yet taken, toward a supranational welfare state that was to perform basically the same function as its national predecessors, only for integrated Europe as a whole, and that would gradually penetrate and absorb the national systems that had preceded it. Taking the end-point for granted, on the assumption that integration could lead only to replication of the familiar on a larger scale, resulted in the typical discussions on the 'social dimension' of integrated Europe, which essentially were about the question of whether the glass was already half full or still half empty. The answer depended on the point of view, the interests one felt sympathetic with, and how patient one was willing to be. Throughout, however, given that the Community's 'really existing' social policy seemed so minimal in comparison to what it was supposed to become, it was discussed much more in terms of what it was not, or not yet, rather than what it was – which largely explains the analytical shallowness and the normative-declaratory tone of most of the debate. Overcoming this requires that the basic institutional properties of European Union as we now know them be taken into account, which in turn implies breaking once and for all with the teleological federalism that has informed most of the past debate. As soon as this is done, and indeed only then, the empirical realities of European integration begin to matter and make sense, and the historical defeat of the Social Action Programme of the 1970s and the 'social dimension' project of the 1980s can be taken seriously – instead of being treated as by definition no more than a contingent temporary delay in the functionally inevitable progress of federal European welfare state-building. Once it is recognized that the political and economic regime that is developing in Western Europe, whatever it may be, is a new kind of animal that is altogether different from the national state, especially in its relation to the economy, the problem in analysing European social policy changes from how empty or full the glass is, to what kind of glass we are dealing with and what purposes it may serve.

To set the stage, the present chapter begins with a brief recapitulation of the main institutional properties of the European Union as they have evolved over several decades. One central insight that will be derived from this is that European social policy will for a long time, and for all practical purposes forever, be made simultaneously at two levels, a supranational and a national one, with complex interactions between them as well as among the national systems included in the international order and situated in the integrated economy that underlies it. Proceeding from here, the chapter will then look separately at the two levels of social policy-making, beginning with the supranational and moving on to the national. In both cases, it will make an attempt to identify the kind of policies that are most likely to develop given the constraints and opportunities embodied in the institutional framework.

The institutional framework of European Union

The future shape of European social policy will be circumscribed by six fundamental conditions that have, in one way or other, worked their way into the *de facto* constitution of post-Maastricht European Union:

1 *From the Luxemburg Compromise to the Union Treaty, the member states of the Union have with surprising success defended their position as the masters of their community.* Rather than nation-states becoming obsolete and being absorbed into and superseded by new, federal-European institutions, the developmental path of European unification has remained strictly under intergovernmental control.[63] While integration did progress, every step along the way came at the price of further assurances for member states of their supremacy over all other forces within the Union's developing international-domestic polity. Steps that would have undermined this

supremacy were mostly not taken, and considerable legal and institutional inventiveness was deployed to enable integration to proceed without damage to national sovereignty, or indeed to use integration to fight off challenges to the latter emerging, above all, from growing economic inter-dependence. In the process the Community's character as an intergovern-mental arrangement was continuously reinforced – an arrangement that, rather than replacing national with supranational sovereignty, to the contrary typically served to enable national states to assist one another in protecting as much of their sovereignty as possible, in large part turning the Union into a mutual insurance arrangement for nation-states under rising interdependence.

Generally, even though European nation-states have lost the capacity to govern 'their' economies and impose a political will on the play of market forces, they have managed to remain the most important political organizations and foci of collective identity. While losing more and more of their internal sovereignty over their economies, nation-states retained their external sovereignty over international relations, which turned out to be an increasingly important political resource in a rapidly internationalizing world. In this way, while internationalization weakened the control of the nation-state over the national economy, at the same time, and contrary to the expectations of neo-functionalist integration theory, it provided it with powerful means to obstruct the development of supranational sovereignty. Even in Western Europe there is as a result today no alternative to the nation-state as wielder of public power, in spite of the fact that it has largely lost the ability to apply such power domestically for other than market-supporting or market-conforming purposes.

The successful resistance of the nation-state to supranational governance draws legitimacy from its historical association with democracy and 'cultural diversity'. Although the market has grown far beyond the scope of democratically organized political and cultural identities, electorates still regard national democratic politics as their principal source of protection, not least from economic dislocations caused by 'market forces', and per-ceive supranational governance as an undemocratic imposition of external control. The growing gap between the scale of democratic legitimacy and that of the international market as an integrated economic 'community of fate' notwithstanding, defenders of the nation-state continue to find it easy to convince citizens that in the absence of a common political identity at European level, and even though nationally confined sovereignty in an internationalized economy is in effect fragmented sovereignty with respect to the political control of markets, supranational governance cannot be democratic and would replace inevitably nationally based citizen participation with bureaucratic rule.[64]

2   Due to the survival of the nation-state as the pivotal political entity in integrated Europe, *European social policy will for the foreseeable future be made in a two-tier polity*, consisting of a set of supranational and inter-national institutions, on the one hand, and a number of sovereign nation-

states, on the other. Rather than absorption of the latter into the former, the making of social just as, increasingly, any other policy in Europe will therefore involve complex 'nested games' proceeding simultaneously in the international and, presently, twelve national political arenas – resulting in a patchwork of heterogeneous national policies constrained and modified by international rules and market interactions. As the allocation of jurisdiction over the two levels is controlled not by supranational sovereignty or by a functionalist dynamic of transnational state formation, but by the collectivity of member states sharing a common interest in preserving as much of their sovereignty as possible, the vertical dimension of upward delegation of authority and downward intervention in national regimes will remain far less important in the European two-tier polity than the horizontal dimension of interaction between national systems.

3 *Economic governance through fragmented sovereignty and international relations is more suited to market-making by way of negative integration and efficiency-enhancing regulation* (Majone 1993) *than to institution-building and redistributive intervention, or 'market distortion'.* This is because the removal of barriers to cross-border trade and mobility is less threatening to national sovereignty and less demanding of democratic legitimation than the creation and enforcement of rights and obligations of citizenship, especially the modification of property rights and the institutionalization of social rights to a minimum level of subsistence. As the example of 'mutual recognition' has shown, international market-making may advance largely through deregulation, which can be achieved by adopting by international treaty relatively simple rules of cooperation between independent national states, supplemented if necessary by narrow commitments to international enforcement.[65]

Limiting integration to the removal of trade barriers fits the interests of nation-states and the logic of intergovernmental cooperation, as it can mostly be accomplished without investing supranational bodies with sovereignty of their own. Negative integration of transnational markets can in principle be institutionalized as a default option that enters in force unless a unanimous joint decision among participant states is made to the contrary. By contrast, imposing common standards on markets or regulating their social outcomes by placing a floor under them requires a positive decision, often one leading to institutional development, which under the rules of intergovernmentalism can be vetoed by just one participating state. The fact that the Council, on behalf of the member states and in the name of national sovereignty, retains ultimate control over Union legislation thus has fundamental consequences for the European political economy in general and European social policy in particular.

Excluding social intervention in markets from common concerns accommodates the fact that democracy and citizen participation continue to reside in the member states. Distributive and redistributive politics require democratic legitimation. The way the European Union is designed, such legitimation remains beyond its reach. European-wide rules of social protection, e.g. effective rights of workforces to information, consultation and codetermination, are thus laid open to the objection not just that they impose inefficient 'rigidities' on what is to be a 'flexible' economy, but that they pre-empt the only democratic participation rights on offer, those vested in the sovereignty of individual nation-states – depriving European-wide redistributive 'inefficiencies' of their only possible justification, that they are the democratic will of the citizens.

Moreover, while joint market-making does require states to give up control over their economic borders, and in this sense does involve a loss of sovereignty, this is easy to accept today even for the most sovereignty-conscious of nation-states. In the 1950s and 1960s, the formation of the European Economic Community may have advanced the integration of the European economy beyond what it would have been without political intervention. But the relaunching of the European Community in the 1980s was more the ratification of an independent, market-driven process of internationalization, not just of trade but, most importantly, of capital markets, technologies and production systems. In this situation, 'completing' or, for that matter, joining the 'internal market' was and is not really something on which countries had and have much of a choice. To prosper at the end of the twentieth century, national economies must be part of the rapidly advancing global division of labour, and the most elementary assistance their governments can offer them is to remove any 'artificial' barriers to this. Even traditionally neutral countries like Sweden or Austria had no alternative to joining the European Union if they wanted their economies to be admitted to an increasingly international production system, coordinated by multinational companies that control the allocation of crucial productive investments and supplier contracts and want to be certain that their choices will not be interfered with by national borders and the vagaries of national politics.

4 *The desire to preserve national sovereignty in an internationalized economy gives rise to a historical coalition between nationalism and neoliberalism.* Nation-states embedded in a competitive international market and exposed to supranationally ungoverned external effects of competing economies are strongly tempted to protect their institutional integrity by devolving responsibility for the economy to 'the market' – using what has remained of their domestic sovereignty to limit, as it were constitutionally, the claims politics can make on the economy, and citizens on the polity. As a matter of fact, in many countries today the ongoing disengagement of politics from the economy is presented to the citizenry as the only economically rational political response to economic internationalization, especially to international competition, and the only promising way of defending the national interest in economic survival.

Moreover, whatever the *economic* merits of deregulation, deploying internal sovereignty to liberate and accommodate market forces instead of domesticating them, ending once and for all the use of public power for market-correcting purposes, may have become the only *political* programme that can still be nationally imposed on internationalized national economies without jeopardizing the integrity of the national state. If citizens can be persuaded that economic outcomes are, and better be, the result of 'market forces', and that national governments are therefore no longer to be held responsible for the economy, national domestic sovereignty and political legitimacy can be preserved even in conditions of tight economic inter-dependence: as nation-states offload their economic responsibilities to the 'world market', their own obsolescence in relation to the latter becomes less visible.[66]

In institutional terms, the affinity between nationalism and neo-liberal domestic and international market-making derives from decision rules under intergovernmentalism that effectively require unanimity, in practice even in areas where international treaties may allow for some kind of majority voting.[67] As Margaret Thatcher has shown by skilfully fighting the Community's 'social dimension' with national and neo-liberal arguments in turn, the defence of national democratic sovereignty – of the freedom of the 'Parliament at Westminster' from interference by the 'bureaucrats in Brussels' – and the defence of the freedom of transnational market forces from political intervention may be one and the same thing. Under the rules of intergovernmental diplomacy, any country can veto any decision *if it is willing to live with a non-decision*, i.e. with the preferred outcome for a neo-liberal economic policy. In other words, in the unique politics of integrated Europe as a domestic–international political system, all that the social interests opposed to a 'social dimension' need is the support of one national government concerned, if not about a 'free market', then about national sovereignty – whereas the proponents of a positive supranational social policy require not a majority of countries, but unanimity.

5 *The national fragmentation of democratic sovereignty within a competitive market and the continued dominance of the member states in the political system of European Union reinforce notions of national interest*, in stark contrast to older expectations of growing common European interests. This holds not least for the formation of interest groups, which by and large remain confined by the fragmentation of the international political system to their national bases, effectively incapacitating the main engine of supranationalism in neo-functionalist theory. Rather than the growth of a federal European state being driven by centralization of group interests in response to economic internationalization, European interest groups remain closely adapted to the political constraints and opportunities offered by fragmented sovereignty and intergovernmentalism, where positive decisions at transnational level can be made only unanimously and can be prevented by no more than one national government vetoing them; where supranational bodies have few resources at their discretion; and where legal and organizational support is safely available only at national level. Moreover, even when supranational interests do organize, they have to compete for influence in the polity of the Union with the

member states, whose superior constitutional status and organizing power places them at invincible advantage.

The stunted development of European interest groups represents another powerful obstacle to federal European welfare state formation, since it prevents the rise of supranational corporatism as a second generative mechanism of social policy. European employers in particular have no interest in advancing positive integration or European-level social intervention; with respect to common social policies that go beyond market-making, their interests are best served by non-decisions, i.e. by what intergovernmentalism is most likely to produce on its own. Also, with employers unavailable as European-wide interlocutors, unions, while fundamentally interested in supranational economic and social regulation, are thrown back to their national organization and national economic and institutional interests.

As the constitution of the Union is controlled by national states, these are in a position to keep European-level participation of organized social interests strictly within the limits of intergovernmentalism. By, among other things, refusing supranational institutions like the Commission budgetary and policy jurisdiction, and thus the means to make supranational organization and participation rewarding, e.g. by bribing employers into negotiating in good faith or punishing them for not doing so, member states can ensure that they themselves remain the most important targets of interest group action and that they can continue to claim the political dividends of successful adjudication of interests, not least by defending nationally defined interests in the international arena.[68]

6   Rather than moving towards a functionally integrated and territorially consolidated state, or state-like entity, the European Union is developing into *a collection of overlapping functionally specific arrangements for mutual coordination among varying sets of participating countries*. In Eurojargon, this is often referred to as a 'Europe of varying geometries', where some member states group together for shared purposes on a voluntary basis, leaving out others that do not want to take part.[69] Examples are the Schengen Agreement, the Social Protocol attached to the Maastricht Treaty, and the European Monetary Union envisaged for the end of the century, all of which join different subsets of member states for purposes far narrower than those of a supranational state.

Varying the 'geometry' of integration uniquely fits the principles of intergovernmental cooperation among sovereign nation-states, where no state can be forced to participate in common ventures, and unanimity is required for joint decisions and commitments. The result of integration of this kind is a menu of options for limited voluntary involvement in a set of distinct, functionally specific international regimes – adding up to an international order that allows countries to contract in or out of a variety of joint governance arrangements in accordance with nationally defined interests. Far from being an intermediary step on a road towards supranational state formation, a cafeteria, *à la carte*, self-service, *Zweckverband* or joint venture system of governance of this sort is likely to obstruct the evolution of integrated sovereignty since it prevents issue cross-trading and allows countries to act on their interests by exit or non-entry, rather than by voice, compromise and redefinition of interests.

In summary, while the internationalization of the European state system and the European political economy are progressing at a rapid pace, this is not accompanied by a reconstitution of the interventionist national welfare state at supranational level. Indeed the present transformation is so funda-mental that traditional models and concepts have become misleading. While European nation-states are ceding important economic functions, either to the market or to international institutions, those functions have *de facto* long been lost due to the internationalization of the economy. By cutting those losses and formally disengaging themselves from their economies, nation-states have surprisingly managed to consolidate their position both as masters of the international system and as the principal foci of political identification and democratic legitimacy.

As European nation-states 'pool' their sovereignties in order to protect them, the density of international regulation increases, creating illusions of growing supranational statehood. In reality, however, instead of rebuilding the interventionist national state at supranational level, such regulation almost exclusively serves purposes of market-making or market accom-modation. As international institutions are created with the purpose of protecting the integrity of national regimes, the internationalization of the European political economy is ratified and expedited by a myriad of international regulations that extract it from national control and thereby deregulate it. It is in this context that European social policy is made, as the combined outcome of joint intergovernmental decisions at the supranational level and the fragmented use of sovereignty vested in interdependent national political arenas.

Supranational social policy under intergovernmental constraints

The development of European Union social policy reflects closely the con-straints and opportunities embodied in the institutional structure of the Union as it evolved and solidified over the years. Four influences in particular came together to produce what has become a complex and often confusing *mélange* of policies and institutions at European level, forming a social policy regime *sui generis* that defies easy categorization and differs fundamentally from what exists in national welfare states:

(a) the *member states*, with their interest in building an international labour market and, at the same time, preserving the national found-ation of social rights of citizenship as well as the integrity and political stability of their respective domestic regimes – as reflected in an ambiguous and evolving 'treaty base' for Community and, today, Union social policy;

(b)   the – weak – impact of a *coalition* of political interests in supranational
       state-building, with social-democratic and trade union interests in a
       market-modifying, redistributive social policy at supranational level,
       and the, often no more than symbolic, concessions the dominant
       national–neo-liberal coalition had to make to it;
(c)   various rulings of the *European Court of Justice*, which from early on
       pursued a distinctive ingrationist agenda of its own;
(d)   and the activities of the *Commission as a political entrepreneur* trying
       to make the most of the Union's limited political jurisdiction and
       administrative capacities, in part by developing new tools of regula-
       tory intervention that promised to have at least some integrating and
       unifying impact even under strong intergovernmental constraints.

The impact of nationalism

The nation-states that created and continue to govern integrated Europe
have themselves for long been highly developed welfare states that derive
much of their domestic political legitimacy from their social policies.
Contrary to what is sometimes suggested, this makes them less rather than
more likely to agree to a supranational European welfare state due to the
manifold domestic interests that have over the years become attached to the
national provision of social welfare (Pelkmans 1985). Transferring jurisdiction over social protection to the Community or endowing the Community with a capacity to collect contributions or taxes, pay out benefits or
provide social services was therefore never seriously considered. All of these
remained and remain firmly vested in member states.

What the Community was instead charged with by the Treaty of Rome
was developing a new kind of social policy, one concerned with market-
making rather than market-correcting, aimed at creating an integrated
European labour market and enabling it to function efficiently, rather than
correcting its outcomes in line with political standards of social justice.
Community jurisdiction on social protection was as a consequence limited
from the beginning to work- and employment-related matters, excluding
'such classic social policy issues as pensions, unemployment, housing,
family, the disabled and the young' (Henningsen 1989: 56). Moreover, the
majority of Treaty articles and Union legislative measures in the social
policy area were and continue to be concerned with freedom of movement
of labour across national borders. As Juliet Lodge puts it, member states
designated Union social policy to deal with 'technical matters' such as
'factor mobility, labour mobility, industrial relations and technical aspects
of social security necessary to foster labour mobility in a customs union',
rather than with matters of 'social conscience' (1989a: 310).

Arguably a market-making social policy is not really one at all, as it is
concerned only with the civil right to enter in contracts and not with
industrial and social rights relating to their outcomes.[70] In fact some of the
main conflicts over European-level social policy were about demands for

market-correcting to be grafted onto market-making policies, or for the latter to be transformed into the former. However, to the – limited – extent that the Treaties seemed to lend themselves to this, it soon turned out that while the Community's original social policy mandate did contain certain ambiguities, on the whole these reflected no more than initial uncertainty among member states on how much homogeneity between national systems was needed to make an integrated European labour market work, and to protect countries with advanced systems of social provision from being politically destabilized by economic competition from countries with lower social costs. Language in the Treaty of Rome demanding a 'harmonization' of living and working conditions stems from this, and so do the Community's mandate to foster 'dialogue between management and labour' and the Treaty commitments to 'harmonization' of national social security systems and equal pay for women and men – the latter two having been included in the Treaty to alleviate concerns of the French government that the social policies it had to have for domestic reasons might put its economy at a competitive disadvantage.

Conveniently, it soon was found that differences in living standards did not obstruct market integration; that the common market worked well without tripartite concertation at European level; that social-security harmonization was not just intractable but also not required to keep the more advanced countries competitive, and so the respective Treaty article was soon forgotten; and that French laws on equal pay for men and women did not ruin the French economy. Community social policy as a consequence early and increasingly abandoned harmonization, first in practice and later, in the 1980s, also in rhetoric, and, in line with the institutional biases of intergovernmentalism, confined itself more and more to removing obstacles to mobility, especially of manual workers, between national, and still nationally governed, labour markets. In this it could leave national systems basically as they were, intervening in them only to the extent necessary for building interfaces between them, e.g. by obliging member countries to let workers from other member countries enter freely to seek work and to eliminate any legal discrimination that might impede the free movement of labour across national borders.[71]

In subsequent years, while the bulk of Community social policy remained concerned with cross-border mobility and market-making, considerable attention was also devoted to finding new ways of protecting the political stability especially of the countries with more advanced national social policy regimes.[72] Originally the natural response of hegemonic countries, first of France and then of West Germany, to perceived competitive pressures on their domestic social policy settlements had been demands for, again, harmonization. Both countries had to realize, however, that generalizing their respective 'models' to the rest of Europe ran up not just against the sheer technical complexity of the matter, but also, and more importantly, against the economic and institutional nationalism of the other countries – not to mention the sea change in economic policy during the

1970s and 1980s in favour of 'deregulation' and 'flexibility'. But here too it turned out that there were functional alternatives to harmonization, in the form of – often highly complex – supranational legislation designed to insulate national social policy arrangements against politically unmediated external interference. Instead of institutionalizing general and uniform supranational rights and obligations of social citizenship, a large part of Community social policy thus became concerned with 'coordination' of different national regimes and policies (Henningsen 1989), abandoning the perspective of convergence of national systems.

Today examples abound of European social policy legislation that serves not to create uniform social rights or obligations for participants in the integrated European labour market, but to protect the viability of member states as formally sovereign political entities. Often such legislation is highly complex, like the proposed directive which, on German pressure, would require firms from one Union country that send workers to work in another to pay them local rather than home country wages under a so-called 'territoriality principle'; the purpose is to preserve the complicated and expensive system of wage setting and collectively negotiated, levy-based 'social funds' in the German construction industry against pre-emption by non-German firms selling construction services in Germany. Another case is the envisaged possibility for member countries to limit the choice offered to large firms by proposed European company law between alternative systems of workforce representation to the existing national system, thereby preventing domestic firms from exiting from national industrial relations systems, or importing foreign models into them. Similarly, supranational obligations for multinational companies to provide information to workers in branch plants outside a firm's home country, e.g. on plant closures, are designed to close the gap in national control that results from closure decisions being taken exterritorially by corporate citizens of other sovereign states. While typically such legislation is accompanied by impressive integrationist rhetoric, it is in reality concerned with protective insulation of national regimes and the political stability of the nation-state.

The failure of harmonization

It is true that there were also attempts to take Community social policy beyond intergovernmental market-making and the mutual defence of national sovereignty. The first of these was the Social Action Programme of 1972, which, in spite of the narrow Treaty base, was widely perceived as announcing the arrival of a comprehensive market-correcting social policy at European level. Responding to the worker unrest of the late 1960s and, later, the deep restructuring of the European economy in the aftermath of the 'first oil shock', and drawing on long-dormant Treaty commitments like those to 'harmonization' of working conditions, the Programme aimed at unified, centralized governance of integrated labour markets, harmoniza-tion of labour standards and workplace participation rights at the highest, mostly West German, level, and Europeanization of collective bargaining.[73] The initiative was driven by social-democratic governments that at the time happened to be in office in key countries, and by unions intensifying their efforts at international organization; it also linked up with the older federalist state-building agenda harboured in particular in the Commission.[74] Other motives behind the Programme were, again, those of countries with high levels of social protection that were trying to preserve their social policy regimes by spreading them to the rest of Europe.

The same coalition also supported the second wave of social policy proposals, the so-called 'social dimension' that was attached in the late 1980s to the 'internal market' programme. This time the political power of labour and social democracy was weaker, and European social policy depended even more than in the past on riding on the coat-tails of the state-building project. That project, in turn, as promoted especially by Delors and inspired by the German 'social market economy', relied as its main vehicle on an assumed functional necessity for markets to be socially regulated (Streeck 1995). Hampered by the experience of the demise of the Social Action Programme in the early 1980s,[75] as well as by the need to enlist the support of business for relaunching the integration process, the Commission limited its initiative to essentially the same issues that had been addressed by the Programme, while trying to rewrite the old legislative proposals so as to make them acceptable to both business and the member states.

It is now widely recognized that, apart perhaps from a few symbolic concessions to the state-building forces in the Union and to what is called the 'Europe of working people',[76] the second initiative was even more thoroughly defeated than the first. The details have been presented elsewhere (Streeck 1995) and require no recapitulation. Ultimately, the reasons why the European social policy coalition failed to shift the evolution of the European Union in the direction of a federal welfare state have to do with the Union's basic constitutional structures. International diplomacy and intergovernmental relations are far from an ideal channel for the articulation of social interests in redistributive social policy. Even apart from the continuing national orientation and weak supranational organization of European social interest groups, any Union-level social policy project must pass through the needle's eye of the Council, where it must compete for attention with a wide range of other subjects. Many of these are more amenable to diplomatic treatment, or in any case more important for international relations – compare a country's inflation or interest rate, with its many external effects on other countries, to its level of unemployment benefit. Also, unlike, for example, trade or security policy, social policy has no lobby outside the Union that would demand attention for it and make the Council move it up on its agenda.

In addition, of course, the fact that integrated Europe is not a polity like national polities means among other things that Union-level social policy is not made by a parliament. Unlike in national systems, there is in the

European Union no possibility for social policy ever to become the subject of an electoral contest between 'left' and 'right' parties. In fact, under intergovernmental decision-making, requiring unanimity – *de jure* or *de facto* – whether or not a social policy proposal is supported by a majority of countries, and what size that majority is, is irrelevant, as one opposing vote is enough to prevent a decision. Moreover, as has been pointed out, there is also in the political constitution of integrated Europe no place for integrated collective bargaining that could prefigure or substitute for legislation.

Encapsulated federalism

Surveying the results of four decades of European-level social policy-making, there is no denying that they include elements of – weak – federalism, notably in the areas of equal opportunity for women in employment and of health and safety at work. But these owe their origin to peculiar circumstances unlikely to occur again, and on closer inspection turn out to be safely encapsulated. Of the ten directives that were passed under the Social Action Programme, three were concerned with equal opportunity for women in the workplace, and all of them had 'discernible impact on Member states . . ., which were forced to introduce enabling legislation' (Addison and Siebert 1991: 602). Moreover, the Commission successfully 'brought enforcement procedures against a number of Member States' (Addison and Siebert 1991: 602). Three factors in particular account for the exceptional effectiveness of Community policy in this area. First, the Commission was able to draw on the by then almost forgotten legislative resource of the Treaty of Rome mandate to establish equal pay for women and men, and deploy it for purposes never anticipated by the Treaty signatories.[77] Second, equality between men and women at work has not traditionally been central to national states' social policy concerns, and was therefore unclaimed territory that the Community could relatively easily enter in an effort to expand its jurisdiction and enlarge its constituency. And third, sexual non-discrimination fits a civil as much as a social rights agenda, and its political support extended well into the professional middle classes, making it difficult for national governments to be perceived as opposing Community initiatives in the area.

Four other of the Social Action Programme directives dealt with *health and safety*, and on them agreement of national governments to Community-wide rule-making seems to have been even easier to secure. Although at the time 'proposals concerning health and safety required unanimity in Council, they proved much less controversial than other Commission proposals, possibly because of reticence on the part of Member States to embrace the notion that the right to have lower health standards is a valid means of labour market competition' (Addison and Siebert 1991: 602). Reflecting the experience of the 1970s, workplace health and safety later became the only social policy area that was placed under qualified-majority voting in the

Single European Act. Subsequently, in the context of the social dimension wave of Community social policy, health and safety became the sole example of harmonization 'not . . . of the lowest common denominator type, but maximalist in character' (Teague and Grahl 1991: 226ff).

Again, there are peculiarities here that make 'spill-over' unlikely. Mutual recognition of national health and safety regulations, which would have been the alternative to federal regulation, would not only have put pressure on some countries to lower their standards in order to remain competitive. While this might have been welcomed in the Thatcherite spirit of the time as an economically if not physically healthy supply-side shake-up, or shake-out, nationally different health and safety standards also acted as trade barriers in an important product market, that for production machinery. As long as machines had to meet different national safety standards, there was in effect no common market for them. Federalization of the issue through qualified-majority voting made it possible in 1989 to pass the Machinery Directive, which harmonized health and safety standards for the design of new machinery (O'Cleireacain 1989: 17) and thereby in effect created a Community-wide free market in production equipment.[78]

A new European social policy regime?

Outside the two areas of encapsulated federalism, and apart from binding international commitments to open up national labour markets, European-level social policy must make do with a minimum of compulsory modification of both market outcomes and national policy choices. This has led its advocates to describe it as an innovative, 'flexible', 'decentralized' and democratic alternative to both hard regulation and no regulation at all. But what really distinguishes the emerging European from traditional national social policy regimes is its low capacity to impose binding obligations on market participants, and the high degree to which it depends on various kinds of voluntarism. In particular, supranational European social policy, as a product of both intergovernmental constraints and sometimes inventive attempts especially by the Commission to work around these, allows countries to exit from common standards where their polity or economy will not sustain them (*cohesion by exemption*); gives precedence to national practices and contractual agreements between market participants (*unity by subsidiarity*); tries to enlist the subtle, cajoling effects of non-binding public recommendations, expert consensus on 'best practice', explication of the common elements of national regimes and mutual information and consultation (*governance by persuasion*); offers actors, public and private, menus of alternatives from which to choose (*governance by choice*); and hopes to increase the homogeneity of national regimes through comparison by electorates of their situation to that of citizens in other countries (*governance by diffusion*).

1 *Cohesion by exemption.* With the increasing size of the Union, varying its 'geometry' may be even more frequently used than in the past as a

means of keeping integration alive while preserving the voluntarism of intergovernmental relations. A central case is the Maastricht Treaty's creation of what is in effect a 'Social Policy Union' of eleven countries, with Britain being given permission to dissociate itself from wide areas of social policy at European level.[79]

Substantively, the scope of the so-called 'Social Policy Agreement' signed by the Eleven at Maastricht is limited to 'implement[ation of] the 1989 Social Charter on the basis of the "acquis communautaire"'. For this purpose, and only for the Eleven, the Agreement amended the Treaties to extend qualified majority voting to five subjects:

(a)   improvement in particular in the working environment to protect workers' health and safety;
(b)   working conditions;
(c)   the information and consultation of workers;
(d)   equality between men and women with regard to labour market opportunities and treatment at work;
(e)   the integration of persons excluded from the labour market.

The Agreement also specified a category of issues that will continue to require unanimous decisions, if only among the Eleven, including 'social security and the social protection of workers', 'protection of workers where their employment contract is terminated', and 'representation and collective defence of the interests of workers, including co-determination'. Finally, the Agreement 118(6) states that the changes in the Treaty 'shall not apply to pay, the right of association, the right to strike or the right to impose lock-outs', which remain excluded from supranational deliberation even under unanimity and among the Eleven.

For a while it was believed that the British 'opt-out' would give a strong boost to Union social policy by setting it free from the threat of a British veto. But this overlooked the fact that exemption is now likely to become a routinely accepted device to reconcile the desire of some countries to have, for whatever reasons, a common floor of standards, with the desire of others to remain below that standard. One consequence of this will be further fragmentation of European social policy, with different subjects being dealt with by differently demarcated 'sub-unions' under varying decision rules.

In addition, the existence of a separate Social Policy Union within integrated Europe creates a host of constitutional and political complexities that are bound to encumber policy-making among the Eleven. Not only will the jurisdiction of the Court over legislation passed under the Agreement be challenged. Moreover, to the extent that the Eleven may decide to impose social costs or obligations on firms under their jurisdiction, these may appeal to the Court against what could be construed as a competitive disadvantage against British firms, which would remain free from such obligations while continuing to enjoy unlimited market access throughout the Community. Also, if the Eleven passed a works council directive,

British multinationals, while in all other respects corporate European citizens, would technically be as exterritorial for the purposes of the directive as American multinationals – which would re-create inside the European Community the Europe–United States problems that helped defeat the first Vredeling proposal (DeVos 1989).[80]

In practice, however, none of this may ever be brought to a test. Federalist optimism on the British opt-out disregarded the inevitable interdependence between Community and British social policy. In integrated Europe such interdependence is much more likely to work in favour of the less than of the more regulated system, with the British exemption from Union social policy likely to impose strong limitations on the substantive policies that can be adopted by the Eleven. In part, this is because the Eleven will want to avoid testing to the end the capacity of European institutions to deal with the uncertainties of divided social policy governance. Also, given their revealed priorities of monetary and, perhaps, foreign policy integration, political prudence will tell them not to let internal diversity grow divisive. Governments will furthermore be under pressure from firms in their countries to keep the difference between their social obligations and those of their British competitors narrow.[81]

2 *Unity by subsidiarity.* Where countries do not ask to be exempted from common social policies, the principle of 'subsidiarity', which has in recent years assumed growing prominence and legal status in integrated Europe, ensures that national practice remains largely undisturbed by authoritative supranational interference. In Catholic social doctrine where the concept originated, subsidiarity implied a duty on the part of higher levels of governance to enable smaller units at lower levels to conduct their affairs in responsible 'social autonomy'. Part of this duty was to see to it, if necessary by active intervention, that more 'organic' units like firms or parochial charities were able to resolve problems themselves that otherwise might have become problems for the society as a whole.

By contrast, in the European Union, especially in the post-Maastricht period between the Danish referenda, the concept came to mean a general presumption of precedence of lower over higher levels of governance, wher the Union was to be allowed to regulate only matters that could not be equally effectively regulated below the European level. In the concessions made to the Danish and British resistance to Maastricht, this translated into a doctrine of *laissez-faire* with respect to whatever 'lower levels' of governance may or may not do. Subsidiarity thus *de facto* changed from a Catholic social into a liberal concept – the difference being that the former requires a strong central state mandating and enabling less encompassing social formations to govern themselves in the public interest, whereas the latter implies a weak state acting only at the request of sovereign constituencies.[82]

Subsidiarity is invoked in European usage to claim precedence for two very different kinds of lower-level self-governance: territorial and functional. In reality, however, with the absence of supranational state capacity that could enable and empower organized interests at European level, it is almost exclusively the much better endowed nation-states that benefit from it.[83] The space for functional subsidiarity – for the devolution of public power to the 'social partners' at European level – is narrowly limited, regardless of the co-decision procedure instituted by the Maastricht Agreement on Social Policy for the eleven members of the 'Social Policy Union'. In part this is because of the unwillingness of the employers to negotiate binding agreements with unions at European level. But it is also due to the nation-states themselves, which have written the rules of 'subsidiarity' so that they favour states over organized social groups, and empower the latter only to the extent that 'national diversity' and intergovernmentalism are not affected.[84]

In effect, given the *de facto* deregulatory consequences of ungoverned interdependence between national regimes, the institutionalization of subsidiarity to protect national practice from supranational governance benefits yet other modes of 'lower-level self-regulation', in particular corporate hierarchies and private markets.[85] Just as nations, large multinational firms are better organized and more capable of acting on their own, without public facilitation, than social groups, including their own workforces. How *laissez-faire* subsidiarity blends into voluntarism is exemplified by the Union's gradual retreat, in the name of self-regulation, from mandatory legislation on information and consultation rights for workers, to 'European Works Councils' established by voluntary agreement between management and workforces of large firms. By leaving the institutionalization of information and consultation procedures to 'free' negotiations, without enabling the weaker party, labour, to make the stronger party, management, negotiate in good faith, the new, European-style subsidiarity leaves social relations in the integrated market to the mercy of market conditions and economic power relations, blurring the crucial distinction between self-governance under subsidiarity and non-governance under a self-regulating market. Subsidiarity, in this definition, comes down in practice to two principles: whatever may exist at the national level is there by right; and where nothing exists at all, this is so either by economic reason or, again, by right.

3   *Governance by persuasion*, in particular by *recommendation, expertise, explication* and *consultation*. In the absence of majority rule and with strong intergovernmental inhibitions against overruling dissenting member countries, European bodies have increasingly made use of *non-binding recommendations* instead of binding directives. An example is the *de facto* replacement under the Delors presidency of the Economic and Social Committee, with its formal, legislation-oriented proceedings, with a 'Social Dialogue' limited to producing informal and non-binding 'opinions'. Ideologically, this is typically defended as reflecting 'recognition of the diversity and heterogeneity of industrial relations and employment practice in the member states' (Teague and Grahl 1991: 231). Recommendations may be of no more than symbolic value, suggesting activism where all that

is produced is a piece of paper. On the other hand, while their adoption is entirely voluntary both for member states and for market participants, they may draw attention to problems as well as ways of dealing with them, which may inspire national legislation or voluntary adoption of 'best practice'. This may be the case particularly in member countries that have no expert bureaucracy or no developed peak organizations of labour and capital.

Similar effects may be expected from committees of experts charged with problems that might otherwise be dealt with in political-adversarial ways. While in the past meetings of experts from member countries were convened primarily in preparation of central rule-making, now the hope often seems to be that joint technical deliberations will informally bring about a convergence of national standards that may render 'hard', formal rules superfluous. While the mechanisms and capacities of this kind of governance are not well known, that hope should not in principle and altogether be dismissed. German experience, for example in areas like health and safety, work organization and product standardization, would suggest that politically divisive issues may be defused by turning them over to groups of experts from 'all interested parties' charged with jointly establishing the technical 'state of the art' (*Stand der Technik*). Voluntary self-regulation results to the extent that actors are averse to lagging behind publicly established standards of good practice – be it out of a cultural commitment to technical excellence; for reasons of 'image' and prestige; to avoid conflict or liability suits; or in the anticipation that sooner or later the *Stand der Technik* will in any case become a formal norm.[86]

Similarly, supranational standards may be created by *explication* of the commonalities of already existing national standards. The most prominent example of this in the social policy field is the Charter of Fundamental Social Rights of Workers, issued in 1989 by the European Council in the form of a non-binding 'Solemn Declaration'.[87] On the surface, the Charter would appear to be not much more than a comparative labour law exercise extracting the least common denominator from national regimes. Supranational rules that are merely a compilation of rules already in force in all member countries do not have to be made formally binding; in this sense the weak formal status of the Charter follows logically from its content.[88]

Non-bindingness need not mean that explication of commonalities will always be without consequence. A collectively authorized catalogue of shared rules may make it more difficult for individual countries to move below present common standards. Moreover, there may be gaps between a country's formal rules and its actual practice that its national system of law enforcement may be too weak to close. To the extent that such a country's government cannot prevent such rules being included in a joint document, citizens or authorities seeking more effective enforcement may find it easier to mobilize public pressure.

Fourth, *governance by consultation* refers to mutual information and deliberation, on a mandatory or voluntary basis, as a substitute for legally mandated power-sharing and joint decision-making. This principle has long been employed within the Community itself, where the rights of the European Parliament are basically limited to being informed and heard by other bodies. In social policy, governance by consultation now seems to have become the preferred model for labour–management relations at the European enterprise level, where the Community is unable or unwilling to create legally enforceable codetermination rights and instead focuses on labour–management information and consultation.[89]

The situation is similar at the European and the sectoral level where the Delors Commission has instituted the 'Social Dialogue' in an effort to generate trust and cooperation through information-sharing and regular discussion. Even under the co-decision procedure of the Maastricht Treaty, the results of such consultations can become formally binding only by specific agreement between business and labour. Short of this, the effect of consultation depends on its contribution to a rational clarification of interests on both sides, by forcing groups to put forward presentable state-ments of their objectives and to make a case to each other as to why prevalence of their position over that of others would be in the 'public interest'.

4 *Governance by choice.* Community law increasingly offers national governments or market participants a choice between alternative ways of complying with it. Examples in social policy are the revised drafts of the Fifth Directive on Company Law and the European Company Statute, and certainly the proposed European Works Councils directive. Instead of prescribing a uniform mechanism of workforce participation, the directives offer firms and countries menus of alternative models from which they may choose to satisfy legal requirements.[90] Which alternative is chosen is left to national political choice, the preferences of market parties, especially management, and the relative strength of management and labour in a given institutional or economic setting.[91]

5 *Governance by diffusion.* To the extent that neo-voluntarism expects convergence across national borders, its privileged mechanism for this is regime diffusion through a multinational political market (Teague and Grahl 1991: esp. 231). A government that refuses to agree to high common European standards for health and safety or working hours, for example, may be attacked by its opposition for not letting its citizens enjoy the same rights as other Europeans. To avoid this it may prefer to fall in line with the other countries.[92] Also, short of common European legislation, coun-tries may come under domestic pressures to follow non-binding European recommendations or adapt 'best practice'. Similar pressures may be brought to bear on multinational employers by workers comparing their rights and benefits to those of workers in the firm's foreign plants.[93] Political regime diffusion must, however, compete with economic regime competition; while the former may create pressures to raise national standards, the latter may militate toward lowering them.

Neo-voluntarism in social policy represents a break with the practice of the European national welfare state to create 'hard', legally enforceable status rights and obligations for individual citizens and organized collectivities acting in, taking advantage of and being disadvantaged by market relations. Compared to welfare state interventionism, neo-voluntarism is much less statist, reflecting the European Union's lack of state capacity. In this sense, it entails a shift of social policy-making from the state to 'civil society'. However, unlike neo-corporatism, where strong quasi-public organizations of social groups are enabled by an interventionist public policy to negotiate and correct market outcomes, neo-voluntarism returns allocational decisions to private actors in private markets, with no possibility previously to readjust their political and organizational resources.[94]

National social policy in international context

What are the consequences of European integration for national social policy regimes, embedded as they have become in the internal market and the two-tier system of European social policy-making? While social citizenship in Europe remains nationally based, national social policy-making is increasingly becoming subject to powerful external constraints. These originate in the vertical dimension of the transnational two-tier polity, where they take the form of international obligations to adjust the national welfare state to requirements of cross-border mobility of workers, as well as in the horizontal dimension, where they result from the external effects and competitive pressures placed by an integrated economy on fragmented political sovereignty. Harmonization having been abandoned – except, to some extent, for the two isolated instances of encapsulated federalism – three kinds of constraints seem to be particularly relevant for national social policy in Europe today:

1 *Obligations in international law to enable cross-border mobility of labour.* A large and growing share of domestic social policy-making in European Union countries today is concerned with adjusting national law to the needs of international labour market integration. Typically this consists in the translation in national law of directives adopted by the Union. Social policy of this kind is mostly limited to what Scharpf (1993) has described as standardization of the interfaces between national systems, which is less politically and institutionally demanding than harmonization of national rules or the creation and enforcement of a body of directly applicable supranational law. All that is required of member countries is that they make movement of workers in and out of national labour markets as easy as movement within them. Apart from this, national 'sovereignty' and 'diversity' can remain intact.

At the same time, Union legislation and, in particular, the European Court of Justice have consistently expanded the concept of what constitutes obstacles to cross-border mobility, thus compelling member countries to spend considerable legislative and political effort on removing them. Rewriting national law to remove mobility barriers may be a technically exceedingly complex exercise, which contributes to the current discontent among national politicians with integrated Europe, in part because the attention and political capital national legislatures have to devote to the 'completion of the internal market' go at the expense of a wide range of other, potentially more politically rewarding areas of social policy.

What is more, international commitments to market-making may limit the substantive options of national social policies in surprising ways. Since withholding social benefits from non-nationals may always be construed as obstruction of cross-border mobility – and, even more so, of the individual rights of 'European citizenship' that the Court has liberally read into member countries' obligations to allow for mobility of labour – social policies that are politically or financially viable only if limited to national citizens will be increasingly difficult to uphold or pursue. For example, if Germany tried to reduce old-age poverty among women by introducing a high minimum pension, the increased benefits could probably not be withheld from former foreign workers living in their countries and drawing small German pensions for short spells of employment in Germany. This, however, would likely make the measure too expensive, and in any case would make it politically vulnerable. More generally, with all national social-security benefits potentially available to an infinite number of non-nationals, national social policy projects will in future have to be scrutinized for their financial and political compatibility with international commitments to cross-border mobility, with some likely to be ruled out as incompatible.

2   *Growing interdependence with actors in other national systems.* In an integrated economy governed by fragmented sovereignty, the operation of national regimes and the pursuit of nationally defined interests are to a significant extent conditional on the actions and reactions of external agents. This may be perceived as a threat to the sovereignty of national states and the integrity of their social policy regimes, as in the case of a foreign-based multinational company violating national plant closure legislation. As nation-states are highly sensitive to the danger of their legal systems being circumvented under protection of exterritoriality, they may decide to drop regulations that have ceased to be enforceable with national means. Where a deregulatory response of this kind is not politically possible, they may instead seek agreement with other states on some sort of 'pooling' of sovereignties, under which states help each other to restore the effectiveness of their respective legal orders. As pointed out above, common interests of nation-states in protecting fragmented sovereignty may give rise to supranational legislation obliging firms to respect local law ('territoriality principle'), creating supranational rules for multinational firms, or indeed 'harmonizing' national regulations. As the European experience demonstrates, it is paradoxically in the defence of national sovereignty that nation-states seem to be most likely to subject themselves to supranational regulation.

Where such regulation is not possible, another way of dealing with interdependence is horizontal coordination across national borders. Today, a growing share of the activities of national social policy actors, in particular interest groups, is devoted to building informal, issue-specific networks for mutual information and consultation with counterparts in other European countries. Participation in such arrangements is entirely voluntary, and is entered into only if it is perceived to be in line with nationally defined interests. As exit and non-entry are always possible, the geometry of coordination varies widely from issue to issue. Also, the resources used are exclusively nationally based, with participants from the better-endowed countries likely to exercise hegemony. Coordination networks cannot make binding decisions or impose obligations, and will as a rule side-step controversial issues on which it is clear that there can be no unanimous agreement.[95] For social interest groups, recourse to horizontal coordination represents a weak substitute for consolidated formal organization at supranational level, one that reproduces within European organized interests the voluntarism of the international system with its variable geometry, intergovernmental decision rules and soft forms of commitments.

3 *Competition between national systems for mobile production factors.* Under fragmented sovereignty, mobile production factors may easily emigrate from jurisdictions that impose high social costs or regulatory burdens on them, to others that do not. Pressures for what has been called 'competitive deregulation' – or, for that matter, 're-regulation' – result especially from the possibility that firms that are subjected by their home countries to broad social obligations may suffer disadvantages in international markets, and in response move jobs to lower-cost regimes. In the absence of European-wide harmonization of social obligations at a high level, this forces national governments to conduct their policies, social as well as economic, in line with imperatives of international 'competitiveness', as gauged by their attraction for mobile investors. As governments under fragmented sovereignty have little or no ability to control market participants, economic intervention becomes limited to provision of support to investors as an incentive to enter, or not to exit, the national system.

National competitiveness depends not just on costs, although these are important. Investors may also feel uncomfortable with procedural rules, like those that firms have to obey under codetermination. In any case, the ascent of national competitiveness to become the dominant objective of national policy reflects the fact that, under fragmented sovereignty, governance regimes, rather than containing competition, are themselves exposed to it. One consequence of this in social policy is mounting pressures to shift the financial base of the welfare state from employer contributions to general tax revenues, which for its sheer complexity alone would for a long time displace most other items on national social policy agendas. Also, cost-intensive new legislation, like the German *Pflegeversicherung* (long-term care insurance), will become increasingly difficult to pass. Even where re-regulation or outright deregulation of national social policy regimes can be avoided, competitive pressures are likely to result in power shifts inside them in favour of more mobile participants, especially capital, forcing governments and labour to be more 'reasonable' in enforcing existing regulations or trying to expand social protection.

Less direct although probably even more fundamental consequences for national social policy-making can be expected from competition law and the Maastricht Treaty's provisions on economic and monetary union. By ruling out 'state aids', the post-1992 competition policy has already made it difficult if not impossible for countries to subsidize domestic industries for the protection of employment. Competition policy also militates toward the privatization of hitherto nationalized sectors that have often been used to shelter parts of the national workforce. For the future, economic and monetary union require that member countries make their monetary and fiscal policies compatible with those of the other members, with the Treaty's criteria for accession to and continued participation in monetary union including low levels of inflation, budget deficit and public debt. Moreover, while fiscal policy remains nominally under national control, it will be narrowly constrained in that public borrowing will be limited under the Treaty to 3 per cent of GDP, and central banks are no longer allowed to extend credit to governments.[96]

Responsibility for 'economic convergence' under fragmented sovereignty lies exclusively with individual countries, which in many cases will for a considerable time have to commit themselves to rigorous stabilization and austerity measures that will inevitably involve cutbacks in – direct and indirect – welfare state spending. At the same time, economic union rules on fiscal policy and public debt pre-empt some of the classical instruments of national full employment policy. In fact, while an integrated federal European state could conceivably put its monetary and fiscal policies at the service of objectives other than monetary stability, as long as sovereignty remains fragmented, the only policy member countries can in the common interest be allowed to pursue is a monetaristic one. *Nota bene* that the Union's competition rules and convergence criteria do not require countries not to exceed a certain level of unemployment, or to provide for a minimum level of social protection.

It may be true that the Maastricht Treaty's provisions on economic and monetary union no more than ratify a development that has long taken place in the realities of the global economy: the demise of the European nation-state's 'Keynesian capacity'. But it is certainly also true that the Treaty makes observance of the laws of the international capital market a matter not just of political prudence, but of formal international obligation. Moreover, by limiting the choices available to national economic policy, and enshrining such limits in intergovernmental arrangements like the future European Central Bank that are insulated from political-democratic pressures, the Treaty provides national governments with additional reasons why they can do nothing to restore full employment, other than adjusting the labour market regime and the national welfare state to the imperatives of economic competitiveness.

Generally, national social policy in the institutional and economic context of European Union is likely to move between two alternatives, both rather different from the social-democratic welfare state of the postwar period. First, nation-states situated in an integrated economy may defend their authority and protect their remaining sovereignty by relieving themselves of economic responsibility and devolving control over the economy from the polity to the 'market'. As such deregulation requires sometimes quite dramatic political action, it can help sustain the appearance of internal sovereignty, although in reality it is aimed at dismantling it. As has been pointed out, deregulation can also be presented to the electorate as the only economically competitive political response to the constraints of internationalization. If carried to the end, as in the case of Thatcher, such a policy would combine market-driven industrial restructuring, large-scale privatization, retrenchment of social protection, restoration of managerial authority, downwardly flexible wages and working conditions, disablement of organized interests, especially trade unions, and the promotion of a large low-wage and low-skill sector to absorb some of the unemployed.

The alternative response, that of what may remain in the 1990s of social democracy, neo-corporatism and social partnership, is the construction at national level of coalitions to 'modernize' the national economy, with all other objectives subordinate to that of increasing national competitiveness. Post-social-democratic cooperative re-regulation can draw on the institutional and economic nationalism of labour movements prevented from acting at the supranational level by lack of state capacity and employer interlocutors. It may also count on the employers, whose main interest is to forestall supranational state formation and European-level economic intervention; who therefore benefit from labour being contained in national political circuits; and who can be certain that, in the face of external competitive pressures and because of their capacity to exit, they will be the alliance's senior partners. Finally, national governments can hope to increase their support from both business and labour for defending shared national interests in the international arena, thereby defending their own legitimacy as well and further reinforcing the national organization of politics and the intergovernmental character of international economic governance.

In both versions of national social policy in an integrated Europe, national sovereignty and democracy remain formally intact while their use and substance change significantly. Under neo-liberal deregulation as well as under cooperative re-regulation, national governments refrain from imposing hard legal obligations on market participants, especially on business, either because of a general belief in the merits of withdrawal of the public power from the market, or because international treaties and factual conditions have already *de facto* confined the possible purposes of public intervention to the creation of incentives and the removal of deterrents for mobile investors. Similarly, nationally based democracy is in both cases constrained by a need not only to respond to competitive pressures before responding to citizen demands, or to define the latter in terms of a technically correct response to the former, but also to observe the guide-lines on national competition, employment and fiscal policies created by nation-states for themselves by intergovernmental agreement. As factual and international legal constraints on national policy become more strin-gent, national governments of whatever complexion, just as the supra-national regime they have built, become dependent on the voluntarism of the marketplace, having lost recourse to the hard law that used to be the principal tool of economic state interventionism in the past.

In conclusion

European integration has added a second, supranational level of social policy to the national welfare state. Expectations, however, that supra-national social policy would gradually absorb and replace national social policy have not materialized. Far from replicating the national welfare state, the European Union has developed into a polity *sui generis*. Citizen-ship, including its social and industrial extensions, remains firmly vested in national states, and supranational jurisdiction over social policy is limited by intergovernmentalism to market-making and a few instances of encap-sulated federalism. Apart from these, supranational social policy, lacking the signature capacity of the national welfare state to create enforceable rights and obligations of citizenship, is confined in its reach by its depen-dence on the voluntarism of both sovereignty-conscious member states and interest-conscious private market participants.

That there will be no supranational European welfare state to absorb the national welfare states does not, however, mean that integration leaves the latter unaffected. A supranational social policy regime limited to market-making, forces national social policy to devote significant political resources to the opening of national borders. It also requires national actors pursuing nationally defined interests to develop new methods of mutual, issue-specific international coordination as a substitute for centralized organization and authoritative governance. This extends the voluntarism of intergovernmental decision-making into the relations between nationally divided interests in European civil society. Moreover, unable to impose harmonized social standards on national systems, supranational voluntarism fails to contain competition between them. With market integration laying national welfare states open to unprecedented competitive pressures, nationally confined economic and social policies become dependent on the voluntary co-operation of mobile production factors, forcing governments to rely more and more on the provision of incentives and inducements for the latter.

In the process national social policy regimes and the national social compacts that sustain them are bound to be fundamentally transformed.

With fiscal and monetary policies insulated from popular political pressure, and in particular unavailable for labour-market-correcting, redistributive purposes, national polities are increasingly finding themselves forced to follow the lead of the emerging supranational polity and move away from hard obligations to soft incentives, and from social-interventionist to liberal democracy. As democracy remains vested in nationally demarcated political communities – where it provides strong legitimation for national sovereignty – it must generate support for policies that, simultaneously, conform to international obligations to open up national borders for international markets; respect international guidelines for monetary and fiscal policies that preclude any return to a Keynesian full employment policy at national level; redesign national economic and social policies to accommodate internationally mobile 'market forces'; and generally accept the need for politics to withdraw from authoritative interference with the economy, through either deregulation or re-regulation. How democracy will fare when the loss of its ability to protect society from the vagaries of the marketplace is fully realized by its citizens remains to be seen.

Appendix: unions and employers in the European Community: on the logic of transnational class politics

The neo-voluntarist bias of European Community social policy, and the corresponding rise of economic competitiveness to dominance in national social policy regimes, are explained by two factors: the intergovernmental limitations imposed by the nation-states on the Community's jurisdiction and decision-making, and a particular asymmetry in the interests and capacities of labour and capital in the internationalizing European economy, in relation to each other as well as to intergovernmental policy-making.

Social policy, in the European Community as in national states, is made not just by governments, but also by organized social classes. In the Community, however, class politics is far more complex. This is because the constituents of both classes, labour and capital, have a choice between *class* and *national* interests and strategies, and the corresponding organizational forms and political alliances. Class interests of *labour* seek supranational protection against 'competitive deregulation' of national systems, and generally against competition between these for internationally mobile capital, with the resulting pressures on wages and working conditions (Figure 4.1, cell 1). National interests, on the other hand, seek to outcompete labour in other countries on investment, export markets and employment (economic nationalism), and to defend the integrity of established national industrial relations systems against supranational re-regulation and the effects of international interdependence (institutional nationalism; cell 2). Among *capital*, class interests are to remove barriers to mobility of capital and labour across national borders, without in the

Interests pursued in		
	Class strategies	National strategies
Labour	Supranational protection against competitive deregulation; prevention of social system competition for mobile capital (1)	National prosperity through high competitiveness of domestic economy; stability and autonomy of national industrial relations (2)
Capital	Removal of barriers to mobility and market expansion, without 'market distortion' by supranational welfare state (3)	Power shift in national systems in favour of enterprises and investors through competitive deregulation (4)

Figure 4.1   *Social interests and interest-political strategies in transnational social policy*

process having to accept 'market-distorting' redistributive intervention or the development of welfare-state-like international institutions (cell 3). Capital's national interests, by comparison, lie in strengthening the position of enterprises and investors in national economies through competitive deregulation, and generally in adjusting national economic and institutional conditions to business needs (cell 4).

Closer inspection of the strategic options available in a transnational system of interest politics reveals that capital finds it structurally easier than labour to pursue its transnational class interests, since it can do this by either not acting at all, or continuing to act exclusively at national level. Labour, on the other hand, can pursue its transnational class interests only if it manages to define positive common objectives; build a transnational capacity for collective action; and overcome the logic of non-decision inherent in the intergovernmental system. It is this differential significance of action and non-action that governs the transnational class politics of European social policy, and accounts for its results.

The principal reason for the structural superiority of capital at trans-national level is that the interests it has at that level are overwhelmingly negative in character, i.e. either require no more than comparatively non-demanding market-making policies of 'negative integration', or are best satisfied by non-decisions. Both kinds of decisions, however, are exactly what intergovernmentalism is most likely to produce on its own, for reasons of its own. For capital, the very deficiencies of intergovernmental decision-making are therefore a political asset. Insofar as the structural bias of inter-governmentalism towards market-making can be presented as protecting national 'cultural diversity' and democratic sovereignty, the particularistic interests of capital as a class, and the selectivity of intergovernmental decision-making that favours them, may in addition come to benefit from strong universalistic legitimations.

Unlike the class-political interests of capital, those of labour require positive political decisions and central regulations capable of suspending social system competition. These, in turn, demand strong supranational institutions capable of central regulation of the integrated market as a whole, and overriding national regulations. Their development, however, is stunted by the very constellation of national sovereignty and transnational interdependence that is described by the notion of 'fragmented sovereignty'. Centralization is unlikely because it will meet the resistance of the nation-states determined and well positioned to defend their sovereignty; because, given the way decisions are made in the Community, it would be bound to result in political immobility; and because it would come in conflict with the only available mode of democratic legitimation, which is and will for long be nationally based. With respect to supranational institution-building, that is to say, the class interests of labour are at a twofold structural disadvantage: they require unanimity – or at least a qualified majority – among governments, whereas business interests in non-decisions need no more than the support of one ('veto') country; and they lack legitimacy in a transnational economy in which the development of economic identities, e.g. of multinational firms and networks of firms, has, very likely irreversibly, outpaced the development of a common political identity.

The same asymmetry that characterizes the relationship between transnational class interests and intergovernmental decision-making controls the bilateral relations between capital and labour. Here too capital is privileged by the fact that it can achieve its class interests by non-action, while the class interests of labour depend for their realization not just on their own transnational organization, but also on the willingness of labour's opponent, capital, to organize itself as an interlocutor capable of negotiating binding agreements. Exactly this, however, European employers have consistently refused. UNICE, the peak association of European employers, has no powers to negotiate on behalf of its members, and is not seeking any since its organizational weakness represents a political strength in its relation not just with the Commission, but also and in particular with European unions.[97] This is because where regulations and decisions are to be produced by bilateral negotiations, interests in non-regulation and non-decisions are best served by functional, if not physical, absence: better by silence than by voice. Not only in international but also in industrial relations is there a strategy of the 'empty chair'. For interests in negative integration, non-organization is the best organization, all the more so since it requires no effort and conveniently ensues from non-action as a default condition.

In the reality of Western Europe, transnational non-organization of class interests means their continuing national organization. The ideal transnational organization of capital, in this sense, consists of its already existing national organizations. Employers can best pursue their transnational class interests if they participate in organized class politics, to the extent they (have to) do so at all, exclusively at national level, thereby pre-empting the development of transnational corporatism as a market-regulating mechanism; protecting cross-border economic activities against political infringement; and representing and reinforcing inside national social policy regimes the competitive pressures emanating from the integrated transnational market.

While for the transnational class interests of capital, confinement of collective interest politics in national organizations and strategies is the preferred condition, this abandons the class interests of labour to the unfavourable decision logic of the intergovernmental system, with its bias for negative and non-decisions. Still, European labour has without much resistance resigned itself to being limited to class-politically suboptimal national strategies, and not just because of the impossibility of central negotiations without a counterpart willing and able to negotiate. In addition, at least four reasons can be identified why the Community's intergovernmental 'decision trap' (Scharpf 1988) and the non-organization of European employers at supranational level have been so successful in keeping organized labour locked in its national starting positions:

1   The considerable differences in the prosperity of European national economies tend to result in European-wide labour standards being perceived by workers and unions in poorer countries as devices to protect their fellow workers in richer countries from investment and employment losses. Such standards are, therefore, only half-heartedly supported, and are if necessary undercut. This is particularly likely where common social policy minima are not economically underwritten by a redistributive structural policy at European level, paid for by the richer countries and aimed at raising the productivity of the poorer ones, to enable them to compete under high general labour standards. Policies of this kind, however, happen to be notoriously difficult to agree on in an intergovernmental decision-making system, like that of the Community. In their absence, economic nationalism (Figure 4.1, cell 2) is the most plausible strategy for, already nationally organized, worker interests, both in the weaker as well as in the stronger countries – with the latter sometimes seeking protection for their domestic employment by trying to extend a supposedly universalistic 'social dimension' to the integrated market.

2   European unions have formed and grown as national organizations, in unison with European nation-states and as part of their transformation into democratic welfare states. Within these they are by and large securely lodged. Supranational unions encompassing the transnational internal market cannot hope for a similarly supportive symbiosis with state institutions. Moreover, whatever state-like structures may emerge in the Community, they will certainly be quite unlike most national states, forcing on unions painful changes in organizational routines, with uncertain consequences for the career prospects of existing staff. Also, because of the high

heterogeneity of the national systems involved, any internationalization of industrial relations must affect national labour interests differentially, and indeed is bound to favour the organizations and interests of those countries that serve as a model for the supranational system. The same 'logic of diversity' (Hoffmann 1966) that sets apparently insurmountable limits to the supranational integration of nation-states thus reproduces itself in the realm of collective interest organization.

For European national union movements, supranational integration of industrial relations is inevitably saddled with uncertainty about its effects not just on the balance of power between capital and labour in general, but also on the relative position of each union's members compared to union members in other countries. The result is an institutional nationalism determined to defend the integrity of existing national institutions and organizational forms, and willing to accept internationalization only to the extent that it does not undermine the stability and autonomy of national institutions, or disadvantage nationally institutionalized interests (cell 2). The resulting limits to integration within European labour as a class are the same as those between European nation-states: in both cases, they reflect the defence of, however residual, national sovereignties and action capacities in the face of growing economic interdependence against centrally determined reorganization with its uncertain consequences for the internal stability and international position of national systems. Even among unions, that is, all rhetoric to the contrary notwithstanding, 'subsidiarity' is far more popular than harmonization or centralization, in spite of its suboptimality for an effective pursuit of transnational class interests.

3 Economic and institutional nationalism of labour can be rewarded and reinforced by strategic behaviour of capital. As an alternative to the pursuit of transnational class interests, employers can offer unions national cross-class alliances, both to promote the competitiveness of national economies in the internal market and to defend national institutions against supranational interference. Such coalitions do not conflict with the transnational class interest of capital in unregulated international markets. Indeed they advance these, in that they divert labour from pursuing *its* class interests, and thus make supranational corporatism even more unlikely. Here again, for capital, unlike for labour, national action is also international action.

In addition, the embedding of national modernization coalitions between capital and labour in an internationally integrated market exposes such coalitions to competitive pressures. Under conditions of economic globalization, these improve the positions of employers and investors within national industrial relations systems even in the absence of formal deregulation. As the expansion of integrated markets without an integrated state proceeds, employers can expect to become more than ever the dominant partners in cooperative labour relations within the old nation-states, if only because they represent the internationally more mobile production factor. For competing national cross-class alliances to become the interest-political rule, all that is required is the refusal of a single country's labour movement to participate in transnational class formation and organizational integration. Since offers by employers of national cooperation for international competitiveness can expect to be favourably received, given labour's already existing disposition towards economic and institutional nationalism, this condition is highly likely to be met. If unions in just one important country withdraw from transnational collective action to join a competitive–cooperative national modernization coalition, all other national unions are forced to do the same. Once more, the principle applies that to realize its interests, labour requires unanimity, whereas capital needs no more than the absence of unanimity.

4   The governments of European welfare states derive an important part of their legitimacy from mediating and reinforcing compromises and coalitions between social groups with conflicting interests, especially between capital and labour. They will therefore as a rule support employer offers to unions of national modernization alliances, and will be prepared politically to subsidize them. One way in which governments can make participation in such alliances attractive to unions is by promising in return to help them defend the integrity of national industrial relations systems against supranational interference.[98] Given the specific decision-making logic of the intergovernmental system, this is not difficult for governments to do. Nor is it costly, as the preferences of national governments prominently include the independence and sovereignty of national institutions, strongly motivating them to defend their own, privileged role in mediating social peace, and to refuse supranational institutions the legitimacy premium potentially derivable from such mediation.

5

Social Movements and the Changing Structure of Political Opportunity in the European Union

Gary Marks and Doug McAdam

To an observer of the contemporary world it might seem obvious that social movements and revolutions are, first and foremost, political phenomena.[99] In light of the momentous changes wrought by the Eastern European revolutions of 1988–9 and the myriad nationalist movements currently operating throughout the former Warsaw Pact countries, it would seem the height of folly to deny political status and significance to social movements and revolutions. And yet, barely twenty-fve years ago, the prevailing academic view did just that. Reflecting the conceptual dominance of the collective behaviour perspective, social movements were seen as, at best, a form of 'pre-political' behaviour; as warnings to those in power of emergent strains in society (Smelser 1963). Accordingly, movements were depicted as more ephemeral and expressive than enduring and instrumental. Indeed, on the issue of rationality, the classic movement theorists were quite explicit. Movements were motivated more by a need to cope with the psychological stresses occasioned by 'strain' than by the straightforward pursuit of political/material ends. Given this view, social movements were left, in William Gamson's paraphrase of the traditional view, to 'the social psychologist whose intellectual tools prepare him to better understand the irrational' (1990: 133). So it was that sociologists (and the occasional psychologist) came to dominate the study of social movements, while their colleagues in political science eschewed the subject.

The 1970s, however, were witness to a significant paradigm shift in the study of social movements and revolutions. Fuelled by the turbulence of the 1960s and 1970s, scholars such as Peter Eisinger (1973), Charles Tilly (1978), William Gamson (1990) and John McCarthy and Mayer Zald (1973, 1977) rejected the classical collective behaviour perspective in favour of a more explicitly political view of social movements. At the heart of the emerging 'resource mobilization' and 'political process' perspectives was the assumption of a close connection between institutionalized politics and the ebb and flow of social protest. This close connection was reflected in both the dynamics of collective action and the historical origins of the 'modern social movement form'.

Regarding the dynamics of collective action, the argument was straight-forward. Social movements and revolutions were thought to emerge and develop in response to changes that rendered institutionalized political systems increasingly vulnerable or receptive to challenge (Tilly 1978; McAdam 1982). As Peter Eisinger argued, 'protest signifies changes not only among previously quiescent or conventionally oriented groups but also in the political system itself' (1973: 28). Thus, a close causal relationship was posited between institutionalized and movement politics.

Just as important to the emerging 'resource mobilization' and 'political process' perspectives on social movements was the fundamental assertion that what we know as the modern social movement form arose historically in response to the emergence of the modern nation-state (Tilly et al. 1975; Tilly 1978). The centralization of power in the emerging national state and its legitimation of a public civic culture gave rise to new forms of interest aggregation and articulation to replace the private corporatist forms characteristic of the *ancien régime* (Sewell 1990; Tarrow 1994). So social movements were linked not simply dynamically, but historically, to the rise of the modern nation-state.

While we are critical of, and will later take issue with, the prevailing top-down view of this historical process, we concur with the underlying theoretical premise: shifts in the structure and geographic locus of insti-tutionalized power can be expected to be accompanied by simultaneous changes in the structure and locus of mass politics. When we shift our focus from the historical rise of the nation-state to contemporary events, this general proposition has important implications for thinking about the consequences that are likely to follow from the new transnational forms of governance that appear to be emerging today. Though by no means the only example of this trend, we will none the less focus our attention on the emerging European Union and the EU process more generally. This restricted focus is due both to space constraints and to the limits of our expertise. We simply know the EU case better than any other contem-porary example of the broader trend we seek to understand.

Our general argument is straightforward: to the extent that European integration results in the replacement or, more likely, the decline in the importance of the nation-state as the exclusive seat of formal political power, we can expect attendant changes in those forms of interest aggregation/articulation historically linked to the state. In addition to the modern social movement, these forms would include trade unions and interest groups. Here we are not merely making the standard definitional point that the boundaries between these forms – social movements, parties, public interest lobbies and unions – are inherently fuzzy. Rather we are arguing that the conceptual coherence of these categories is itself historically contingent and, in light of current trends, increasingly problematic. That is, the distinctions that we associate with these forms are inextricably linked to the historical rise and refinement of a *national* system of politics within which these distinctions were negotiated and subsequently institutionalized. So the generic labour union exists as a distinct form and coherent political entity only within the context of the nation-state. And if, indeed, institutionalized power is shifting away from the nation-state, then we would do well to relax the conceptual boundaries between these historically circumscribed political forms. Just as guilds, religious orders and other politico-organizational artefacts of the *ancien régime* had no standing in the emerging nation-state, neither do the rigid distinctions between interest groups and social movements mean much in the context of the EU. All stand in much the same relationship to the integration *process*. They share the status of 'challenging groups' which hope to contest and shape the emerging institutions and philosophy of the EU.

This emphasis on the emergent, contested nature of European integration stands in stark contrast to the typically top-down accounts of the rise of the modern state. So before we turn our attention to an assessment of the likely impact of European integration on the political prospects of several contemporary 'challenging groups', we will want to revisit critically the prevailing argument linking the origins of the nation-state to the development of the social movement form.

The emergence of the modern state and the national social movement

In recent years scholars such as Charles Tilly (1982), William Sewell (1990) and Sidney Tarrow (1994) have argued that what we know as the social movement emerged in response to the rise of the modern state. This is not to say that there was little or no collective action prior to the emergence of the nation-state, only that the *form* and *characteristics* of that action were very different from those we associate with contemporary social movements and revolutions.

Under the *ancien régime*, popular protest activity had four defining characteristics. First, it tended to be local in origin and scope. So rather than marching on the capital, peasants seized local grain stores. Rather than orchestrating national boycotts, the aggrieved citizenry drove the local magistrate out of town. Given the decentralized nature of power preceding the rise of the national state, it made sense to attack local rather than national targets. More to the point, the 'national' did not yet exist in anything like the form we know it now. Second, collective action tended to be reactive rather than proactive. Third, it was typically spontaneous instead of planned. And finally, popular protests were ephemeral rather than enduring.

According to the prevailing account, the rise of the modern state changed all of this. The key to the transformation was the dramatic increase in centralized authority vested in the national state. As the state came to exercise increasing control over more and more aspects of daily life, it also came to be seen as the appropriate target of collective efforts to promote or resist change in society. So, over time, popular protest took on a more national, rather than localized, character.

All well and good. Certainly the basic punch-line of the story seems correct. The rise of the modern state clearly is associated with a significant shift in the locus and nature of collective action. What is much less convincing is the top-down, state-centric view of the process linking these two outcomes. The idea that state formation shaped the subsequent development of institutions we now associate with the nation-state strikes us as an overly simplified gloss on a contested, reciprocal process. While social movements and the political institutions of civil society grew in response to the rise of the modern state, it makes sense to conceive both civil society and the modern polity as the outcome of a prolonged, contested and, above all, mutually interactive process of political restructuring. In our view, then, the modern, democratic state was as much an outcome as the architect of this emergent process.

While it is not our intent to sketch the definitive 'revisionist' account of this process, we can offer two sorts of 'evidence' in support of our alternative perspective. The first is simply a historical observation. It is not the case that state structures occur chronologically prior to the political forms noted above. Rather they typically develop apace of one another. This is perhaps clearest in the French case, where prototypical movement groups and/or political parties – as represented by the various revolutionary factions – coexist with embryonic state structures.

To give one example among the many that could be offered here, trade unions in most Western societies developed national federations to campaign better for basic legal freedoms so that they could bargain in the labour market more effectively. But once such federations were established they took up a range of functions, including lobbying for substantive state legislation of working conditions, maximum hours and minimum wages, etc. To the extent they were successful, they created the basis for further demands and legitimated a political strategy for achieving basic union goals. While there are wide variations across European countries in the institutional configuration of trade unionism and the political channels that were available to workers, it is clear that the causal arrows from union-building to state-building go in both directions. As trade unions were creating peak organizations better to influence authoritative decision-making, so they sought to extend the reach of the state. The second piece of evidence we would offer in support of this alternative perspective concerns the fundamental shift in the ideological foundations of government that accompanied the rise of the modern state. We think this shift bears the imprint of the kind of emergent, contested process we are describing. Indeed, the legitimating account of the modern, democratic state is nothing if not a product of popular contestation.

Above we characterized collective action in the *ancien régime* as local, reactive, spontaneous and ephemeral. By contrast, in the modern, democratic context, popular protest tends to be national in focus, proactive, planned and enduring. We can account for the geographic shift in the locus of protest on the basis of the more centralized nature of governmental authority in the modern state. But that is only part – and arguably the less important part – of the story. For had the modern state simply adopted the legitimating ideology of the *ancien régime*, we might have seen a shift in the locus of collective action, but almost certainly no change in its form and typical characteristics. But the collapse of the old order occasioned not only a shift in the scale and locus of governmental authority, but also a thorough discrediting of the ideological account on which it and the 'family' of corporatist groups empowered by that account rested.

In their place there arose the modern state and the variety of organizational forms – including social movements – so familiar to us today. In turn, this distinctive organizational topography reflects the very different legitimating frame that developed apace of the process of state formation. Whereas the earlier monarchical states rested on the notion of divine right, the modern democratic state governed at the behest 'of the people'. This latter account legitimated the rise of a *public* civic culture to replace the privatized system of corporatist charters characteristic of the *ancien régime*. Under the terms of this new system, it was not so much groups which survived at the behest of the state as the reverse. The state's claim to legitimate authority depended upon it being seen as a responsible steward vis-à-vis various 'client' publics. The key point is that this sea change was not the product of unilateral state action, but rather was imposed on the emerging states by the embryonic predecessors of these various 'client' publics. So Girondists and Jacobins in France, Sons of Liberty in the American colonies and their counterparts elsewhere were as much the architects of the modern nation-state as its offspring.

This view of the contested, reciprocal nature of the relationship of regimes to popular politics reflects more than our reading of history. It reflects as well our interpretation of contemporary events in Europe. There, under the aegis of European integration, a new 'multi-level polity' would appear to be emerging in response to precisely the mix of top-down institution-building and bottom-up contestation described above. The ultimate impact of this process is far from clear. What is certain is that just as the shift from the *ancien régime* to the modern nation-state had implications for the locus and forms of collective action, so too does integration create new constraints and opportunities for European social movements.

European integration: implications for states and social movements

European integration offers social scientists any number of fascinating topics for study. But among the most interesting to us concerns the potential of the process to set in motion the same broad transformation in governance structures and attendant organizational forms that we now associate with the rise of the modern nation-state. How likely is this to happen? Clearly, the final outcome of integration is uncertain. However, fundamental changes have already taken place, and while their causes are subject to debate, the locus of decision-making and the direction of change are reasonably clear. In this section we will review the character of the emerging European polity and what it implies about possible future changes in the spatial character and form of social movements. We begin, however, with a brief history of European integration.[100]

The European Economic Community (EEC) was established by six countries, Belgium, France, West Germany, Italy, the Netherlands and Luxemburg, in 1958, in an effort to 'lay the foundations of an ever closer union among the peoples of Europe'. The impetus for the EEC lay chiefly in the experience of the Second World War and the overriding desire to quench, or at least moderate, the intense nationalisms that fuelled successive and ever more destructive wars among the European powers. The founders of the EEC wished to enmesh European countries in a web of interdependencies that would encourage the growth of supranational loyalties as governments and peoples experienced the benefits of co-operation. The postwar decades provided a unique window of political feasibility for this ambition. Western Europe was desperately trying to rebuild its economic base, and European integration was trumpeted as a pragmatic step in this direction. In the context of the Cold War, traditional antagonisms among the old imperial powers of Western Europe diminished as their sense of collective vulnerability to the Warsaw Pact grew. In response to these and other unique pressures and opportunities, the European Economic Community, as founded in the Treaty of Rome, was a mixture of supranational idealism and practical measures for economic cooperation.

The past thirty-eight years have been characterized by extended periods of stasis, most recently the years of 'Eurosclerosis' from de Gaulle's reassertion of member state veto power in 1965 to the early 1980s, punctuated by periods of institutional recasting, as in the Single European Act (1986) creating an EU-wide market for goods, labour and capital, and the decision at Maastricht in December 1991 to proceed with monetary union by the year 1999. Up to the present, the EU has not had a formal constitution; its development has been guided by irregular and *ad hoc* institution-building to reap collective benefits in particular policy areas (Marks, forthcoming). In recent decades the original idealistic component of the EU has been very much overshadowed by hard-nosed bargaining among the executives of member states to achieve specific, mostly economic, benefits.

The question of how one should describe the governance structure of the EU has been the subject of intense debate between those who focus on the development of a European capacity for supranational decision-making and those who focus on member state control of institutional development (Caporaso and Keeler 1993; Marks 1993; Marks et al.

forthcoming). The debate is compounded by disagreement about how to explain institutional outcomes, and by the implicit assumption on the part of many academic observers of the EU that it is more important to explain where the European Union may eventually end up than its current political dynamics.

However, these debates hide substantial agreement about how decision-making in the EU has actually developed. Virtually all observers agree that national states no longer monopolize policy-making in a growing number of areas (Schmitter in this volume). Decision-making is increasingly shared among institutions operating at different levels of government, at the subnational and supranational levels as well as the national level.

Early proponents of the EU foresaw a polity in which states would wither away, but the past four decades have not seen anything of the sort. Member state executives have played the decisive role in the treaties and major pieces of legislation that specify the outlines of the present structure (Moravcsik 1991). Treaties, including above all the original Treaty of Rome and the Maastricht Treaty, actually formalize the monopoly of existing states as the recognized legal bodies in the process of institutional creation in the EU.

However, when one shifts from the high politics of treaty-making to policy-making in individual policy areas, the role of national states and their political executives is far less sharply defined. Here, one sees diverse policy networks made up of member state executives, their civil services, national courts and other state agencies, including subnational governments at various levels, interacting with diverse private or semi-public groups and EU institutions (Nugent 1995; Mazey and Richardson 1993; Marks et al. forthcoming). Member state institutions are almost never excluded from such networks, and they continue to provide most of the key actors in the process of policy implementation. But this should not cloud the novelty of the present situation, which is that national political institutions no longer monopolize decision-making in a number of important fields of policy. EU institutions now influence decision-making across most spheres of public policy, and they play a role that is as large, or larger, than national institutions in regulating regional development, agriculture and agricultural subsidies, capital flows, international movement of labour, competition and the regulation of trade in goods and services. In addition, subnational institutions at the regional and local level play an important role in diverse areas of policy provision, and in some countries, particularly in Belgium, Spain and Germany, they play a wide-ranging and decisive role in policy formulation.

The most powerful institution at the EU level remains the Council of Ministers, which is dominated by the executives of the member states. But since the Single European Act of 1986, which ushered in the integrated market, decision-making in the Council on a range of issues, including the single market itself, has been by qualified majority. The number of votes for each state ranges from ten for the four largest countries (France,

Germany, Italy, and the United Kingdom) to two for the smallest, Luxemburg, making a total of eighty-seven votes in all with a minimum of sixty-two votes necessary for qualified majority. Under this system, decisions in the Council are determined by member state executives collectively but not individually, a situation that is ambiguous – and frustrating – for those who wish to pin down sovereignty by identifying a final and ultimate source of authority in the EU.

Alongside the Council are three institutions, the European Commission, the European Court of Justice and the European Parliament, which are more or less independent of member states. The Commission, the most powerful supranational institution in the EU, serves both as political executive (alongside the Council) and as civil service. The European Court of Justice is, by virtue of the principle of primacy, the court of last appeal on Union law, and the European Parliament is a legislature whose powers have grown significantly over the past decade, though they are constrained in relation to those of national legislatures.

The creation of what we have called a multi-level polity has resulted from a centripetal process in which decision-making has spun away from the national level, both up to the EU and down to subnational governments. The development of the EU is, in terms of locus of authority, a mirror image of that of the development of the modern nation-state. The overall direction of power redistribution in the process of state-building from the thirteenth to the twentieth centuries was towards the centre. The monopolization of legitimate authority, the creation of a secular hierarchical system of justice, the deepening and widening of taxation, all pressed decision-making towards the national level. This process was greatly intensified with the rise of nationalism across Europe and the identification of centralized extraction, provision of welfare and control of various sectors of the economy and society with the interest of the nation as expressed by the state.

Given the duration of this development and the movement in some programme areas towards further centralization – this time at the EU level – it is tempting to see European integration as a further step in this process. But the spin-off of decision-making away from the state over the last three decades has been just as visible in the shift down to the subnational level as it is in the shift up to the European level. Governments across Western Europe have experimented with ways to deconcentrate administration and even decentralize decision-making to mollify ethno-linguistic minorities, to bring policy provision nearer policy receivers, to cushion demands on the state and to reduce the central tax burden (Keating 1988). Over the last three decades Belgium has been transformed from a unitary into a federal polity; Italy, France and Spain, previously highly centralized political systems, have created a comprehensive layer of regional government; and Greece, and to a more limited extent Portugal, have moved tentatively in the same direction, partly in response to the financial advantages of participation in the EU's structural policy. Only Germany, which is a federal polity in a culturally homogeneous society, has moved steadily in the opposite direction. Ireland remains highly centralized, though there are pressures for the creation of regional government, and in the United Kingdom Prime Minister Thatcher restricted the autonomy of subnational governments and resisted demands for devolution, though these are unlikely to dissipate in the future.

Given the process of institution-building in the EU and variations across policy areas, one should not expect uniformity of response on the part of social and political groups. No uniform structure of political opportunity has developed, or even shows signs of developing. Institution-building in the EU is taking place in the absence of a strong legitimating myth or ideology – indeed, this is one of its most important characteristics. The process is an *ad hoc* one, leading to greater heterogeneity of policy regimes rather than one overarching model (Mazey and Richardson 1993). As a result, the impact of the EU on various 'challenging groups' – including social movements – has, to date, been highly variable. Indeed, it is hard to make general statements about the 'system' as a whole. One can, however, discern beyond the specifics of particular cases two general factors that shape the unique mix of constraints and opportunities available to any given group: (1) the relative structural access a group has to EU institutions; and (2) the general policy receptivity of the Union – particularly the Commission – to issues salient to the group. Together, these two factors serve to specify, for any given group, its structure of 'EU-level political opportunities'.

But the political impact of the EU on any given group is not solely a function of Union-level structures and attitudes. These structures and attitudes serve merely to define a new external environment for a group. How successful a group is in adapting to and interacting with this environment is more a function of its internal characteristics. Of particular relevance here is the way inherited institutions and ideologies may constrain a group's ability to exploit whatever EU-level opportunities are available. That is, the link between political opportunity and movement response is not at all reflexive. To the extent that a movement is wedded to the existing political order, i.e. is oriented to a national system of law, a national system of membership incentives or belief structures, etc., so we would expect to find powerful sources of resistance to institutional adaptation (Krasner 1988).

Together, these two sets of factors – EU opportunities and internal organizational constraints – have shaped the overall impact of integration on any given group or movement. When combined they yield a two by two diagram (Figure 5.1).

In the remainder of this chapter we will use this basic conceptual framework to assess the impact that integration has had on three major European movements. The focus on internal constraints will also allow us to evaluate which of the four are in the best position to mobilize effectively in the future.

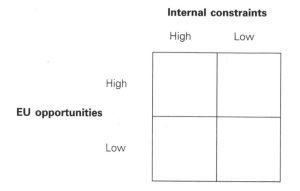

Figure 5.1   *Internal and external context of transnational mobilization*

The labour movement

Trade unions have been profoundly influenced by the EU and the widening of market competition in Europe. However, they have found it very difficult to adapt to these new circumstances by building transnational organizations to extend their national bargaining leverage to the European arena. European integration has restructured the political and economic contexts in which unions operate, but the ability of unions to adapt to and exploit those opportunities is constrained by their history.

All trade unions attempt to increase their members' wages, improve their working conditions and create a favourable social and political context for workers. However, the character of union organization differs widely across Western countries. In countries where unions developed gradually since the nineteenth century in a relatively non-repressive legal climate, union organization reflects the accretion of early craft unions, organized exclusively by occupation, a later and competing layer of industrial unions, organized by industry irrespective of occupation, and a subsequent layer of general unions, composed of unskilled workers irrespective of occupation or industry. The British Trades Union Congress is made up of some one hundred overlapping craft, industrial and general unions, reflecting the accretion and survival of diverse organizations over the past two centuries. At the other extreme are union movements that have been purposefully created or re-created after some fundamental political disjuncture. German unions were re-established after the Second World War along industrial lines. The DGB, the principal German union federation, contains just fifteen unions with mutually exclusive memberships.

Diverse political and religious cleavages across Western Europe have compounded these organizational contrasts with competing socialist and communist union movements; Catholic, Protestant and non-denominational movements; and unions organized along ethnic lines. Finally, there are wide variations in the extent to which white-collar and professional employees are organized in dominant blue-collar unions or form separate unions.

The result is a diverse mosaic of organizational forms at every level of industrial relations: in the workplace, among individual unions and among union federations. The organizational structure of union movements reflects particular national historical trajectories, and, given the diversity of historical experience across Western Europe, the study of union movements is a study of historically rooted variation (Marks 1989).

In addition, union movements have come to depend on national political and legal systems to mobilize members, structure collective bargaining and create opportunities for legislation. Unions were deeply affected by the creation of the modern nation-state and national markets, and as a result they are embedded in distinctly national structures of political opportunity. In the nineteenth century and first half of the twentieth century, trade unions across Western Europe were transformed from organizations representing workers in particular localities and regions to national organizations bargaining routinely with employers at the national level. As national product markets developed, unions followed by placing their own organizations on a national basis so that they could encompass the supply of workers in the relevant product market in order to minimize employers' fears that by acquiescing to union demands they would be undercut by non-unionized employers.

In this period unions developed intensive political strategies to gain national political influence. Across Western Europe unions came to devote considerable financial and organizational resources to pressure governments to legislate improvements in their members' working lives. Unions formed national federations to coordinate their political efforts and most unions have maintained close links to labour or socialist parties. Unions came to pursue a dual strategy, pressing their demands for improvements in wages, working conditions and welfare in politics as well as directly in the labour market.

The relationship between unions and the national state has operated in both directions. Not only did unions respond to the development of the modern nation-state by nationalizing their own organization, but they were also key actors in creating the state by campaigning for political inclusion, welfare reforms and state intervention in the economy. In the process, unions were intermeshed with the political system in which they operated. As organizations that are extremely sensitive to legal constraints on their ability to organize workers and use their labour market power to mount boycotts, strikes, etc., unions in all industrial societies have invested immense time and effort in gaining legal rights. Every union movement in Western Europe is embedded in a legal system that determines its ability to exercise economic muscle, its rules concerning leadership selection and, even more critically, the conditions under which it can organize and compel free-riders to join its organization.

These factors make it very difficult for unions in different countries to coalesce along international lines. Yet the costs for unions of not doing so are great. In the first place, unions face a drastic loss of bargaining power vis-à-vis employers. Many medium and most large companies in Western Europe have placed their organization on a multinational basis and so are able to outflank unions in one country by relocating, or threatening to relocate, to another country where the workforce is less organized (Streeck in this volume). Even in industries where transnational firms are weak, unions are pressured if the product market is subject to international competition. To the extent that a union wins wage concessions from unionized employers, so those employers find themselves at a disadvantage in competing with non-unionized employers. So for example, Air France workers gained only a pyrrhic victory in thwarting a recent management plan 'restructuring' employment because their efforts were directed at a single airline competing in an increasingly competitive international market. To the extent that unions do not encompass all competing firms in the relevant product market, they undermine the international competitiveness of the firms they organize.

One way to summarize the problem is to say that unions are less flexible than the firms they bargain with. The logic of capital ownership and organization is essentially anational. Firms provide their shareholders and employees with selective material incentives that travel without too much difficulty across national borders. Firms establish subsidiaries or merge with or take over firms in other countries with comparative ease. If they wish to constrain the transnational dynamic of capital ownership, governments have to enforce specific regulations to that effect. Unions, in contrast, have to strive actively to create transnational organizations. The economic benefits that unions provide, such as job security and higher wages, cannot be targeted selectively to their members, but improve the position of all those in the relevant labour market, whether members or not. Hence, unions usually rely on some combination of the legal system, social norms and ideological incentives to induce potential free-riders to join the union, and these tend to be nation-specific. Unions are expressions of particular communities rather than vehicles for private gain and, as a consequence, do not have the option of expanding transnationally by buying the property of a foreign union. Unions are nationally rooted in a way that is quite alien to the corporation.

The chief response by unions to European integration has been to establish an umbrella organization, the European Trade Union Confederation (ETUC), which encompasses union federations in EU and potential EU countries. The ETUC, which was formed in 1973, represents forty federations in twenty-one countries (the EC-15 plus Cyprus, Iceland, Malta, Norway, Switzerland and Turkey), with a combined membership of 44 million workers, accounting for 86 per cent of the total unionized workforce in those countries (Visser and Ebbinghaus 1992).

Given the existence of competing union federations in most of the targeted countries, the coverage of the ETUC is impressive and a clear advance on previous international union organizations – the socialist European Free Trade Union Confederation, the Christian World Confederation of Labour and the communist *Comité Permanent* – which were exclusive, sectional organizations. However, the ETUC is a feeble peak organization. It has just thirty-five full time staff, less than a fair-sized individual union, let alone a national union federation. It is a loose confederation of sixty-one union federations and confederations, many of which have very little power over their own member unions. Because it is so diverse, the ETUC tends to take a lowest common denominator position in representing union interests in the European Union.

On some important issues the ETUC is split between unions located in richer countries, which push for high uniform wages, benefits and health and safely regulations, and unions in poorer countries, which resist uniform standards because they are aware that their comparative economic advantage within the EU lies partly in the lower taxes that employers pay in their countries (Lange 1992).

The ETUC is too decentralized to play a constructive role in collective bargaining. The chief stumbling block for transnational union organization in particular economic sectors is that the coverage and type of unions differ substantially across countries (Visser and Ebbinghaus 1992). In some countries there are several competing unions within a particular sector; in other countries unions encompass parts of several sectors. There are also wide variations in the extent to which white-collar workers and managerial staff are unionized and in their type of organization. In some sectors they belong to monopolistic industrial unions, in others they have their own unions or entirely separate federations. Finally, as noted above, unions in different countries are enmeshed in very different legal frameworks covering collective bargaining.

These differences have severely limited the ability of unions to form effective transnational organizations. At present there are fifteen sector-specific European Industry Committees in the EU with varying types of membership and coordination, the most effective of which are the European Chemical and General Workers' Union and the Metalworkers' and Miners' Inter-Trade Committee. But no European Industry Committee has been able to press employers into formal bargaining at the European level. In most cases employers are able to block the possibility of transnational collective bargaining by simply failing to give their own transnational organizations sufficient authority over their national constituents, and unions lack the coordinated economic muscle to force employers to negotiate at the European level.

Unions in the EU are trapped between the demise of autonomous national political economies which their organizations were built to cope with, and their inability to shape the new regimes that are replacing them (Streeck and Schmitter 1991; Klausen 1992). The social contracts that they shaped in their respective countries have been undermined by several forces over which they have little control, including the 1992 Project of market integration. They are outflanked by multinational companies that can threaten to relocate to areas beyond their organizational reach. And their efforts to recapture their political and economic power at the European level have been resisted both by employers and by some member states, above all the United Kingdom (Rhodes 1992, 1995). The main thrust of European integration so far has been in creating a European-wide economic space rather than regulating that space through coherent social policies or building strong supranational institutions of European governance. Hence, unions are faced not simply with the task of gaining favourable decisions, but with the far more exacting challenge of creating institutions to reassert political authority over market outcomes.

The incoherence of unions in the EU severely constrains the possibility of social democracy based on institutionalized class compromise practised in central and northern Europe in the decades after the Second World War. In these countries union movements were legitimated and strengthened by the ability of national union federations to exchange wage restraint for social, industrial and welfare reforms. The institutional conditions for such exchange are absent in the EU. Not only is a coherent transnational union movement absent, but the European polity is extremely fragmented, reflecting diverse member state interests and an institutional structure based on a complex distribution of power across the European Council, Commission, Court and Parliament. Even if unions were strong and united, there is no coherent European government that could engage them in supranational bargaining.

Regional movements

The EU has been viewed as a creation of coherent states wishing to achieve particular goals that benefit them individually. This is the approach taken by intergovernmentalists, and it is an influential, perhaps the most influential, view of the EU among scholars in the field. It is supported by the fact, as noted above, that the member states, or, to be more precise, the national executives of member states, are the principal participants in the treaties and major pieces of legislation that undergird the EU. As noted above, the Treaty of Rome recognizes states, and states alone, as the constitutional representatives of their respective countries. This line of thinking underlies the recent application of two-level games in analysing institutional creation in the EU (Moravcsik 1993). At the international level there is a game in which individual states interact with each other. At a second level, there are domestic games nested within each state which influence the state's bargaining position and which therefore must be taken into account in predicting systemic outcomes of the Union as a whole.

In this chapter we argue that this conception of the European polity is inappropriate for understanding social mobilization. Trade unions are seeking to build transnational links so that they can bargain with employers and influence legislation at the European level, and, as we discuss in the next section, new social movements, particularly environmental movements, have established a real European presence. But it is the experience of regional movements that provides the strongest case against the view that member states remain the nexus between domestic politics, on the one side, and international relations, on the other. The mobilization of regions directly in the EU challenges the capacity of national governments to aggregate and represent domestic interests as if they were the buckle that joined two games played in two separate sets of political arenas.

Despite the legal fiction of unitary states embodied in the Treaty of Rome and in successive treaties, most states in Western Europe are arenas in which ethno-territorial groups and subnational governments contend for authoritative competencies. In several countries territorially organized groups within states demand an enhanced role in deciding affairs not only in their own communities, but in the EU as a whole.

Regions have mobilized in the EU along three avenues (Marks 1992, 1993). Many have set up their own offices, staffed and funded autonomously or with the help of businesses in their territory, to give themselves independent voice and access to information (Salk 1993).[101] Second, alongside these regional offices there are a growing number of interregional organizations, many of which encompass regions in different states. Finally, regional governments have sought to extend their formal role in the Union, and have succeeded in instituting a consultative Committee of the Regions composed of local and regional representatives across the EU.

Why have regional governments been drawn to Brussels (Marks 1992, 1993)? As the policy activity of the EU has expanded, so it touches on the affairs of subnational decision-makers across Europe. They need to know what potential policies are coming through the European pipeline and how those policies may affect them. They demand information, and they want to provide information to relevant policy-makers at the European level so that their specific concerns may shape regulation. For its part, the European Commission is hungry for information, particularly from non-central state sources. Regions are steered towards Brussels to gain predictability and control in their institutionally complex world, and in the Commission and Parliament they have a set of interlocutors who are happy to engage in informational exchange. In general, the greater the policy competencies of subnational actors, the more intense their need for information and influence. So we find that every German *Land* has an office, alongside the majority of Spanish, Belgium and French regions. Where subnational governments are weakly articulated, as in Greece, Ireland and Portugal, they are absent from Brussels.

Regional distinctiveness is also an inducement to organize autonomously at the European level. Regions having a distinctive culture or longstanding political differences with their respective national governments are likely to try to foster autonomous channels of informational exchange because they do not want to rely exclusively on national channels. The efforts of such regions are intensified by their fears as well as their ambitions. Regional governments are acutely aware that the institutional structure of the EU has been shaped by treaties drawn up by the central executives of member states. Subnational governments that are entrenched in their respective federal states are drawn to Brussels to prevent their domestic political position being outflanked by national executives operating beyond their reach in Europe.[102] German *Länder* have managed to gain observer status on the Council of Ministers and individual *Länder* are now mandated by the German government to represent its position on certain issues in meetings of the European Council. But such concessions only provide the *Länder* with a shadow of the powers they exert in the German constitution, both individually, and collectively through the *Bundesrat*. Spanish regions, including the Basque Country and Catalonia, play an even smaller role in formulating or constraining the Madrid government in the EU. German and Spanish regions are mobilized defensively, to attain a constructive role in Europe commensurate with that they already have in domestic politics. One of the priorities for regional governments in both countries is to compel their respective national governments to accede them more formal power in the EU.

Under the terms of the Maastricht Treaty, regional and local government representatives across the EU participate in a new Committee of the Regions which has formal consultative status in the EU's political process. Beyond and beneath this, regional governments have created a labyrinth of transnational networks linking regions based on industrial specialization, geographical location, transnational cultural ties and a common political role. These include the Association of European Regions, the Conference of Peripheral Maritime Regions, the Associations of Regions of Traditional Industry, the European Association of Border Regions, the Union of Capital Regions, Associations covering the western, central and eastern Alps, the Jura and the Pyrenees, the Association of Frontier Regions and the Coalfields Communities Campaign.

In pursuing their goals in the EU, and in trying to transform it in a regionalist direction, regional movements are themselves transformed. The possibility of regional empowerment in Europe has influenced culturally distinctive regional movements away from the demand for full national independence toward the demand for greater autonomy in the context of the EU. As policy-making has shifted away from national executives up the supranational level and down to subnational governments, so the issue of nationality appears separable from the demand for an independent state. In reducing the stateness of the European polity, the development of the EU has diverted ethnic groups away from a focus on forging a separate state as their ultimate goal. The 1992 Project creating a common market for goods, services and labour has provided regionalists with the security that demands for decisional autonomy need not have a negative effect on wider trade and economic ties.

The Commission has fostered regional ties through structural policies targeting economic investment in the poorer regions of the Union. These structural policies are designed and implemented in conjunction with representatives of governments in the affected regions as well as with national government officials. Direct contacts between the Commission and subnational governmental representatives take place on a daily basis both in the regions and in Brussels. Around 240 committee meetings involving Commission, national and subnational representatives to monitor the development programmes were held in the regions of the EU in 1992 (Commission of the European Communities 1992a). By participating actively in the EU's structural policies, subnational governments have developed vertical linkages with the Commission that bypass member states and challenge their traditional role as sole intermediary between subnational and supranational levels of government.

Formal institutional changes in the Union reflect the organizational mobilization of regions and their demands, voiced most powerfully by the German *Länder*, for a more visible political role. At Maastricht, the member states agreed in a Protocol attached to the Treaty to expand the Consultative Council of Regional and Local Authorities, set up by the Commission in 1988 with consultative rights over the formulation and implementation of regional policies, into a Committee of the Regions on lines parallel to the Economic and Social Committee with an increased membership (189 as against 42 for the Consultative Council) and widened consultative scope (Commission of the European Communities 1992b: Arts 189a, 189b and 189c). The Protocol directs the Council of Ministers and Commission to consult with the Committee of the Regions on regional issues. In addition the Committee can forward its opinion to the Council and Commission 'in cases in which it considers such action appropriate'.

This new chamber is merely the most visible expression of a diverse and growing number of mostly specialized transnational organizations representing subnational governments. Horizontal linkages among regional and local governments within and across countries have been created and intensified in response to new opportunities for political access in the EU.

These transnational efforts are *ad hoc*, as are the individual efforts of regions to gain representation in Brussels, yet they are considerably more effective than the efforts of trade unions to create a transnational organization because the challenges regions face are not nearly as severe. Market integration does not threaten the organizational basis of regional governments, as it does unions. Regional governments are able to respond to the threat and promise of European integration both individually, by setting up European offices, and cooperatively, through transnational alliances. Trade unions, as detailed above, are compelled to build authoritative decision-making bodies to bargain effectively with employers, and these compromise the autonomy of the constituent national unions. The creation of an effective European union movement is traumatic for national movements, while the creation of effective regionalist movements in the EU involves innovation and elaboration of existing regional organization in a new direction.

The Commission, for its part, has consistently encouraged the activities of regional governments at the EU level. The mobilization of regional governments serves as a counterweight to the entrenched power of state executives, and the Commission is eager for political allies to moderate state executive domination in the EU. Moreover, regional governments and their representatives in Brussels provide a source of information to the Commission outside regular state executive channels. As a small organization with vast responsibilities, the Commission has to rely on externally generated information, and it seeks as diverse an informational base as possible.

Regional governments have extended their reach into the EU in impressive fashion. But like the other cases dealt with in this chapter, their ability to exploit new political opportunities is conditioned by their organizational roots. Subnational governments that are weak in their national political systems lack the resources to establish autonomous offices in Brussels. While all seventeen German *Länder* and most French *régions* are represented, there are no subnational governments from Portugal or Greece. Finally, regional mobilization in the EU reflects the individualized character of constituent subnational governments. Almost all of the offices in Brussels represent individual regional governments, and the dense web of transnational organizations at the European level does not compromise the autonomy of the individual constituents.

New social movements

Finally, we want to assess the impact of the emerging EU structure on a third type of movement, the so-called 'new social movements' (NSMs). Before we do so, however, a few thoughts on the controversy surrounding the use of the term are in order.

The literature on NSMs defies easy summary. Not only is it voluminous, but, as tends to happen with any broad theoretical perspective, there is little consensus among the writers associated with the approach. In identifying the qualities that define a movement as 'new', different writers stress very different features. Some emphasize the 'postmaterialist' or otherwise distinctive values of the movements (Inglehart 1977, 1990; Offe, 1985); others point to the non-traditional organizational and decision-making forms associated with the movements (Brand 1990; Dalton et al. 1990); still others to the central importance of new collective identities in the NSMs (Melucci 1980; Touraine 1981).

Nor do NSM scholars agree on which movements merit the designation and which do not. Virtually all include the women's movement, the environmental movement, the anti-nuclear movement and the Third-World Solidarity movement, but others argue that the peace movement, the student movement, the gay and lesbian movement, the squatters' movement and even the kind of regional movements discussed in the previous section should be included as well. In short, there is little consensus, even among proponents of the approach, on the qualities that define the new movements as new, or on the specific struggles that make up the category.

Critics have charged that this lack of definitional consensus betrays the underlying poverty of the concept (Calhoun 1992). The sharp distinction drawn between the 'old' class-based movements and the 'new' post-materialist movements is simply untenable and ignores the many 'new' features of the 'old' labour movement (Tucker 1991), the many conventional features of the NSMs (Rochon 1990) and the strong links between the NSMs and previous activist traditions (Kriesi and van Praag 1987). We agree with the general thrust of these criticisms. We see little in the values, goals, tactics or organizational forms of the NSMs to suggest that they represent a qualitatively new type of social movement.

The only sense in which the movements are new is that their contemporary manifestations have their roots in the late 1960s or early 1970s (though some did not really develop until the early 1980s). What marks the movements as distinctive, then, is not so much their qualitative uniqueness, as their shared roots and continuing affinity with the political and counter-cultural New Left of that period. This alone marks them as an important category of movement for our purposes. As the dominant 'movement family' (della Porta and Rucht 1991) throughout Western Europe over the past twenty-five years or so, the NSMs have proven to be a potent force for social change in many countries. Accordingly, we need to assess the impact of the emerging EU structure on this class of movements. In doing so, we will restrict our attention to two specific struggles: the environmental and anti-nuclear movements.

The environmental movement

Of the four movements under discussion here, none has been as advantaged by developments at the EU level than the environmental movement. The earliest expression of this receptivity came with the Union's proclamation of 'a common environmental policy' at its 1972 summit meeting in Paris. More concretely, in recent years the Union has initiated four major environmental action plans aimed at various aspects of the environment, including: 'the prevention and reduction of atmospheric, water or soil pollution; action against noise nuisances; management of waste and dangerous chemical substances and processes; promotion of clean technologies; [and] preservation and . . . restoration of the natural environment and habitats' (Wistrich 1989: 72). The Union has also participated as a signatory in a number of important international conventions aimed at curbing pollution in international waters.

Virtually all of the major EU institutions betray the imprint of this generalized pro-environmental emphasis. Most importantly, the Commission itself has been consistently progressive on environmental issues, often opposing the stated positions of powerful member state governments. This disjuncture speaks to the increasing independence of the Commission from the narrow interests of the member states who appoint its members. In effect, there has emerged a distinctive Commission perspective that tends to transcend the mere aggregation of national positions on issues. And one of the clearest and most consistent components of this Commission perspective is progressive environmental policy. The Commission has provided the 'environmental lobby' in Brussels with financial support presumably as a way of increasing the pressure on the Union to be responsive to environmental issues (Rucht forthcoming).

Nor is the Commission the only EU institution to prove receptive to environmental concerns. The 1972 declaration of a common environmental policy paved the way for legal challenge on environmental issues. In fact, only trade and commerce rank ahead of the environment as a focus for EU-level court cases. The European Court of Justice in Luxemburg has heard the majority of these cases, and, like the Commission, has come to be regarded as pro-environment in its interpretation of the law.

Finally, the European Parliament has evidenced a strong environmental consciousness. Much of the credit for this stance must go to the sizeable number of Greens represented in Parliament and to their strategic role in the majority left coalition.

To date, then, environmentalists have confronted a Union that, with the exception of the European Council, has shown itself to be both attitudinally sympathetic and structurally open to the interests of the movement. How has the movement responded to this apparently favourable structure of political opportunities? Suffice to say, European environmentalists have been aggressive in their efforts to take advantage of the Union's structural openness and attitudinal receptivity. They have, in fact, sought to utilize all of the institutional channels touched on above.

Encouraged by the Commission's environmental sympathies and various forms of EU sponsorship, the movement has established a strong lobbying presence in Brussels. The lobby is comprised of four major organizations, several lesser groups and at least a half-dozen specialized environmental 'networks'. The four major organizations are the European Environmental Bureau (EEB), the European office of Friends of the Earth (SEAT), the World Wildlife Fund and Greenpeace. The EEB was established and continues to be funded directly by the EU, while the other three organizations derive a portion of their budgets from programme and grant funds available on a competitive basis under the terms of various Union programmes. In 1990 some ECU50 million was available to these and other groups for projects or research aimed at protecting the environment (Wistrich 1989: 73).

Besides these fund-raising activities, these and the smaller groups and networks which comprise the lobby engage in the kinds of educational, information-gathering and direct lobbying efforts that we associate with their national-level counterparts. Radical environmentalists have been critical of the 'professional' form the movement has taken at the EU level, and especially of the willingness of these groups to accept EU funds, but the criticism speaks to the very real presence of the movement in Brussels and the close ties that exist between these groups and actors at the Union level.

As previously noted, the movement has also pursued its goals through both the European Court and the European Parliament. In doing so environmentalists have simply applied the legal and electoral strategies developed at the national level to the EU. Legal challenge has been arguably the dominant weapon in the arsenal of national environmental movements. And with the success of the Greens in Germany, 'electoral environmentalism' has gained adherents as well.

This last observation goes a long way toward explaining the success the movement has enjoyed in the face of the emerging EU structure. Not discounting the favourable sympathies of many EU officials, the fact remains that there exists a real affinity between the tactics practised historically by the movement and the institutional openings afforded environmentalists by the emerging EU structure. Most national environmental movements in Europe – and especially the German exemplar – have been dominated by a combination of legal, electoral and lobbying strategies; the precise mix encouraged by the relative openness of the European Court, Parliament and the emerging policy community in Brussels.

Here again, then, we see that the political implications of EU for a given movement are conditioned as much by the internal constraints on the movement's response to integration as by the structure of EU itself. So while labour's efforts to respond to the EU challenge continue to be hampered by the sedimented layers of *national* level organization and the historic importance of the strike as labour's ultimate weapon – a weapon not yet available at the EU level – the relative youth of the environmental movement and the elective affinity between the movement's tactics and the structure of EU institutions have clearly had a salutary effect on its efforts to influence Union policy. The same cannot be said for our other new social movement.

The anti-nuclear movement

Given the obvious similarities between the anti-nuclear and environmental issues it might seem logical to expect the anti-nuclear movement to benefit from a comparably favourable structure of political opportunities at the EU level. After all, both issues are environmental at root and, as such, concerned with threats that fail to respect national borders. If ever there were any doubts on this score, the accident at Chernobyl should have erased them. No corner of Europe was entirely spared fall-out from the accident. Given this clear demonstration of interdependence, one might have expected the same kind of generalized receptivity to the issue that EU has shown with regard to environmental matters. This has not been the case. In contrast to the Union's handling of the environmental issue, the EU has yet to declare a common nuclear or broader energy policy. In his thorough survey of EU involvement in various policy areas, Schmitter (this volume) includes energy as one of the areas least subject to EU control. Nor does he expect this to change. Projecting to the year 2001, Schmitter continues to list energy policy as one of only five issue areas (out of a total of twenty-eight) over which he expects the national states to retain the lion's share of control.

To understand why nuclear (and, more generally, energy) policy has remained largely immune from EU control, one needs to understand a bit more about the extreme divergence among member states in their past and current policies regarding nuclear energy. The Union includes countries with diametrically opposed positions on the issue and it is this wide range of opinion that has discouraged EU involvement in the area. France and the Netherlands define the extreme poles of the implied policy debate on the issue. France has been and remains heavily dependent on nuclear power as a source of energy, and, as such, is decidedly pro-nuclear in its official policy. The Netherlands, on the other hand, has yet to build a nuclear plant and remains an outspoken opponent of such facilities.

Given the well-established, strong and opposing nature of these views, member state governments recognized early on that nuclear policy was one issue on which they were very unlikely to reach agreement. Accordingly, as Schmitter's survey shows, it has remained a non-issue in EU policy circles. As the functional executive and legislative arms of the Union, neither the Council nor the Commission has proposed any serious initiatives regarding the issue. Further, the lack of legitimate EU authority in the area has rendered the European Court effectively off-limits to anti-nuclear activists intent on pursuing a legal strategy. Finally, the European Parliament is also neutralized as a possible target for movement pressure. Lacking Council or Commission initiatives in the area, sympathetic Members of Parliament are denied even an advisory forum on the issue. In short, where environmentalists have found attitudinal sympathy and structural openings at the EU level, the anti-nuclear movement has encountered the opposite. The strong and divergent national views on the issue have permeated the Council (and to a lesser extent the Commission), and effectively organized the issue out of EU's broad policy agenda.

Lacking any real opportunities for EU-level mobilization, the anti-nuclear movement has been as conspicuous by its absence in Brussels as environmentalists have been by their presence. A check of the official directory of organizations maintaining offices in Brussels shows nary a single anti-nuclear organization represented. Nor, as noted earlier, has the movement been able to press its case via any other EU institutions. Neither the European Court nor the European Parliament has afforded anti-nuclear activists alternative venues for pursuing movement goals. Indeed, as long as individual nation-states retain a virtual monopoly over nuclear policy, the movement has little reason to mobilize at the EU level.

Unlike labour, however, the anti-nuclear movement would not appear to be constrained by any internal impediments to transnational union. Indeed, the movement would seem to share the same characteristics that have allowed environmentalists to mobilize so quickly. First, anti-nuclear activists have always known that theirs was inherently an international, rather than a national, issue. Eliminating the nuclear threat in one's home country would hardly solve the problem. Second, the movement is a relatively young one. In addition, like the adherents of most new social movements, anti-nuclear activists have long eschewed traditional bureaucratic forms of organization. In combination, then, the relative youth of the movement and its philosophic commitment to non-traditional organizational forms have prevented any real institutionalization of the movement at the national level. Instead national movements have tended to remain loose networks of adherents rather than enduring coalitions of formal movement organizations. Moreover, these adherents have always been attuned to events elsewhere and in contact with their counterparts in other countries. In this case, then, it seems clear that the relative powerlessness of the movement at the EU level is owed almost exclusively to the lack of institutional access afforded by the current EU structure, rather than to any ideational or organizational features of the movement itself.

Summary of the cases

The cases discussed here nicely illustrate the highly variable nature of the effects of EU on different social movements. With reference to Figure 5.1, the movements most likely to benefit from the emerging EU structure are those which enjoy a certain receptivity/openness at the Union level and which are not handicapped in their efforts to mobilize transnationally. Two of our examples – regional movements and the environmental movement – fall into this category. Two other cells – the upper left and lower right – represent somewhat indeterminant outcomes as regards the movements in question. The lower right-hand cell is restricted to movements that are ideologically and organizationally well suited to transnational mobilization, but which, to date, have been afforded few structural opportunities at the EU level. It is here that we would place the anti-nuclear movement. Finally, most disadvantaged by the shift of power to the EU level are those movements which seem both ill suited to transnational mobilization and whose interests find little resonance in the Union. The labour movement would seem to be saddled with these twin deficits. On the opportunities side, European unions have been handicapped by economic integration and the multiplication of new institutional sites for collective bargaining and lobbying. As Fligstein and Mara-drita (1993) have noted, integration has, so far, reflected the desire of business interests and national leaders to remove all cumbersome barriers to the free movement of capital, labour and materials. Given this central agenda, is it any wonder that labour's interests have not been built into the basic structure and underlying philosophy of the EU? Unions still have the weapon of the strike and they retain considerable political influence in many European polities, but these traditional sources of power have declined in value as product markets have widened in scope beyond the organizational reach of entrenched unions.

As daunting as is the challenge confronting the movement at the EU level, the movement also faces considerable internal constraints on its ability to mobilize cross-nationally. Critical here are historically rooted national orientations. The fate of workers has been intimately linked to national institutions – above all, national unions, national labour laws, national collective bargaining procedures, etc. – forged over decades of struggle. The result has been the persistence of insularity and defensiveness among unions – qualities that have made effective transnational organization immensely difficult to achieve.

Conclusion

We began this chapter by applying a perspective developed in recent years by Charles Tilly and others concerning the close historical connection between the rise of the modern state and the subsequent development of the national social movement to the contemporary process of European integration. If, as many observers believe, integration is slowly shifting power away from the nation-state, should we not also be able to discern corresponding changes in the locus and form of social movement activity? What, then, are the implications of European integration for European social movements and for a more general understanding of the relationship between institutionalized politics and social movements?

We are unable to answer this question authoritatively because the final shape of the EU is still uncertain. The past development of the EU is characterized by fundamental discontinuities as well as continuity, and it would be hazardous to assume that one could extrapolate current developments into the future. But European integration has already transformed political agendas, relations across levels of government and patterns of decision-making, and, as a result, has changed the political environment for most political movements and interest groups.

Our understanding of the causality of social movement change must encompass the variable pattern of multi-level governance in the EU and the ongoing efforts of groups to change, as well as respond to, the emerging structure of political opportunities. The groups we have described in this chapter are not just corks on the tides of history, but actively seek to shape the institutional structure of the European polity. They do this strategically, as in the concerted efforts of regional governments in Germany and Spain to gain a formal place in EU decision-making. When a movement decides to press its demands within the EU rather than at the state level, this has institutional as well as substantive policy implications, for it enhances the legitimacy of the European polity as an arena for authoritative decision-making.

While state executives continue to control the broad outlines of institutional creation in the EU, they are no longer the final arenas for policy determination. State executives play a major role in policy-making, but they do so in the context of a multi-level polity that encompasses actors above and beneath the state.

What does multi-level governance portend for European social movements? The answer, in our view, is as complex as it is fascinating. Consistent with the perspective sketched here, we expect – in fact, can already discern – significant changes in the locus and form of social movements as a result of European integration. However, the contemporary restructuring of formal political power has a distinctly different character from the earlier process of state formation. The rise of the nation-state meant everywhere a centralization of power. In contrast, European integration combines elements of continued state authority with the creation of decentralized subnational power and the development of supranational decision-making bodies. The practical significance of this difference should be obvious. Whereas the classic nation-state tended to define the 'structure of political opportunities' for *all* challenging groups, the emergence of a multi-level polity means that movements are increasingly likely to confront highly idiosyncratic opportunity structures defined by that unique combination of governmental bodies (at all levels) which share decision-making authority over the issues of interest to the movement. So instead of the rise of a single new social movement form, we are more apt to see the development and proliferation of multiple movement forms keyed to inherited structures and the demands of mobilization in particular policy areas.

In short, as our examples illustrate, the effects of the EU have been highly variable. In some cases, such as the anti-nuclear movement, the unwillingness of member nations to transfer any real policy authority to the EU has left the movement dependent on whatever openings or leverage it can muster at the national level. In other cases, significant policy authority has been transferred to the Union, but in such diffuse fashion as to pose real tactical problems for the movement in question. This would appear to be the case with regard to the labour movement. In still other instances, movements have clearly benefited from a general receptivity or structural openness to their issues on the part of the EU. Both the environmental movement and the various regional movements would seem to fall into this category. Both issues – environmental protection and regional participation – were accorded legitimacy by the Union early on and, more importantly, have received significant institutional sanction and support.

In contrast to the process of state-building, then, the impact of European integration on popular movements has been anything but uniform. We would also be remiss if we suggested that, as important as these effects are, the fate of European social movements were solely a product of their impact. On the contrary, consistent with our critique of state-centric accounts of the rise of the movement form, the relationship between the EU and social movements is clearly a reciprocal one. This is true in at least two ways.

The effect of the EU on social movements has been shaped by their capacity to *respond* to structural constraints and opportunities. In general, as our examples show, those movements with the longest and most nation-centric histories face tangible constraints in their efforts to seek transnational links with other like-minded movements. By contrast, those movements of more recent origin – and especially those whose histories have granted them a certain expertise with the tactical forms favoured at the EU level – tend to transcend their national roots rather more easily than their older counterparts.

Second, as we have emphasized throughout, European integration is very much a process, the destination of which remains in considerable doubt. The ultimate shape of the Union will depend on years of contestation, negotiation and compromise by a wide range of actors. We can expect that social movements will be among those engaged in this ongoing process, gradually transforming the broader structures of institutionalized power, even as those emerging structures reshape the form and practices of social movements.

6

Imagining the Future of the Euro-Polity with the Help of New Concepts

Philippe C. Schmitter

The Single European Act (SEA) came in with a whimper; the Maastricht Treaty (MAT) with a bang. When the former was initialled in 1985 and ratified in 1986, even quite knowledgeable observers discounted its import-ance. There was very little in the Act that did not just repeat obligations previously assumed in the Treaty of Rome (if not acted upon); moreover, the member states had a past history of signing sonorous agreements to 'relaunch' the integration process that produced little effect. The national governments which signed the SEA seemed not to have been fully cognoscent of the full implication of its provisions, nor could they have foreseen the unprecedented response they evoked within the business community and, eventually, the public at large.

The negotiation of the MAT was a much more scrutinized affair, and there is evidence that member state participants took the elaboration of their respective national positions much more seriously. It was preceded by a very complex structure of bilateral encounters between heads of state and ministers, as well as a steady flow of 'white papers' and draft proposals from the Commission and two Intergovernmental Conferences (IGCs), one on economic and monetary union, the other on political union, that had been meeting over the previous year.[103] Considering all the hoopla among specialized 'attentive élites', it is perhaps surprising how very little discussion there was among the public at large. Admittedly, the SEA was destined to have a much greater and more immediate impact upon the daily lives of individuals, affecting everything 'from boar-meat to banking', as the *Financial Times* put it. The MAT is focused more on the reform of institutions than the movement of 'goods, services, capital and persons' and, hence, will take more time to produce effects that can be registered by government agencies, interest groups, political parties and social move-ments in the member countries. However much the MAT may contribute to defining the future Euro-polity in the long run, it has not done much for increasing the popularity of the EC/EU in the short run.

When compared with the 'founding documents' produced by Constitu-tional Conventions or Constituent Assemblies at the national level, the MAT comes off very poorly. One looks in vain for a clear statement of purpose, a coherent institutional design or a stirring assertion of rights. Its more than 200 pages consist mostly of articles amending the original European Coal and Steel Community (ECSC), EEC and European Atomic Energy Community (EURATOM) treaties, as well as a hodge-podge of protocols. It is written in an incredibly turgid Euro-speak that defies interpretation.[104] A confirmed neo-realist could read it with joy and conviction since it literally reeks of 'statism', especially in its frequent mention of the role of the Council of Ministers and repeated (but not exclusive) insistence on unanimity voting. Its articles are liberally sprinkled with escape clauses: '. . . these arrangements may provide for derogations where warranted by problems specific to a Member State' (Art. 8b); 'This article shall be without prejudice to the exercise of responsibilities incumbent upon Member States with regard to the maintenance of law and order and the safeguarding of internal security' (Art. 100c); 'Without prejudice to Community competence and Community agreements as regards EMU, Member States may negotiate in international bodies and conclude international agreements' (Art. 109.5).[105]

This ostentatious 'statism', however, should not be allowed to obscure the very significant restructuring of functional and institutional Europe that the MAT seems likely to promote – unless, of course, its provisions remain a dead letter in the face of intransigent national resistance. For the record, my evaluation is that the point of no return has been passed and member states will find it politically impossible to defect from the Community as a whole and increasingly difficult to be 'selective' in the implementation of specific rules and regulations. They may, however, seek to exploit specific exemptions and loopholes that the MAT has abundantly opened for them.

The major 'functional' accomplishment of the MAT consists in its provisions with regard to monetary union. This is a spill-over beyond what was originally envisaged in the Treaty of Rome, although significant intergovernmental cooperation on this issue has been going on since 1972 when the 'snake' was created, and especially since 1978 when eight of the then nine member states formed the European Monetary System (EMS). What is different about the evolving European Monetary Union (EMU) is not only that it establishes a set of deadlines for attaining a much more ambitious goal – nothing less than the creation of a common currency with a critical decision (by qualified-majority vote!) supposed to come in 1996 – but that it does so through the creation of new Community institutions – eventually to be called the European System of Central Banks (ESCB) and the European Central Bank (ECB) – with very substantial resources and competences, *and* it specifies in rather considerable detail the criteria which have to be met in order to bring about nothing less than the convergence of macro-economic performance among the participating countries. If successful, member states will have 'pooled' some of their most sovereign rights by 2001: to issue their own money; to run budgetary deficits; to borrow as much as they please (or can); to set their own interest rates and targets for monetary growth; to alter their rates of foreign exchange; in effect, to pursue any macro-economic policy independent of the other participating member states. There are 'opt-out' and 'ease-out' clauses that can be used either to refuse to join or to force a member to derogate, and it remains to be seen whether individual countries will have the capacity to use the former or whether a qualified majority will have the courage to apply the latter. Nevertheless, once they are locked into Stage III of the EMU, it is difficult to imagine how any state could go back to issuing its own currency or, even, to improving its competitive market position through effective and exclusive national policies.

The MAT also encourages the Council of Ministers to take initiatives in other issue arenas by qualified-majority voting that have either not been dealt with in the past or that have long remained dormant: public health; education; consumer protection; the promotion of 'trans-European networks' in telecommunications, transport and energy; and the development of small and medium-size firms.[106] It places a higher threshold, i.e. unanimity, on its getting involved with such items as environmental protection, industrial policy, energy planning and taxation. Since the early 1970s, the European Court of Justice has interpreted Art. 235 of the Treaty of Rome as providing the implied powers for the Community to take all action 'necessary and proper' for the attainment of its objectives without necessarily amending the original treaty – provided the Council approved such actions unanimously (Weiler 1991: 2443–2447). Since the SEA modified the voting procedures and now that the MAT has issued an extensive licence to explore other arenas, the political (as opposed to the legal–constitutional) limits to EC/EU involvement in virtually all issues of public policy seem to have been relaxed (but not removed). As Joseph Weiler put it in the aftermath of the SEA, what he calls the 'foundational equilibrium' has been shattered: 'unlike any earlier era in the Community and unlike most of their other international and transnational experiences, Member States are now in the situation of facing binding norms, adopted wholly or partially against their will, with direct effect in their national legal orders' (1991: 2403).[107]

Nowhere could this prove more subversive of traditional notions of sovereignty than in the field of external relations. Already the member states had largely given over their right to conduct independent foreign commercial policy and the EC/EU has become a well-established actor in bilateral and multilateral trade negotiations. Presumably, once the EMU has taken hold, it will play a role in the IMF similar to the one it already plays in GATT. But Art. J of the MAT goes farther. It proclaims boldly: 'A common foreign and security policy is hereby established which shall be governed by the following provisions.' Needless to say, the provisions that follow are laced with statisms. Nothing will happen unless and until the European Council, i.e. the assembled heads of government/state, unanimously agrees on the 'principles and general guidelines' (Art. J.8). The ultra-sensitive issue of 'the eventual framing of a common defence policy, which might in time lead to a common defence' (Art. J.4) is very cautiously raised and referred to the Western European Union (WEU) for elaboration and implementation – with the caveat that decisions 'shall not prejudice the specific character of the security and defence policy of certain Member States and shall respect the obligations of certain Member States under the North Atlantic Treaty Organization' (Art. J.4). When one reflects back on the many vacuous, past declarations of common EC foreign policy and observes the recent ineffectualness of member state cooperation with regard to the the civil war in the former Yugoslavia, it is easy to dismiss all this as mere window-dressing intended to disguise the tough reality – the 'high politics' – that continues to protect the outer shell of existing national states. My reading of the MAT suggests not only that there is something novel and urgent in these commitments to inform and consult, to define a common position, to coordinate representation in international organizations and to engage in joint action vis-à-vis outsiders that may be connected with the growing regional and global uncertainties of the post-Cold War era, but also that there may be an underlying interdependence between the two, ostensibly independent, pillars of the MAT, i.e. between monetary and political union. This is the first time that the EC has negotiated simultaneously rather than sequentially, and done so across such a broad spectrum of issues. I know of no evidence that the two IGCs 'conspired' with each other or that major *quid pro quos* were exchanged to bring about agreement, but it does not take a great deal of imagination to foresee situations in the future in which their *engrenage* could be brought to bear in order to induce national actors to delegate more authority to EC institutions than would otherwise be the case.

In Table 6.1, I have sought to describe the dynamics of the expansion of EC authority across the full range of issue arenas. Using the measurement device invented by Lindberg and Scheingold (1970 – and the scores they proposed for the 'foundational period' from 1950 to 1970), I have added estimates of the impact likely to be produced by the SEA as of the end of 1992 and of the probable effect of the MAT by 2001 – if it is implemented by member states.

The scores in Table 6.1 confirm what was ventured above. There is no issue area that was the exclusive domain of national policy in 1950 and that has not somehow and to some degree been incorporated within the authoritative purview of the EC/EU. Needless to say, this is most evident in economic matters, but one finds '4s' (mostly policy decisions at the EC level) and even a '5' (all policy decisions at the EC level) in the allegedly more sensitive politico-constitutional and international relations/external security areas by 1992–2001. There are, however, three noticeable disappointments at the core of the Common Market: transportation, energy and communications. All would seem intrinsically promising from a neofunctional perspective; indeed, they collectively facilitate the interdependence between other substantive policy areas. And yet, according to the scores in Table 6.1, they had barely been touched by 1970, and were expected to rise to the status of 'only some decisions at the EC level' by

Table 6.1   *Issue arenas and levels of authority in Europe, 1950–2001*

	1950	1957	1968	1970[1]	1992[2]	2001[3]
I Economic issue arenas						
1 Goods/services	1	2	4[4]	4	4	4
			(3)	(3)		
2 Agriculture	1	1	4	4	4	4
3 Capital flows[5]	1	1	1	1	4	4
4 Persons/workers[5]	1	1	2	2	3	4
5 Transportation	1	2	2	3	2	3
				(2)		
6 Energy[5]	1	2	1	1	2	2
7 Communications	1	1	1	1	2	3
8 Environment[6]	1	2	2	2	3	3
9 Regional development[5]	1	1	1	1	3	3
10 Competition	1	2	3	3	3	3
			(2)	(2)		
11 Industry[7]	1	2	2	2	2	3
12 Money/credit	1	1	2	2	2	4
13 Foreign exchange/loans	1	1	3	4	2	4
			(2)	(2)		
14 Revenue/taxes	1	1	3	3	2	3
			(2)	(2)		
15 Macro-economic[8]	1	1	2	3	2	4
II Socio-cultural issue arenas						
1 Work conditions	1	1	2	2	2	3
2 Health	1	1	1	1	2	2
3 Social welfare	1	2	2	3	2	2
				(2)		
4 Education and research	1	1	3	3	2	3
			(2)	(2)		
5 Labour–management relations	1	1	1	1	1	3
III Politico-constitutional issues						
1 Justice and property rights[5]	1	1	1	2	3	4
2 Citizenship[5]	1	1	1	1	2	3
3 Participation	1	1	2	2	2	2
			(1)	(1)		
4 Police and public order[9]	1	1	2	2	1	2
			(1)	(1)		
IV International relations/external security issues						
1 Commercial negotiations	1	1	3	4	5	5
2 Economic–military assistance	1	1	1	1	2	4
3 Diplomacy and IGO membership	1	1	2	2	2	4
			(1)	(1)		
4 Defence and war	1	1	1	1	2	3

Key: 1 = All policy decisions at national level
2 = Only some policy decisions at EC level
3 = Policy decisions at both national and EC level
4 = Mostly policy decisions at EC level
5 = All policy decisions at EC level

continued overleaf

Table 6.1   (*Continued*)

---

[1] Source for the estimates, 1950–1970: Lindberg and Scheingold (1970: 67–71). Their estimates for 1970 were 'projections based on existing treaty obligations and on obligations undertaken as a result of subsequent policy decisions' (Lindberg and Scheingold 1970: 70).

[2] Estimated outcome of the Single European Act based on projections from existing Treaty obligations and obligations undertaken subsequently. Score indicated for this and successive column represents the mode of independently provided evaluations by members of the Consortium for 1992 present at the Center for Advanced Study in the Behavioral Sciences in March 1992: Geoffrey Garrett, Peter Lange, Gary Marks, Philippe C. Schmitter and David Soskice.

[3] Estimated outcome of the Maastricht Treaty based on assumed Treaty obligations and presumed ratification by member states.

[4] Scores in parentheses ( ) represent *ex post* revaluations in March 1992 of the original scores in Lindberg and Scheingold (1970) by members of the Consortium for 1992.

[5] Category not in Lindberg and Scheingold (1970). My estimates for 1950–1970.

[6] Defined as 'Exploitation and protection of natural resources' in Lindberg and Scheingold (1970).

[7] Called 'Economic development and planning' in Lindberg and Scheingold (1970).

[8] Called 'Counter-cyclical policy' in Lindberg and Scheingold (1970).

[9] Called 'Public health, safety and maintenance of public order' in Lindberg and Scheingold (1970).

1992. Energy, an intersectoral and, one would think, interspatial commodity *par excellence*, was judged to remain essentially in national hands through 2001 – along with such other laggards as health, social welfare, political participation and police and public order!

The great leaps forward in the future are anticipated in the mobility of persons and workers (a product of the SEA), money and credit, foreign exchange and loans, macro-economic policy-making (all obviously as a result of EMU) and the coordination of economic–military assistance to foreign countries, diplomatic initiatives, membership in international organizations and matters of external security (presumably based on an optimistic assessment of impact of the MAT clauses on political co-operation and defence policy).

The estimates for 1992 and 2001 are based on the modal response from five independent evaluations. They, therefore, disguise some significant divergences. For example, the most marked one came with regard to competition policy. Most of us scored this a '3', a policy decision about equally distributed at the national and supranational levels, but one scholar gave it a '5', i.e. assigned it exclusively to the EC/EU by 2001, and another a '2', i.e. saw it as remaining a predominantly national matter. The areas of personal and worker mobility, management prerogatives and labour relations, citizenship and voting rights, law and public order and defence and war also brought out persistent differences among us about where the locus of decision-making would lie at the turn of the century. There was no divergence, however, about the general trend, and very few instances of anticipated 'spill-back' to a more national level of authority.

But for someone seeking to peer over the horizon at the future Euro-polity, the most interesting aspects of the MAT cannot be glimpsed from the probable range of activities the Community or Union will be performing in 2001. Rather, they are hidden in its excruciatingly abstruse provisions about institutions and decision rules. In its first paragraph (Art. A), the MAT announces that it is establishing a new entity: the European Union (EU), never subsequently defined but somehow more ambitious and overarching since it will contain the European Community (EC) and be 'supplemented by the policies and forms of cooperation established by this Treaty'. Repeating the opening phrase of the Treaty of Rome, it commits its members to 'an ever closer union among the peoples of Europe',[108] and then adds the dependent clause: 'where decisions are taken as closely as possible to the citizens'. This is an indirect reference to the latest buzz-word in Euro-speak: subsidiarity.[109] In other words, whatever its functions, the EU is to be a dispersed polity where most decisions will presumably be taken (and not just implemented) by other than central supranational authorities. Taken to the extreme (by the British), subsidiarity would permanently exclude Community intervention in a wide range of policy areas designated as 'national'. The concept, however, hints that such a system might have several levels of aggregation, not just two. Subnational, i.e. local, provincial or regional, units might even be favoured over national states with regard to some policies. In common parlance, such a system is often called 'federalist', but apparently the United Kingdom vetoed any explicit mention of this F-word in the MAT.

These common provisions for the EU go, however, to hint at several other features which sound more 'state-like'. For example, they announce the creation of a new 'citizenship of the Union', the intention 'to assert its identity on the international scene', to strengthen 'economic and social cohesion' and 'to maintain in full the *acquis communautaire* and to build upon it' (Art. B).[110] They promise the creation of 'a single institutional framework to ensure the consistency and continuity of . . . actions' and specifically call attention to the EU's eventual 'actions as a whole in the context of its external relations, security, economic and development policies' (Art. C). If one took these pretensions seriously and ignored the caveats, one might be tempted to conclude – erroneously – that a supranational state was being founded.

What actually seems more likely to emerge from the multiple (and by no means coherent) provisions of the MAT is something quite novel – and, perhaps, unexpected. How ironic it would be if the Eurocrats – normally so attentive with regard to identifying unintended consequences and so skilful at turning them into an expansion of their *compétences* – should discover that their preferred design for the Euro-polity was to be the accidental victim of their own efforts! For the MAT opens the way for the institutionalization of diversity – for a multitude of relatively independent European arrangements with distinct statutes, functions, resources and memberships, not coordinated by a single central organization and operating under different decision rules. No doubt, the Commission will work hard to defend the *acquis communautaire*, a single-track and synchronized process and its own concentric role, but this may not be an easy task given the changing external context within which the Euro-polity is emerging.

The MAT abounds in potentially partial and eccentric arrangements. For example, it calls for a 'third stage' European Central Bank (ECB) with very considerable independence, not only from national governments, but also from the EC/EU itself. The field of monetary policy has long pioneered in variable geometry when the European Monetary System went ahead without the participation of several member states, including a major player, the United Kingdom, until 1990. At the present moment, neither Greece nor Portugal participates in it, although they are formally committed to do so eventually. According to the MAT, it will be possible to move ahead to the ECB in Stage III by a qualified-majority vote and with as few as seven members. Countries whose economic performance does not meet exacting standards will be declared 'in derogation' and prohibited from participating in the decision. The United Kingdom asked for a special dispensation and can decide to 'opt out' during Stage II.

Social policy is another arena in which the MAT found it necessary to improvise. Again, the problem stemmed from British intransigence. The Conservative government opposed instating worker rights and welfare provisions through European measures which had been removed from its national practices by the 'Thatcher revolution'. A last minute solution was cobbled together to allow the other eleven member states to 'opt in' to policies which will be decided by qualified majority in a reduced quorum, i.e. without British participation, if they so choose. In a separate protocol, the signatories pledge to use 'EC institutions, procedures and mechanisms', but it is not inconceivable that they might eventually decide to establish a separate European Social Regime, say, for the administration of common pension or unemployment funds. In any case, an unusual precedent has been created that could be applied in other issue arenas.

In the field of foreign policy, for example, the Treaty calls for 'systematic cooperation', but places it outside formal EC institutions and the Treaty of Rome. It even sets up a new permanent 'Political Committee consisting of Political Directors', a sort of embryonic Foreign Office, in Brussels to which 'the Commission shall be fully associated' (Art. J.8) – but not control. In a parallel fashion, the member states resorted to working through the Western European Union (WEU), an organization existing since 1954, for defence issues. The WEU will be opened to new members (but none will be compelled to join) and eventually become the 'defence component' of the EU, but its relation to existing EC institutions seems very loosely defined – and deliberately so.

One could go on with other potentialities for partiality and eccentricity in the MAT:

1   A new advisory Committee of Regions is created with representatives
    from (unspecified) subnational units (Art. 198a) which, when combined

with the promise of a substantial increase in funds for economic and social cohesion (Annex I, Protocol 15), could develop into a circuit of influence bypassing the national level of aggregation.

2 The European Parliament is granted important new powers: to form Committees of Enquiry (Art. 137b), to request that the Commission take specific initiatives (Art. 137a), to receive petitions from individual European citizens and 'legal persons' (Art. 137c), to appoint an independent Ombudsman (Art. 137d) and, most significantly, to enter into an exceedingly complex co-decision procedure (Art. 189b) for a wide range of issues whereby, should the Euro-deputies persist by an absolute majority in rejecting a Council decision, even a unanimous one, they can effectively veto its passage.

3 The signatories 'invite' the European Parliament and the member state national parliaments to form and meet as often as necessary in a new representative assembly, the Conference of the Parliaments or *les Assises.*

4 An EU-wide organization for police cooperation (Europol) is established, as well as an unnamed 'Coordinating Committee' consisting of senior national government officials which is empowered to make recommendations for action in such highly sensitive areas as asylum rights, visa requirements, immigration policy, drug trafficking, commercial fraud, judicial cooperation in civil and criminal matters, and terrorism.

5 Within the eleven-member agreement on social policy is inserted a strange 'proto-corporatist' provision that encourages the Commission to facilitate the 'dialogue' and 'balanced support' of management and labour in drafting policy initiatives that could pre-empt EC measures and lead to independent private contracts implemented through either Community or national procedures (Annex I, Protocol 14, Arts 1–4).[111]

The above items were not listed because they are all likely to make some major contribution to the 'institutionality' of the EC/EU. Some are clearly slated for political oblivion; others may remain only as minor nuisances. Together, however, they amount to a substantial increase in the complexity of both the systems of representation surrounding the Euro-polity and the levels of decision-making within it. A greater variety of non-state actors are going to be drawn into some regular (if not always very potent) relation with the EC/EU and it is going to take the coordination of more collectivities to produce EC/EU policies. Subgroups of member states will be able to threaten more plausibly than before to go ahead on their own – within or even outside the Community framework. Individual countries in unanimity situations, and even minimal blocking coalitions in qualified-majority ones, may become more reluctant to insist on their 'sovereign rights'.

Together, these potentialities for partiality and eccentricity could circumscribe the role of member states well beyond the formal treaty prescriptions that still assign a preponderance to the European Council or the Council of Ministers simply because national government leaders and representatives will have to make concessions – side-payments, if you will – to various entities that can obstruct the passage even of the measures they unanimously want or imperiously need. In some cases, the only power of these semi-independent bodies is to clog the channels with rival proposals or to delay in issuing their approval, but the European Parliament's newly acquired capacity to veto (and not just hold up) directives could well be crucial in this regard, especially if the less powerful bodies can learn how to cooperate with it.

The MAT may have changed the trajectory of European political integration and opened up a range of possible (but not ineluctable) outcomes that were not previously apparent to or desired by either national or supranational actors. Instead of the coherent system of checks and balances long awaited by Euro-federalists, it could encourage the development of a hybrid arrangement for presences and absences in which member states, specific industrial sectors, subnational polities and supranational organizations will be able initially to pick and choose the obligations they prefer and only later discover which are compatible with each other. It is as if 'Europe' – having been previously invited by its nation-states to sit down to a light snack of regional cooperation and by its supranational civil servants to a copious *prix fixe* dinner of centralized governance – suddenly found itself before a *repas à la carte* prepared by several cooks and tempting the invitees with diverse, but unequally appealing, arrangements for managing their common affairs!

Imagining futures for the Euro-polity

The foregoing interpretation of the MAT is, to put it euphemistically, speculative. It has involved reading a very turgid, incoherent and hastily cobbled together text from a self-confessedly biased theoretical perspective. A neo-realist would have seized upon the frequent references in the Treaty to member states, the European Council and the Council of Ministers (i.e. bodies supposedly controlled by these 'sovereign' units) and to unanimity voting criteria, and proclaimed it a victory for the state system. Granted that a few policies and procedures seem to place member states in the potentially embarrassing position of having to conform to collective norms of which they do not explicitly approve, but that should soon be rectified. When 'push comes to shove', i.e. as soon as real consequences begin to emerge and impose future constraints on national decision-making, the irreducible state-ness of the European system will assert itself. The EC/EU will either be reduced to the status of an intergovernmental regime or be converted into an agency of a newly hegemonic *Viertes Deutsches Reich*.[112]

Presumably, a neo-rationalist would quickly arrive at the conclusion that the MAT is a suboptimal solution to the problem of providing 'European public goods' and, hence, destined to be a temporary and ineffectual aberration until the competitive logic of market exchanges and transaction costs have either undermined its misguided efforts at collective regulation or compelled its signatories to resort to hierarchical, i.e. supra-statist, coercion in order to punish the inevitable free-riders and opportunists. By neither of these two standards should the MAT have much of a lasting impact upon the integration process, much less provide a *Vorbild* for its future political institutions.[113]

My hunch is that the MAT does offer us at least a glimpse of a different possible outcome – a stable European political order based neither upon intergovernmental organizations nor upon a supranational state. Which is not to say that the MAT, itself, will not be substantially transformed in the near future. As the outcome of a hastily assembled compromise, it is an intrinsically incoherent document. There are abundant signs that national governments are having second thoughts about what it does (or does not) contain. Its ratification by national parliaments has been much more difficult than in the past and could even trigger the *politicization* of mass publics that has been so long awaited. The Eurocrats in the Commission clearly have strong reservations about the proliferation of institutions and policy options embodied in it, and will do whatever they can to push the eventual outcome in a more single-tracked, synchronic, concentric and statist direction. But what if these centripetal forces are successful only in modifying specific decision rules or policy domains, not in changing the underlying 'format' of the Euro-polity as prefigured by the MAT?

Try to imagine a polity that did *not* have the following:

(a) a single locus of clearly defined supreme authority;
(b) an established and relatively centralized hierarchy of public offices;
(c) a predefined and distinctive 'public' sphere of competency within which it can make decisions binding on all;
(d) a fixed and (more or less) contiguous territory over which it exercises authority;
(e) a unique recognition by other polities, membership in international organizations and exclusive capacity to conclude international treaties;
(f) an overarching identity and symbolic presence for its subjects/citizens;
(g) an established and effective monopoly over the legitimate means of coercion;
(h) a unique capacity for the direct implementation of its decisions upon intended individuals and groups; and
(i) a predominant ability to control the movement of goods, services, capital and persons within its borders;

but *did* have the capability to take decisions, resolve conflicts, produce public goods, coordinate private behaviour, regulate markets, hold elections, respond to interest pressures, generate revenue, incorporate new members, allocate expenditures, send and receive diplomatic representatives, conclude international agreements and even declare and wage war! If you can do this, you will have succeeded in at least mentally superseding the limits imposed by the nation-state upon our habitual ways of thinking about politics, although it may still be difficult for you to imagine how such a 'post-sovereign, polycentric, incongruent, neo-medieval' arrangement of authority could possibly be stable in the longer run.

Admittedly, the MAT itself is not a very clear guide, but if it is combined with other phenomena that have been literally written into the integration process from the start, it may be possible to provide a sketch of what this unprecedented (and perhaps unwanted) form of political domination might look like. Its core lies in the growing dissociation between authoritative allocations, territorial constituencies and functional competences. In the state model (but not invariably in the praxis of states), the exercise of public authority in different functional domains is coincident or congruent with a specific and unique territory. When one arrives at its physical borders, the legitimate exercise of coercion in all these domains ends. The polity on the other side has, in principle, no right to command obedience in any domain on one's own side – and there presumably exists no super-ordinate entity exercising authority over both sides.

But what if either the functional or the territorial domains (and even more if both) were not congruent with the same authority? What if there were a plurality of polities at different levels of aggregation – national, subnational and supranational – that overlapped in a given domain? Moreover, what if these authorities did not have exclusive functions or well-established hierarchical relations, but negotiated with each other in some continuous way to perform common tasks and resolve common problems across several domains?

Our language for discussing politics – especially stable, iterative, 'normal' politics – is indelibly impregnated with assumptions about the state. Whenever we refer to the number, location, authority, status, membership, capacity, identity, type or significance of political units, we employ concepts that implicitly or explicitly refer to a universe featuring sovereign states and 'their' surrounding national societies. It seems self-evident to us that this particular form of organizing political life will continue to dominate all others, spend most publicly generated funds, authoritatively allocate most resources, enjoy a unique source of legitimacy and furnish most people with a distinctive identity. Although we may recognize that the sovereign national state is under assault from a variety of directions – beneath and beyond its borders – its 'considerable resilience' has been repeatedly demonstrated.[114]

But what if the issue were not the outright demise of its peculiar brand of 'high politics' and replacement by the 'higher politics' of a new sovereign supranational Euro-state? What if something qualitatively different were evolving that would blur the distinction between 'high' and 'low politics' and eventually produce a new form of multi-layered governance without clear lines of demarcated jurisdiction and identity? How could we identify these emergent properties, and what would we call them?

My hunch is that we will need a new vocabulary to pick up such developments – initially, at the level of discrete and novel arrangements as they emerge in the ongoing practice of EC/EU institutions and, eventually, at the level of general configurations of authoritative decision-making and policy implementation once they begin to form a more coherent whole.

The first need is already being fulfilled on a daily basis by 'Euro-speak', the *Volapük intégré* that is constantly being invented to describe *ad hoc* or *de jure* solutions to Community problems. Originally, these expressions had a distinctively neo-functionalist cast, e.g. *l'engrenage, le 'spill-over', la méthode communautaire, l'acquis communautaire* and *la supranationalité*, but recently they have increased greatly in number and seem to be emanating more and more from European jurisprudence or treaty provisions, e.g. subsidiarity, proportionality, additivity, complementarity, transparence, *compétences*, direct effect, unanimity, qualified-majority voting, co-responsibility, transposition, *géométrie variable, juste retour*, mutual recognition, home country control, co-decision, pooled sovereignty, opting out, opting in, economic and social cohesion, sustainable convergence, Euro-compatibility, balanced support, and so forth.[115] There are even a few terms that seek to describe the process of integration as a whole and/or its eventual outcome, e.g. *'comitologie'*, the way in which Commission drafts are subjected to an extensive exchange of views among national administrators, interest representatives and Eurocrats until a consensus position is reached and a policy proposal put forth; 'troika', the system of collective executive power through which the President of the Council of Ministers during the six-month term in office of his/her country is associated with the preceding and succeeding presidents; 'concentric circles', the assumption that all institutional development within the EC/EU revolves around a single administrative core, i.e. the Commission, and eventually leads to accretions of its *compétences*.

I doubt if the second need, i.e. for labels to identify the general configuration of authority that is emerging, can be fulfilled by simply aggregating inductively items from Euro-speak as they are invented and take hold. These may provide valuable hints about distinctive properties of the supranational integration process, but they cannot be expected to add up to coherent description of its possible outcome. Heretofore, the portmanteau term for this has been *federation*. Not only, as I mentioned in Chapter 1, does this common label disguise a fairly wide range of institutional formats, but it also strongly implies the existence of an orthodox sovereign state at its core – regardless of how political authority and identity may be shared among its subnational territorial constituencies.[116]

In order to provoke a discussion, I propose to resort to the creation of ideal types, rather than attempt to piece together constructive types from pre-existing efforts at state-building or regional integration. Moreover, I will give to the results of this deductive exercise neo-Latin appellations – better to remind the reader of the novel arrangements they represent.

The central assumption of Figure 6.1 is that all forms of modern politics

	Territorial constituencies	
	Variable Tangential Egalitarian Differentiated Reversible	Fixed Contiguous Hierarchical Identical Irreversible
Functional constituencies		
Variable Dispersed Shared Overlapping	*Condominio*	*Consortio*
Fixed Cumulative Separate Coincident	*Confederatio*	*Stato/Federatio*

Figure 6.1　*Territorial and functional elements in the formation of polities*

are rooted in representation. Where the units of authority have grown larger in area and population, and more heterogeneous in social and economic interests, rulers and ruled have relied increasingly on regularized mechanisms of indirect participation to communicate with each other. *Grosso modo*, these linkages conform to two different principles of aggregation: the *territorial* and the *functional*. Various intermediaries – parties, associations, movements, clienteles, notables – identify with the constituencies formed by these principles and *re*-present their interests vis-à-vis authorities. It is this mix of territorial and functional constituencies, along with their corresponding relations of authority and accountability, that defines the type of polity.

And the emerging Euro-polity is no different. It began with a dual bias:

(a)　toward channelling the representation of territorial interests exclusively through the national governments of member states; and

(b)　toward privileging the development of functional representation through transnational, European-level interest associations.

The deliberate neo-functionalist strategy of Jean Monnet et al. was to concede the former as an inescapable (if eventually mutable) feature of the international system and to build gradually and surreptitiously upon the latter. After some initial successes, this failed for a variety of reasons and the ensuing period of 'intergovernmentalism' from the mid-1960s to the mid-1980s saw even the functional interests being transmitted largely through national territorial channels.[117] Since then, the mix of functional and territorial constituencies/authorities at various levels has shifted significantly within the EC/EU, giving rise to the present uncertainty about the eventual outcome.

Stato/Federatio

According to Figure 6.1, for the *stato/federatio* form to predominate at the European level, both types of constituency should be coincident or coterminous with each other. The territorial boundaries of its authority would be fixed definitively and surround a physically contiguous space. Membership would be irreversible – either because central authority would be deployed to prevent partial defections from specific norms or because outright secession would become too costly for the welfare of citizens. National and subnational units might not disappear – especially in the federalist versions of this outcome – but each would have an assured and identical status within an overarching hierarchy of authority. On the functional side, there would be a fixed allocation of competences among a variety of separate agencies operating within a cumulative division of labour – normally coordinated through a common budgeting process. Given the characteristics of existing national states, the most likely subspecies of the *stato* to emerge in Europe would be something akin to the *Politikverflechtung* and 'co-operative federalism' practised by the Swiss or the Germans, hence the label *stato/federatio*.[118]

Confederatio

A *confederatio* would be a more loosely coupled arrangement in which the identity and role of territorial units would be allowed to vary, while the distribution of functional constituencies and competences would be rigorously fixed and separated in order to protect members from encroachment by central authorities. In it, there would not need to be a presumption of territorial contiguity and an established hierarchy of internal authority. Members would retain their autonomy and be relatively free to enter and exit. Each could negotiate its own differentiated relation to the unit as a whole, but, once a member, would be strictly bound to contribute to the few, cumulative and coincident functions devolved upon central institutions, e.g. common currency, liberalization of trade flows, environmental protection, traffic control, weather prediction and/or collective security. Historically, such polities have been short-lived, namely the United States from 1781 to 1789, Switzerland from 1815 to 1848 or Yugoslavia from the death of Tito in 1980 to 1991. They proved incapable either of defending their variable and dispersed territories from encroachment by others, or of redistributing resources among themselves to prevent the defection of their members. With the recent changes in international security and material welfare, such a solution might be more viable than in the past.

Consortio

The *consortio* is a form of collective action practised more by consenting firms than consenting polities. In it, national authorities of fixed number and identity agree to cooperate in the performance of functional tasks that are variable, dispersed and overlapping. They retain their respective territorially based identities, form a relatively contiguous spatial bloc and accept positions within a common hierarchy of authority, but pool their capacities to act autonomously in domains that they can no longer control at their own level of aggregation. There seem to have been relatively few salient historical examples of this type given its implications for national sovereignty, but one suspects that a detailed investigation of the bilateral relations between any two contiguous states would reveal a large number of 'regional' commissions and task forces designed to cope with specific problems without endangering the international status of their participants. Once these proliferate sufficient to interact with and stimulate each other, then it may be accurate to speak of a *consortio* having replaced strictly state-like relations, say, between the United States and Canada or Norway and Sweden.

Condominio

Finally, the *condominio* would be the most unprecedented, even unimaginable, outcome of all for the Euro-polity since it would be based on variation in both territorial and functional constituencies. Precisely what the state system had taken so long to fix into a coincident interrelation would be sundered and allowed to vary in unpredictable ways. Instead of one Europe with recognized and contiguous boundaries, there would be many Europes. Instead of a Eurocracy accumulating organizationally distinct but politically coordinated tasks around a single centre, there would be multiple regional institutions acting autonomously to solve common problems and produce different public goods. Moreover, their dispersed and overlapping domains – not to mention their incongruent memberships – could result in competitive, even conflictual, situations and would certainly seem inefficient when compared with the clear demarcations of competence and hierarchy of authority that (supposedly) characterize existing national states. While it seems unlikely that anyone would set out deliberately to create a *condominio* – and no long-lasting historical precedents come to mind – one can imagine a scenario of divergent interests, distracted actors, improvised measures and compromised solutions in which it just emerges *faute de mieux* and rapidly institutionalizes itself as the least threatening outcome. According to my admittedly biased and speculative reading of the Maastricht Treaty, this may even be the most probable trajectory for the EC/EU – unless emergent trends and subsequent events deflect its course in the near future.

The imprecision of theory

None of the prevailing theories of integration can predict which (if any) of the above four ideal types will be closest to the Euro-polity that is emerging. All focus on process not outcome. All presume that integration will eventually lead to some kind of stable institutionalized equilibrium, but fail to specify how and when this can be expected to occur.

Neo-functionalists, by defining the process largely in terms of the transfer of sovereignty to a single, more encompassing, 'regional' centre of authority and, thereby, focusing attention on the alternatives of intergovernmentalism and supranationalism, seemed to imply that something like a *supra-stato* was the probable outcome – provided, of course, the mechanisms of *l'engrenage*, transnational interest politics and *l'Eurocracie* were sufficient to overcome the propensity for inertia and self-encapsulation.[119] Neither they nor the neo-realists seemed to have imagined that the EEC/EC/EU might end up somewhere between these two extremes.[120]

Ironically, their predecessors – the pure functionalists – might have pointed them in a different direction. David Mitrany insisted on what he called 'technical self-determination':

> . . . the function determines its appropriate *organs*. It also reveals through practice the nature of the action required under the given conditions, and that way the *powers* needed by the respective authority. The function, one might say, determines the executive instrument suitable for its proper activity, and by the same process provides a need for the reform of the instrument at every stage. (1966: 72–73, emphasis in original)

Following this premise, Mitrany went on to deny 'the habitual assumption . . . that international action must have some overall *political authority* above it' (1966: 75, emphasis in original) and, in effect, provided a sketch for what we have called above a *consortio* at the global level.

What neither Mitrany nor others seem to have imagined is the possibility that not just functional domains might vary, but so might the resource bases, governance arrangements and levels of commitment across territorially defined participants. The very fact that Europe began its integration 'at sixes and sevens' should have alerted theorists to this likelihood. Since then varying subsets of member states have either threatened to go or have actually gone ahead on their own, most notably in the area of monetary cooperation with the 'snake' and the EMS, and more recently in internal security with the Schengen Agreement. As we discussed above, the MAT opens up whole new realms of possibility for variable geometry, some of which may be lodged in relatively autonomous Euro-cratic bodies and even be placed outside the jurisdiction of the European Court of Justice.

The processes of 'association' and 'enlargement' have always introduced an element of ambiguity in defining exactly what were the territorial limits to EC/EU authority – and the agreement on the European Economic Area (EEA) makes this issue even more complicated by compelling non-member states to adopt Euro-norms and obey Euro-directives without having been full participants in the process of their elaboration.

If this were not difficult enough to comprehend, a whole new dimension to the territorial question is emerging, namely subsidiarity, or what level of aggregation should be relevant in deciding and implementing which EC/EU policies. Until recently, everyone took it for granted that the natural and irreducible spatial constituencies were defined by sovereign national states – in their existing and highly unequal configuration.[121] This is how voting quotas, financial contributions, nominations for European Commissioners and Judges, seats on the Council of Ministers, and so forth, are distributed. Indeed, the orthodox assumption held that the creation of the EEC actually served to strengthen the role of national states over lesser political units (Sharpe 1989).

Subsequent changes from below in the territorial distribution of authority within these states (Tarrow et al. 1978; Mény 1982; Keating 1988) and from within in the magnitude and distribution of Community regional funds (Marks 1992) have resulted in a veritable explosion of attention by subnational political units to the integration process. Regions, provinces, municipalities and even whole 'unrepresented nations' (e.g. Catalans, Welsh, Basques and Bretons) have opened up quasi-embassies in Brussels and sought to establish direct contact with EC/EU officials to influence the distribution of structural funds and the direction of sectoral policies. They have been forming associations, alliances and commissions across national borders and pressing for the special status of *Euro-regiones* that group adjacent units from different countries. It would obviously be premature to suppose that this flurry of activity and the creation of informal channels of subnational representation will succeed in 'outflanking' the heretofore dominant position of national member states within the EC/EU, and eventually drive the outcome toward a *condominio* in which varying and overlapping scales of territorial aggregation would interact with varying and overlapping domains of functional competence, although the recent insertion in the MAT of a 'Committee of Regions' does enhance that probability.[122]

Inserting the intervening conditions

But the MAT is not a self-implementing document and a great deal can occur before Europe has its next *rendez-vous* with institutional reform. David Marsh (1991) of the *Financial Times* caught the impending dilemma especially well: 'The challenge for the Community during the rest of the 1990s will be to manage its own enlargement and meet the expectations vested in it from outside – without disrupting the finely-tuned balance of interests and opportunities among its present 12 member states.' As we shall see, the neo-functional perspective can be of some help in anticipating and interpreting those delicate interdependencies within the ranks, but it tells us very little about how interactions with external actors are likely to influence the eventual outcome. For the sake of brevity, I propose to concentrate upon four factors – two endogenous and two exogenous – that I believe will contribute the most to determining what type of Euro-polity will emerge.

1 *Implementation*. The EEC/EC has long suffered from an 'implementation deficit'. Much less touted than its 'democracy deficit', this incapacity to elicit reliable compliance with supranational regulations and directives has placed an invisible, but none the less effective, limit on the scope and efficiency of Community action. The main reason for this is quite obvious, namely its almost exclusive reliance upon agencies of national and subnational governments for the enforcement of supranational norms (Azzi 1985; Seidentopf and Ziller 1988).[123] Not only has the number of reported infractions (as measured by court cases) been increasing consistently, but as the EC/EU widens its policy domain to include more sensitive regulatory and distributive issues that directly involve individual firms and communities, there is every reason to expect that the incentives for 'selective defection' (read, cheating on specific obligations) are going to increase exponentially. At some point, the breakdown in compliance could threaten the legitimacy of the whole Community effort.

So far, member states seem to have stuck, by and large, to the obligation of *pacta sunt servanda*, but the same cannot be said of their local and regional authorities. In the coming years the Commission – faced with a rapid expansion of its administrative tasks and strong resistance to augmenting its budget and staff – will be tempted to rely ever more on these subnational agents for the implementation of its policies – hence, the attractiveness of developing linkages of representation, subsidization and accountability that circumvent the national level of governance and make local and regional authorities more willing participants in Community programmes. Needless to say, member states will resist this and may even prefer that the Commission (or other relatively independent Eurocracies) acquire a greater capacity for directly monitoring performance and punishing offenders to prevent both cheating by competing countries and a diminution of their respective monopolies on territorial representation and authority. Somehow, I suspect, from the resolution of these internecine struggles over implementation, the EC/EU will be pushed toward acquiring at least some of the properties of a *stato*, a *consortio*, a *confederatio* or a *condominio*.

2 *Politicization*. As spill-overs have occurred and raised the level of supranational authority, neo-functionalists have long expected an increase in the controversiality of the integration process. Wider and wider groups are being affected; more and more policy attention has centred on Brussels – why have the relevant publics, especially those in political parties and social movements, not expressed greater concern? How can it be that approximately 50 per cent of all legislation now being passed by national parliaments involves the transposition of EC norms (Lodge 1989a: 38) and so few seem to be aware of this fact?

In the 'benevolent' scenario, the timing and content of politicization would have been controlled by the Eurocrats and their interest group allies. Blocked in their aspirations by the resistance of national politicians to supranationality, they would appeal directly to the publics benefiting from expanded trade, lower transaction costs, cheaper consumer prices, greater personal mobility, regional subsidies, etc., and mobilize them to clamour for an even greater transfer of sovereignty or funds to the emerging centre. In the present 'malevolent' situation, post-MAT, the inverse seems to be occurring, with quite unpredictable effects.

For the first time, the ratification of an EC treaty solemnly (if agonizingly) agreed upon by all twelve governments is in jeopardy. Political parties and social movements that had never focused on Community issues or always acquiesced in them are currently making a fuss and using their opposition to Maastricht to score points against adversaries. Moreover, the MAT seems to have triggered an extraordinary diversity of negative responses: to the loss of a respected national currency in Germany; to the 'threat' of social legislation in Britain; to abortion and the freedom to travel in Ireland; to rights granted to non-nationals to vote in local elections in France; to doubts about promises of regional aid in Spain; to general fear of an expanded European role in foreign and defence policy in Denmark. Should any one member state fail to ratify, the MAT will have to be renegotiated and some new status created to allow the dissenting country to remain in the Community while opting out of a specific obligation.

Moreover, now that the MAT has passed all twelve parliaments and popular referenda in Denmark, Ireland and France, politicization may still not diminish, for there remains the delicate matter of where the additional necessary funds are going to come from and how they are to be distributed among member states. According to Commission estimates, its budget would have to increase by *c.* 30 per cent just to have enough to cover the commitments made at Maastricht – and there are strong signals that the habitual net contributors, the Germans, are in no mood to continue in that role.

It is too soon to tell whether, because of the fuss over the ratification of MAT, EC/EU issues have permanently broken through the barrier of public indifference and begun to influence the course of political careers. Turnout for Euro-elections is still much lower than for national ones – and declining. Few candidates seem to win or lose because of what they do or do not do for Europe – the exceptions being Prime Ministers Thatcher and Major, where not so much the electoral outcome as the coherence of their own party was and continues to be put into jeopardy. As a rule, only highly specialized groups have participated *ex ante* in the abstruse negotiations of EC *comitologie*; broader publics have, at best, been represented *ex post* in the deliberations of the European Council or the votes of their national governments in the Council of Ministers.[124] The European Parliament has seen its power increased marginally in both the SEA and the MAT, but is a long way from providing a mechanism of political accountability or even of symbolic attachment for the citizenry as a whole.

If and when large-scale politicization does occur, its impact may not be what the neo-functionalists anticipated. Instead of providing the critical impetus for a definitive transfer of sovereignty to a supranational *stato*, it could power a nationalist reaction against it, leading to a *confederatio*, or even subnational or sectoral demands for something approximating a *condominio* or a *consortio*.

3   *Enlargement*. The tendency for the EEC/EC/EU to incorporate new members has been one of the hallmarks of its success. Even when it was by all accounts a stagnant enterprise, it still managed to attract new members. Nevertheless, enlargement has rarely been treated theoretically as if it were an explicit part of the integration process.[125] Despite the fact that each successive increase in numbers has brought qualitative changes in rules and policies, they continue to be regarded as essentially fortuitous occurrences. Moreover, since membership has, heretofore, meant the acceptance by the newcomer of all the accumulated Community obligations (the famous *acquis communautaire*), the price for getting in has risen considerably. The longer a given country hesitates about joining, the more it will have to obey policies that it had no voice in producing.

And yet the queue is getting longer. Having held up all deliberations about 'widening' until the Community was sufficiently 'deepened' by fulfilling the obligations of the SEA and taking on the new commitments of the MAT, there is no further excuse for prolonging the issue. The coming years are likely to be overshadowed by a series of 'bloc negotiations'. Those with the adjacent EFTA countries were successfully completed – even if Switzerland decided not to participate after its membership in the EEA was rejected in a popular referendum and if Norway did negotiate a prospective treaty of adhesion which was subsequently turned down by its citizenry. The idiosyncratic cases of Turkey, Malta and Cyprus remain unresolved. The even more problematic candidacies of the former Comecon countries in Eastern Europe (not to mention those of some of the former republics of the USSR) have already generated serious controversy among existing member states. The sheer number of prospective members – as many as thirty to thirty-five, depending on how many pieces emerge from Yugoslavia and how many former republics of the Soviet Union manage to pass the Euro-test – threatens to overwhelm existing EC/EU institutions. Even if only a few get in as full members, their accession will almost certainly produce some changes in voting rules in the Council, in the number of Commissioners, Euro-deputies and judges of the Court, and perhaps even in the mode of selecting the President of the Commission. Those in the first 'round' will raise the average prosperity, contribute positively to Community coffers and generally strengthen the 'Northern or Germanic Bloc' of members with high levels of welfare spending, exposure to the world economy, monetary stability and organized group influence over public policy. Those in the second and subsequent rounds, however, pose a very different set of problems. Even the most favoured among them – the Czech Republic, Hungary and Poland – would greatly increase the heterogeneity of member interests and put a heavy strain on the Community's meagre resources for economic and social cohesion. Their domestic politics are still far from being consolidated and democratic so that it is difficult to imagine how they will fit into the internal processes of the Community, but there is little question that they will make common cause with the existing 'Southern Bloc' in demanding more derogations, dispensations and subsidies.

Until Europe's borders become stabilized – until we know for sure the number, variety and range of those admitted to membership in the EC/EU – it will be difficult to predict what type of polity will govern this ambiguous region of the world. One thing, however, seems relatively clear: the pressure for enlargement will be great and the consequences for failing to cope with it will be considerable. The economic and political stability of Eastern Europe and the former Soviet Union could well hinge upon it – as will the security of Western Europe from the potential hoards of displaced persons that could be triggered by failure. My hunch is that the most likely Community response will be the creation of new forms of 'quasi-membership' that will include the recently liberated states (Eastern Europe and the Republics of the former USSR) and the self-excluded states (Switzerland, Norway, Iceland?) within diverse, functionally based, regional organizations dealing with specific economic, social or environmental issues while according them only an intermediary status in the central institutions of political decision-making. In short, enlargement seems to be pushing the EC/EU toward a *condominio* type outcome.[126]

4   *External security*. Since its inception, the European integration process has been able to free-ride on the politico-military security provided by NATO. Already the decline in American hegemony and shifts in US foreign policy during the Reagan administration had raised questions in Europe about the wisdom of its continued dependence on the Atlantic Alliance. The subsequent end of the Cold War, the disbanding of the Warsaw Pact, the reunification of Germany and the collapse of the Soviet Union radically changed the international context.[127] The short-run consensus has favoured a continuation of NATO and a (reduced) presence of American troops in Europe; the long-run perspective, however, requires that the region develop its own security arrangements. As we saw above, the MAT has taken a first, timid step in that direction by 'empowering' the nine-nation WEU to begin elaborating 'a common defense policy' and encouraging (but not compelling) its other signatories to join.[128]

For understanding likely developments in this exogenous area, integration theory has virtually nothing to offer.[129] Once the European Defence Treaty had been rejected in 1954, making it clear that the direct politico-military route to European unity was barred, the issue disappeared. Whatever 'integrative' effects were produced by NATO – in logistical systems, strategic planning or joint weapons production – they were ignored or discounted. Weapons procurement, indeed all forms of public procurement, were exempted from the process of general trade liberalization. The admission of Ireland, a neutral state, only reconfirmed the widespread assumption that the EEC/EC had and would continue to have nothing to do with security matters.[130]

This, despite the fact that the core of European state-ness and national integration had historically been built around the development of an autonomous 'sovereign' capacity for defence and the creation of each unit's own armed forces exclusively for that purpose. Taxation, conscription, definition of borders, control over the mobility of persons, promotion of science and technology, even policies of public education and health – all reflected this overriding priority.[131] Is it conceivable that the EC could become an effective and legitimate supranational authority without its own armed forces, without even its own capacity to monitor compliance with its norms and to apply coercion when they were transgressed? The viability of either a *consortio* or a *condominio* rests on the assumption that diverse functional tasks can be collectively accomplished while relying almost exclusively on national and subnational agents of policy implementation – supervised by a supranational juridical system which itself depends on the willing compliance of national and subnational courts. Given its very dispersed decisional structure, it is hard to imagine how a *confederatio* could credibly control its own coercive apparatus. Such tasks would be left exclusively in the hands of its component states, although they might agree to act in alliance to resolve particular threats.

The implication seems clear: now that European security can no longer be taken for granted, i.e. now that new threats are surfacing that cannot be contained by existing NATO or bilateral commitments, only the emergence of something approaching a supranational *stato* will be able to accomplish the task. Even if a 'pluralistic security community' is firmly established among EC/EU members, it does not extend beyond their borders. Here is where the other exogenous variable, enlargement, comes into the picture. Presumably, the demands placed upon the EC/EU in the defence area will vary with the members' perception of likely security threats, and this wi'' largely be a function of what happens to the East. Should some combination of full and partial membership – plus substantial Western assistance – help to stabilize economic and political outcomes in the territory reaching from the Baltic to the Adriatic and Black Seas, the pressure for developing an integrated European military command with its attending state-building properties would diminish, and looser forms of collective security and political concertation, such as the CSCE, the Council of Europe, the WEU and/or a revised NATO, could fill the gap.[132]

Alternatively, no amount of 'tinkering' may be sufficient to cope with the disintegration of markets and polities in Eastern Europe and the ex-Soviet Union. Serious, presently unforeseen security threats could emerge 'out-of-theatre', e.g. in the Near East or North Africa. In either of these scenarios, the entire process of regional integration could be jeopardized. European states could revert to *sauve qui peut* strategies based exclusively on national interest calculations, and the recourse to force to resolve potential disputes would again become plausible, tempered only by the mechanisms of the balance of power or the hegemony of a single actor (Jopp et al. 1991; Heisbourg 1992).

If we are correct in assuming:

(a)　that the SEA and, especially, the MAT have imparted an initial bias toward a *condominio*-type outcome, but

(b)　that the above specified endogenous and exogenous conditions may deflect the course of future institutional development from that outcome,

then it would seem that the emerging Euro-polity will be subject to conflicting – if not diametrically opposing – influences and is therefore moving in an indeterminate direction. The impact of implementation problems is particularly difficult to assess, although my hunch is that variation in the functional tasks to be accomplished in different sectors will encourage a *consortio*-type result. Politicization, especially around the ratification process, could bring out *confederatio* characteristics, although the mobilization of subnational territorial units would have a *condominio* effect or of functional domains a *consortio* effect.[133] Enlargement seems clearly associated with the greater likelihood of *condominio*, just as external security could push solutions in the direction of a supranational *stato/federatio*. All this is but an elaborate way of saying that the options for the Euro-polity are still wide open.

The impact on public policy

Neither the SEA nor the MAT is self-implementing. Nor, as we have suggested, do they embody a coherent design. Their eventual impact upon the Euro-polity and its policies will depend on the intervening conditions which we have discussed above, not the least of which has been the growing and irreversible politicization of EC/EU issues. Heretofore, the dominant strategy had presumed a relatively low level of visibility and controversy and the gradual incorporation of specific, not to say specialized, categories of interest. European policy-making had its periodic crises (and extricated itself from them at the last minute with agonizing compromises and complex package-deals), but this took place out of sight of mass publics. Now that the process of national ratification of the MAT has broken that barrier, it will be difficult to return to business as usual. Even the issue of enlargement, which had been handled in such an 'intergovernmental' fashion in the past, has recently stirred unprecedented passions at the national level. And if such controversy surrounds the admission of three to five, rich and irreproachably European countries and the shift in the minimal blocking coalition from twenty-three to twenty-seven votes, try to imagine what it is going to be like to attempt to incorporate an even more numerous set of relatively poor, less culturally unambiguous Mediterranean and Eastern European candidates!

In the MAT, the EC/EU gave itself a *rendez-vous* in 1996 with the major unresolved issue of revising its institutional format. Politicization and enlargement – not to mention growing evidence of its problems in the implementation of existing policies and its blatant failure in efforts at foreign policy coordination with regard to Bosnia-Herzegovina – are putting great strain on existing arrangements. It is not inconceivable that the legitimacy of the entire enterprise could be at stake by the time that the Inter-Governmental Conference renders its final opinion.

Nevertheless, certain features of Euro-policy-making seem relatively well-established and likely to survive whatever format is eventually chosen:

1 *There will be no single dominant style of policy-making for the simple reason that there will be no single Europe.* In each of the multiple, partial and overlapping 'Europes' that are emerging, there will be a distinctive style of collective action depending on the mixture of territorial units and functional constituencies involved. The choice will not be limited to either of the two 'classic' formulae: a 'diplomatic' style characteristic of *confederatii* or a 'federal' style characteristic of territorially decentralized *stati*/*federatii*. Whatever style becomes characteristic of a *consortio* or a *condominio*, it will have to be more open, flexible, heterogenous and issue-specific than corresponding national styles.

2 *Whatever emerges, it will not so much resemble the policy style of any of the existing national member states as constitute something novel.* It will be dictated more by the shifting functional and territorial imperatives of the newly emergent polity than by the nationally engrained habits and preferences of policy-makers and administrators that compose it. This for two reasons: first, the absence of a hegemonic member which can impose its 'style' in a given arena by the superiority either of its resources or of its problem-solving capacity;[134] and, second, the enormous increase in the scale of governance will impose a logic of its own beyond the capabilities of any previous national state apparatus.[135] One should never forget that the 'policy space' of an integrated Europe will be larger demographically and much more culturally and linguistically diverse than that of the United States.

3 Unless the EC/EU manages to acquire a significantly greater direct capacity to generate its own revenues and to implement directly its distinctive policies, i.e. to become more like a *stato*/*federatio* than heretofore, *national and subnational administrations will continue to determine the style of face-to-face authoritative interaction with individual firms and citizens*. European directives and regulations may come to occupy an increasing role in fixing broad policy objectives (and in bringing about their much-needed convergence *pace* the Single European Act), but their effective implementation will still depend on the *bonne volonté* of a very divergent set of national, provincial and local agencies. Under these

conditions, the burgeoning 'implementation deficit' could prove to be even more negative for the legitimacy of EC/EU institutions than the much more talked about 'democracy deficit'.

4   Whatever the mix of national styles or functional imperatives, *European policy-making is likely to be dominated for the foreseeable future by a strong dose of* comitologie, *i.e. by a process of protracted negotiation in functionally specialized committees located at different levels of territorial aggregation.* Voting and, least of all, minimal winning coalitions will be rare, except sporadically at the highest levels; compromise among all participants will be the usual decisional norm, regardless of formal rules. Calculations of proportionality in relation to the intensity of interest (known as '*Sankt Proporzius*' in the Austrian jargon) and reciprocity in relation to successive issues ('log-rolling' in American terms) will ease the degree of acceptance. A great deal will depend upon complex and highly specialized systems of consultation, especially with the socio-economic interests most directly affected. These have been and will continue to be granted privileged access – although not necessarily through their European peak and sectoral associations. There is very convincing evidence that specific firms and even individual businessmen have found their way to the corridors of Brussels. Even though politicization will bring an increase in demands for 'transparency', the whole process will remain relatively opaque to wider publics. Whether *comitologie* among experts and representatives will suffice in its various territorial and functional configurations to ensure legitimacy by the citizenry is an open (and critical) question. So far, the 'democracy deficit' has generated much discussion, but little effective mobilization – and even if it were filled, say, by increasing the *compétences* of the European Parliament, the Commission and other Euro-executive agencies would still be likely to have to rely heavily on the information and compliance of specialized interest representatives.

5   *In the future an increasing proportion of EC/EU conflicts will take place not within Community/Union institutions, but between them.* Each specialized agency with its stipulated functional domain and its specific membership will be tempted to resolve internal disputes between interests by appropriating the benefits for itself and passing on the costs to other European agencies. In the absence of any strong and disciplined pan-European political parties, anything resembling a Euro-government responsible to a single party or coalition of parties or a more serious role for the Euro-Parliament – and, especially, if the Commission's monopoly over the introduction of new policies is weakened – it will become increasingly difficult to ensure compatibility between the policies pursued at the European level. Three mechanisms of collective decision-making, however, could emerge to ensure that *consortio*- and *condominio*-type solutions do not degenerate into utter incoherence:

1   *Hegemony*. Some country or, more likely, core area that is a prominent member of all conceivable 'Europes' could assert its domination and

impose its solutions to the eventual conflicts of *compétence* and interest that are bound to emerge between relatively independent European institutions. The Franco-German axis is the obvious candidate for this, although it has become increasingly fragile in the aftermath of the latter's reunification and would have to surmount rather significant differences in national administrative styles and structures of interest intermediation.

2 *Verrechtligung.* Inter-agency conflicts could be converted into issues of law and turned over to the European Court of Justice for adjudication. To a certain extent, this is already the case, although in the future its efficacy will depend on the willingness of all members of all European institutions to accept the supremacy of a common body of Community law – even in functional domains where they have had no say in the elaboration of these norms. The recent treaty creating the European Economic Area establishes an important precedent in that direction.

3 *Parliamentarization.* If the European Parliament's *compétences* were substantially increased and if all members of whatever European institutions were compelled to become its members and abide by its decisions, then an overarching legislative process could intervene to ensure a minimum of policy coherence. This leaves unresolved the very complex issue of apportionment of seats and voting rights across a varied gamut of issue arenas – not to mention the fact that 'parliamentary sovereignty' is by no means a well-established norm in all European national polities.

If, as I suspect, an integrated Europe will move increasingly in the direction of either a *consortio* or a *condominio*, it will have to break new ground, probably by combining all of the above. The usual solutions of strict issue demarcation in a *confederatio* or of hierarchical inter-agency coordination in a *federatio* will simply not be available.

The EC/EU is still '*un objet politique non-identifié*' and it will be some time before we discover for sure what type of polity it is going to become. The contest between territorially bound national states and functionally defined industrial and service sectors is still unresolved. There are even assertive subnational regions openly demanding greater representation and aggressive transnational firms discretely establishing privileged access. The options are still open, although if the past is any guide the outcome will most certainly be a compromise, possibly a second-best mixture of competing ideals and interests that no one wanted initially, but everyone (or almost everyone) is prepared to live with. The fact that mass publics continue to remain national (or subnational), have little or no identification with Europe as such and tend to regard the politics of the EC/EU as excessively remote and opaque casts a giant shadow over the entire process. It is one thing to imagine a compromised arrangement that member governments and associated interests could live with momentarily; it is quite another to imagine one that individual citizens and social groups not granted special access would accept as legitimate in the long run.

Concluding with some further doubts

As stipulated by the Maastricht Treaty, an Inter-governmental Conference (IGC) is being convoked this year and it will be charged with examining the future objectives and rules of the EC/EU. The compound effects of the Treaty itself and the persistent problems of implementation, politicization, enlargement and external security have been registered; the restricted financial and human resources of the Commission have been pushed to the limit; the multiplicity of decision sites and segmentation of policy domains have undermined the coherence of Community action and brought out the underlying conflicts of sectoral interest; the efforts of subnational political units to worm their way into the process have increased (and, perhaps, crested); the failure of member states to converge in their macro-economic–monetary–budgetary performances is becoming obvious, as are the changes in the pattern of socio-economic cohesion across rich and poor countries; all national governments have become more aware of how much policy autonomy they have lost. In sum, Europe is being forced to confront explicitly the delicate issue of its 'architecture', i.e. the design and coherence of its basic institutions.

This may bring it face to face with the dreaded F-word: *federalism*. There have long been advocates for a federalist solution to the problems of the European state system. Displaced by the neo-functionalism inherent in the ECSC and EEC, and disappointed by the outright failure of the European Defence Community (EDC) and European Political Community (EPC) in the early 1950s, small bands of federalists have nevertheless survived in Europe and persisted in their criticism of the integration process, focusing particularly on its 'democracy deficit'. Virtually all the proposals for institutional reform of the EC that have emanated from the European Parliament (and, especially, from the indefatigable Altiero Spinelli) have been federalist in nature and sought to fill that deficit by enhancing the powers of the Parliament in relation to both the Council of Ministers and the Commission.

Shifting to federalism would represent a dramatic change. The neo-functionalist strategy-cum-theory relies mainly on indirection, informality and incrementalism, even on a certain dissemblance of motives. Infra-national, socio-economic forces are expected to mobilize, to shift the locus of their activity and eventually to constrain national governmental resistance to the granting of further authority to emerging central institutions. The federalist strategy is overtly political and relies heavily on the possibility of reaching a formal and comprehensive agreement specifying the distribution of *compétences* among different levels of governance. Instead of successive shifts, entanglements and amendments, it focuses on the 'founding moment' when governmental, partisan and/or movement representatives meet to draft and approve the constitution for a new supranational *stato/federatio*. Explaining how and when this supreme expression of political will is supposed to come about has long been one of the weak points of the approach, especially in the absence of any evidence of a popular ground-swell of support for such an outcome.[136]

If, however, the EC/EU's *rendez-vous* with institutional design rejects the previous tactic of piecemeal treaty revision and miraculously finds the political will to convoke a full-fledged constitutional assembly, it could be a neo-rationalist's dream. National representatives would deliberate solemnly and reflexively on the pros and cons of adopting different rules and presumably come up with the intergovernmental bargain of all time. Neo-realists might be initially dismayed at the blatant transfer of sovereignty from the institutions they held to be so immutable – the previous national states would become, in effect, mere constituent 'regions' within the new federation – but they might be subsequently heartened when the United States of Europe began behaving in the same way as its multiple, squabbling and aggressive predecessors – only on an enlarged scale.

Such a 'big bang' would neither be predictable *ex ante* nor explainable *ex post* from the neo-functionalist perspective. As we have seen above, it is rooted in the gradual and inexorable formation of an eventual 'European civil society'. Its argument is that only the assertion of transversal cleavages following class, sectoral and professional lines across present national boundaries and their transformation into common, informal practices within private associations, parties, movements, even individual enterprises and firms will be effective in linking economic to political integration in the long run – not intergovernmental bargaining or constitutional drafting alone. This was conceived as the outcome of an almost surreptitious process, not of a highly visible event.[137]

A new and quite unexpected element has been added to this scenario by the radical change in the external context of the late 1980s. With the collapse of bipolar hostility, many of the territorially based units that had been frozen into place by security calculations have been effectively liberated. Various sub- and transnational identities are now free to experiment with different boundaries, alliances and strategies. Moreover, previous economies of scale for producers in large countries have largely disappeared with the existence of a well-established, overarching institution that guarantees market access, property rights, legal protection, product standardization, exchange rates and (perhaps) civic freedoms and democratic processes to even the smallest of its component units. Under the umbrella of EC/EU jurisdiction, it is now possible to demand much greater political autonomy without fearing the wrath and retribution of central national authorities. As a result, the original emphasis on functionally defined lines of interest has now been enlivened and made more complex by the superimposition of newly emergent, culturally defined forms of identity.[138]

In the near future we should have a much better idea about what type of polity the EC/EU will be. To this author the process looks irreversible, even if the specific end-state is still far from obvious. Too many entanglements and commitments have already been accepted. Too high expectations have been lodged in its deliberations. Too many problems no longer seem manageable within national states. Indeed, their politicians and citizens have increasingly looked to the Community to provide the only way out of national political stalemates and suboptimal equilibria. Sending intractable issues abroad to Brussels and blaming it for the need to implement unpopular policies at home has become a standard feature of European politics.

From 1986 to 1996 Europe has gone through a sustained spurt of regional integration – more significant perhaps than the heroic founding years from 1958 to 1965. My hunch, however, is that the EC/EU will still not have found its definitive configuration by then. There will still be a misfit between formal institutions of governance and informal processes of exchange. To put it in the words of Karl Deutsch, trans-European social communication will have vastly increased and become a normal fact of life, but the anticipated trans-European national identity will not yet have emerged and embedded itself in supranational authority (Deutsch 1953; Deutsch et al. 1964; Puchala 1981). The arrangement will still be utilitarian, not affective. Europe will be a nominal 'community of deeds', not a genuine 'community of fate'. The *solidarité* that Jacques Delors (1992) was so fond of invoking and that is so essential for justifying the redistribution of resources from richer to poorer persons and areas within the same political unit will be lacking. Until that becomes a habit superimposed by 'fellow Europeans' upon their multiple and divergent national identities, the Euro-polity will remain intrinsically contingent.

Notes

1. Hence the notion that the international system is becoming 'neo-medieval' has gained some currency. See Bull (1977: 264), for what seems to be the first appreciation of this. For more popular versions, see Eco (1986) and Lapham (1988).

2. For a particularly intelligent use of federalist theory to explore the emergent properties of the Euro-polity, see Sbragia (1992).

3. All deserve the prefix *neo* because they are revised versions of original theories that were much simpler in their causal structures and more demanding in their prior assumptions. Neo-realists and neo-rationalists seem to be much more confident in the generalizability (and logical elegance) of their approaches than are neo-functionalists; therefore, I will in deference refer to the former two as theories and to the latter as a 'perspective' or 'framework' for analysis.

Since writing this section, I have come across Martin Wight (1991), where he outlines three 'traditions' of thinking about international relations: (a) Machiavellian or Realist; (b) Grotian or Rationalist; (c) Kantian or Revolutionary. Leaving aside the appropriateness of his labels, I cannot help but be struck by the degree to which they seem to coincide with the three ways of looking at the more specific topic of regional integration delineated above.

4. An exception would be Robert Axelrod (1984), were it not for the fact that his 'Tit for tat' strategies assume a simple iterative game and not a historically unprecedented experiment involving a succession of novel problems, each with a different pay-off structure.

5. Nowhere is this more marked (and less expected) than in the cases of Robert O. Keohane and Stanley Hoffmann (1991), since the latter was long an eloquent realistic critic of neo-functionalism and the former a leading, if critical, contributor to the neo-realist school. For the earlier work, see Hoffmann (1966) and Keohane (1986). Also Mutimer (1989).

6. Elsewhere, I have defined this 'spill-over hypothesis' in the following way: 'Tensions from the global environment and/or contradictions generated by past performance (within the organization) give rise to unexpected performance in pursuit of agreed-upon objectives. These frustrations and/or dissatisfactions are likely to result in the search for alternative means for reaching the same goals, i.e. to induce actions to revise their respective strategies vis-à-vis the scope and level of regional decisionmaking' (Schmitter 1970: 243).

7. For a case study of entropy and encapsulation, see Schmitter (1969).

8. Joseph Nye (1965) was the first to pick this theme up, but his insight remained unexploited.

9. It undoubtedly helped that in the early 1950s an unusually homogeneous group of statesmen was governing the six original member states. Their common conservative and Catholic background and high degree of mutual trust may have made them exceptionally willing to take '*le saut dans l'inconnu*' that such a novel measure implied. Protestant Britain, it will be remembered, was governed by Clement Attlee and the Labour Party at the time. See Pineau and Rimbaud (1991: esp. 67–101).

10. The scores reported in the cells of Table 1.1 are based on a reading of the extant secondary literature on each of twenty-nine issue arenas. Needless to say, the coverage of these policies by specialists has been uneven, as has been their attention to specific causal agents and processes. The 'yes', 'mixed' and 'no' shadings in the table should, therefore, be regarded as tentative and subject to revision in the future. I am especially grateful to James Kinzer and Matt Tupper for their dedicated help in digesting and coding the data.

11. There has been some disagreement among specialists on the specific role that Jacques Delors, President of the Commission, and his staff have played in the 'crafting' of the SEA and

the MAT. Neo-realists and neo-rationalists, such as Andrew Moravcsik (1991) and Geoffrey Garrett (1992), tend to discount it and to stress the initiatives taken at the European Council Meetings by Kohl, Mitterrand or their respective foreign ministers. For the view of a scholar not contaminated by an *a priori* theoretical stance who stresses the relative autonomy of the Commission and, especially, of its President (but who may be influenced by his status as a participant observer), see George Ross (1992).

12. Research by Roy Ginsberg (1991) on the foreign policy actions of the EC confirms this impression. After classifying the causes of Community action as due either to 'integration' (i.e. functional responses stemming from prior EC policies), 'interdependence' (i.e. political or economic linkages to the global interstate system) or 'self-styled action' (i.e. emanating from the EC's own sense of mission and independence), he observes an overall tendency for the functional explanations to decline consistently and proportionately over time from an initial high in 1976–80 (73 per cent of all foreign policy actions) to 1981–85 (64 per cent) to 1986–90 (57 per cent) – even though their absolute number continues to increase. More and more of the EC's attention in this field seems motivated either by its own autonomous initiatives or by global incentives.

13. Most of what I know about this process I owe to the magisterial article by Joseph H.H. Weiler (1991).

14. Ironically, this need to pay more attention to the role of professional norms and solidarities in the integration process comes close to advocating a return to the original international functionalism of David Mitrany (1966), in which a great deal of emphasis (and hope) was placed on the role of independent experts. Recent work on 'epistemic communities' seems to touch on the same theme, even if the imbrication of national and international lawyers and judges has not (yet) been subjected to its scrutiny. See, especially, Adler and Haas (1992) and Haas (1992).

15. At most, there has been very little written about how different mixes of member states might affect the long-term evolution of European institutions. For some discussion of this issue, see Galtung (1989). Presumably, if a more rigorous theoretical tradition on this subject does develop, it will come from the neo-rationalists, who can draw on an existing (if not very successful) literature on 'optimal currency areas' or the 'optimal size of the firm'. For an effort to apply the theory of clubs and other aspects of economic reasoning to the EEC and other international associations, see Dosser et al. (1982).

16. The pre-First World War period and the 1920s were both times of open capital markets, free world trade and a tendency toward capitalist crisis (Polanyi 1957). In the early 1930s, the major industrial nations responded to the Great Depression with protectionist or even autarkist strategies of competitive devaluation, capital export controls, import restrictions and subsidized exports. As a result, the world economy collapsed. After the Second World War, it took more than two decades of GATT negotiations gradually to re-liberalize international trade, and it took two oil price shocks before the world capital markets were again freed from national control. In retrospect, this gradual transition from closed national economies to an uncontrolled world economy appears to have provided the optimal conditions for 'social-democratic' solutions at the national level. Until the mid-1970s, at any rate, Western European societies were able to profit from the economic dynamism of capitalism while stabilizing its fluctuations through Keynesian macro-economic controls, and correcting its distributive inequities through union power and social-welfare policies (Ruggie 1995).

17. In the neo-Marxist political-economic literature, much is made of declining shares of profit in the postwar decades as an indicator of the unresolvable contradiction between the capitalist economy and the democratic state. But since investment would cease when the rate of return on capital becomes negative, governments and unions would become aware of the risks of a profit squeeze for employment and growth – and economies with neo-corporatist institutional structures are in theory, and were in fact, quite capable of avoiding or correcting this strategic blunder (Wallerstein 1990; Scharpf 1991a).

18. Conversely, national monetary policy does have the power to attract capital, by setting national interest rates above the international level. But in doing so, it will raise the exchange rate, which decreases the international competitiveness of the national economy.

19. In theory, they could still be passed on to consumers through a devaluation of the national currency. However, regulations and wage settlements tend to affect specific branches of industry, rather than the economy as a whole. The loss of competitiveness may thus not be general enough to be fully compensated (from the point of view of the affected industry) by adjustments of the exchange rate. Moreover, under the conditions of global currency speculation, export competitiveness is no longer the most important factor determining exchange rates. In addition, an independent central bank whose primary goal is price stability is perfectly capable of stabilizing the exchange rate at a higher level than would be justified by the international competitiveness of the national economy.

20. Garrett (1992, 1995) interprets the case law of the European Court of Justice in an 'intergovernmentalist' frame as the focal point of a latent consensus among governments, whereas Burley and Mattli (1993) point to the existence of serious conflicts of interest. In their ('neo-functionalist') interpretation, the emphasis is on the relative autonomy of the legal system and its effectiveness as a 'mask and shield' against direct political intervention. See also Weiler (1993, 1994) and Mattli and Slaughter (1995). What Garrett seems to ignore, within his own frame of reference, is the importance of institutional decision rules: the Court (and the Commission, for that matter) is effectively able to impose outcomes that would not find a qualified majority in the Council of Ministers – but which cannot be corrected by the Council as long as the opposing governments are not themselves able to mobilize a qualified counter-majority (or, when the Court's decision involves an interpretation of the Treaty, unanimous action) in the Council.

21. Negative integration was and is pursued by the Commission primarily through 'decisions' and 'directives' under Arts 89 and 90 of the Treaty and through action against national infringements of Treaty obligations under Art. 169. Of at least the same practical importance is the direct application of European law in ordinary legal disputes before national courts and the possibility, under Art. 177, of preliminary rulings of the Court of Justice at the request of any (even inferior) national court. Again, the Council of Ministers is not involved, and national governments will typically appear before the Court only in the role of defendants.

22. According to neo-liberal theorists, the Community was meant to do no more than to establish and safeguard the postulates of economic freedom and undistorted competition in the European market. Hence the expansion of the European mandate, brought about by the Maastricht Treaty, in the fields of environmental protection, industrial policy or social cohesion, is viewed most critically by authors of this school (Mestmäcker 1992; Behrens 1994). In order to minimize potential damage, it is now also postulated that 'the rights of individuals, granted by the Treaty of the European Communities, to participate in commerce across national borders [must] not be encroached upon by measures in the service of the newly established competencies' (Mestmäcker 1994: 286). If this were accepted, the constraints on positive integration would be not only political, but constitutional as well.

23. I will limit myself here to the simplest form of 'intergovernmental' explanation. It is of course true, as has been pointed out by several critics, that actual interaction patterns are much more complex. In addition to national governments (or the ministries represented in specialized Councils), they include at least the 'supranational' Commission and 'subnational' interest organizations and firms as players in connected games. I also do not rule out the possibility that, in order to explain specific decisions, two-level games and perhaps much more complex models must in fact be employed. Pragmatically, however, it still makes sense first to exhaust the explanatory power of simple, and hence transparent, models – and to add further complications only when necessary. And at any rate, the agreement of the national governments in the Council of Ministers has remained the critical bottleneck in EC decision processes.

24. Héritier interprets these conflicts as a 'regulatory competition', where certain 'high-regulation countries' attempt to influence the mode of European regulations in order to reduce their own adjustment costs. In the present context it is useful to point out that this is not the (Prisoner's-Dilemma-like) 'competition among regulatory systems', whose most likely outcome is competitive deregulation. In the processes studied by Héritier, all member states would prefer agreement on European regulations at high levels of environmental protection, but they

differ about the style of regulation that the Community should adopt. Thus, their competition resembles the 'Battle of the Sexes' game discussed below.

25. More differentiated analyses are possible, and may be indispensable in the study of specific cases. In the area of environmental policy, for instance, governments of economically highly developed and ecologically highly impacted countries must respond to the cross-pressures of employment interests in the industrial sector and of environmentally sensitized voters. In less developed countries, by contrast, employment interests may be reinforced by the resistance of consumers to price increases caused by stringent environmental regulations. In either case, of course, government responses should also depend on the relative importance of the affected industries in the country in question.

26. Streeck (1995: 10) is correct in pointing out that process-related environmental and safety regulations may create obstacles to trade in the market for machine tools and production plants. For that reason, he includes these in his definition of 'market-making', as distinguished from 'market-correcting', regulations.

27. Moreover, product-related standardization profits from procedural innovations which minimize the need for consensus in the Council of Ministers by restricting its decisions to the definition of safety principles – whose detailed specification is then left to 'corporatist' committees representing the affected industries and national standardization organizations (Eichener 1993; Voelzkow 1993; Scharpf 1994).

28. Heckathorn and Maser (1987) have labelled this constellation, in which a 'cooperative' solution to the Prisoner's Dilemma requires agreement on one of several options that differ in their distributive characteristics, a 'Divided Prisoner's Dilemma'.

29. In their discussion of environmental policy, Rehbinder and Stewart (1984: 9) focus instead on the distinction between 'polluter states' and 'environmental states'. This appears to be less useful as an explanation of voting behaviour in Brussels, since highly developed countries produce more pollution and also have an interest in more stringent, European-wide, environmental regulations.

30. Naturally, Portugal and Greece (just like eastern Germany – Hank 1994) also have islands of above-average productivity, especially in new plants of multinational corporations.

31. According to surveys conducted by the Swedish employers' association (SAF), overall costs of a man-hour in industry ranged in 1993 between 33 Swedish krona in Portugal, 56 krona in Greece and 204 krona in Germany (Kosonen 1994).

32. Of course, the intensity of price competition varies between sectors. For example, in agriculture, 'Southern products' hardly compete with 'Northern products'.

33. Thus, it is not only the opposition of enterprises that stands in the way of a European social policy (Streeck 1995). Governments in economically weaker states must, on their own account, anticipate and try to avoid the exit option of capital.

34. If the affected branches of industry do not play a major role in the less developed member states, the damage done by European regulations at a high level of protection may be small enough to be compensated by side-payments from the structural and cohesion funds. It is also sometimes suggested that the agreement of some member states to relatively demanding environmental regulations may be a reflection on relatively less demanding practices of implementation.

35. Even though the Maastricht Treaty did generally allow for qualified-majority voting on environmental measures (Art. 130S), any five of the six countries with the lowest wage and non-wage labour costs in the Union (Portugal, Greece, Spain, Ireland, Britain and Italy) can easily muster a blocking minority against regulations that would damage their competitive position.

36. The theoretical background of this proposition can only be suggested here (Scharpf 1970). A need for legitimation arises when decisions override the preferences of some affected parties. Until recently, the European Community was able to rely primarily upon an 'output-oriented' form of legitimacy, for which the maximization of common welfare and the fair allocation of costs and benefits are crucial criteria. But as European interventions have become more frequent, more important and their allocative effects more visible, 'input-oriented'

legitimacy (involving democratic discourse and the democratic accountability of decision-makers) have gained in salience.

37. This is not meant to deny the possibility of non-majoritarian forms of legitimation (Majone 1994a, 1994b; Dehousse 1995). But the respect for expertise, impartiality and procedural fairness which may legitimate the decisions of courts, central banks or American-style independent regulatory commissions is unlikely to do much for the legitimation of the results of political horse-trading in the Council of Ministers.

38. It is often argued that the European Community should not be held to ideal but unrealistic standards of democratic practice which are frequently violated in all member states. In my view, this misses the point. Under modern conditions, democracy can only be defined as a potential or, as it were, a fleet-in-being. It is neither possible nor necessary that *every* matter be dealt with in the full light of public attention, as long as office-holders reckon with the possibility that *any* case may become politicized. When that is assured, the 'law of anticipated reactions' must do the rest.

39. In my view, further increases in the legislative competence of the European Parliament are not the most promising short-term strategy, since they would also render European decision processes even more cumbersome than they are now. Instead, if the President of the Commission were elected by, and fully accountable to, the European Parliament, this would help to focus media attention on a highly visible position of political leadership; it would require parties in the Parliament to present candidates with a European-wide appeal; and it might, in due course, lead to the formation of European-wide political parties (Weidenfeld 1995). As Dehousse (1995) points out, however, the introduction of party-political orientations in the Commission might render its relations to national governments in the Council more difficult than they are now – an argument that finds ample support in the practice of German federalism.

40. Overviews of earlier discussions and actual practices are provided by Nicoll (1984) and Langeheine and Weinstock (1984). There have also been proposals for a 'Europe of relativities' which would generally define common European standards in terms of criteria that are sensitive to differences in the level of economic development. For example, the revenue to be raised by an EC-wide environmental tax might be defined as a percentage of GDP in order to avoid disproportional burdens on the less developed member states (Weizsäcker 1989). Similar models are also being discussed in reference to social policy.

41. Remarkably, negative integration in the European Community includes elaborate injunctions against distortions of competition created by subsidies, preferential public procurement and other forms of 'affirmative action' favouring national producers – but apparently none against the practices of competitive deregulation.

42. The other factor Schmidt (1995: 18) identifies is differences in the 'default condition', i.e. the economic outcomes to be expected if there should be no agreement on 'coordinated liberalization' at the European level. In telecommunications, technical change and international competition would undermine the economic viability of national PTT monopolies, while in electricity, the stability of existing networks would not be affected by purely economic developments.

43. In Germany or Britain, for instance, this might mean that compulsory user charges supporting public television could be successfully attacked as a subsidy distorting competition by private networks, and that the monopoly of private physicians in ambulatory health care could be invaded by American-style health maintenance organizations. While both changes might be considered highly desirable in some quarters, it is also clear that they would not find the support of democratic majorities at the national level.

44. On the other hand, governments which, for domestic reasons, might not wish to agree to a Council directive may actually prefer deregulation by way of Commission directives and decisions.

45. In the electricity field, the Commission has initiated such actions against France, Denmark, Spain, Italy, Ireland and the Netherlands. Also, the drive towards liberalization in telecommunications was initiated by a successful infringement action against British Telecom in 1985 (Sauter 1995).

46. For instance, when the Commission issued its terminal equipment directive under Art. 90 (3), France was joined by Italy, Belgium, Germany and Greece in initiating an (unsuccessful) Art. 173 action against key provisions of the directive. If the directive had not been issued by the Commission, but had been introduced in the Council under Art. 100A, the objecting group would of course have been strong enough to prevent its adoption (Sauter 1995: 101).

47. In fact, as Susanne Schmidt (1995: 25f) argues, the mere possibility of 'uncontrolled' liberalization by the Court may persuade opponent governments to agree to 'coordinated liberalization' through (less far-reaching) Council directives – in the hope that these will be taken into account in the Court's own interpretation of the text of the Treaty.

48. This would not be meaningless, since member state bureaucracies may in fact use European directives to circumvent parliamentary controls at home. The same tendency of constituent governments to promote 'over-integration' at the central level can also be observed in German federalism (Scharpf 1988).

49. Presumably, if an economy has been viable so far, its regulatory costs are reflected in current prices and exchange rates.

50. The major threat to viability of the Danish model, incidentally, comes from European plans to harmonize VAT rates.

51. Here, in my view, is the real reason for the current crisis of European welfare states. Given lower rates of economic growth, rising costs of environmental protection, continued mass unemployment and a growing retirement population, the willingness of blue- and white-collar voters to bear an ever-rising tax burden has become the critical constraint on all policies dependent on democratic legitimation.

52. See Acknowledgements. For the sake of simplicity the authors use the term 'European Union' to describe the former European Economic Community and European Community alongside the present structure.

53. Regional offices have attracted little scholarly attention up to the present. In addition to literature cited elsewhere in this chapter, they have been described in a literature focusing on German offices (see, e.g. Zumschlinge 1989; Fastenrath 1990; Fechtner 1992; Engel 1993). For a recent comparison of offices in Germany and the United Kingdom see Jeffery 1995.

54. The chief contending theory was neo-functionalism, which views the dynamics of European integration mainly in terms of the response of politically influential policy-makers to policy spill-overs, connections across policy areas that would tend to drive the process of integration forward. There is no logical reason for this approach to ignore the role of subnational mobilization in the EU, but, from their standpoint in the 1960s and early 1970s, regional mobilization was nowhere in sight. As Ernest Haas pointed out in 1971: 'There has been very little spillover in the "level" of action, i.e., little progressive penetration from supranational institutions into the lower reaches of decisionmaking at the national and local levels' (Haas 1971: 13).

55. When we speak of regional representation in Brussels in the context of this chapter, we refer exclusively to subnational offices, though, of course, we are aware that subnational or regional governments have several other channels of representation in the EU (for an overview of these channels, see Hooghe and Marks forthcoming).

56. These data have been collected by the authors as part of a survey of regional offices in Brussels.

57. To gain comparability across subnational regions, the European Commission has developed three general categories of territorial unit which in descending size are designated NUTS (*Nomenclature des Unités Territoriales Statistiques*) 1, 2 and 3. These units do not necessarily correspond to levels of government. Each country is divided into three levels irrespective of actual governance structure.

58. Objective 1 of the EU's structural policy is to promote economic development in regions with a per capita gross domestic product of less than 75 per cent of the EU average. Other geographically targeted priorities are objective 2, which is designed to convert regions seriously affected by industrial decline, and objective 5b, which aids rural development. Objective 1 areas encompass 21.7 per cent of the population of the EC; objective 2 areas

encompass 16.4 per cent; and objective 5b areas encompass 5.0 per cent (Commission of the European Communities 1990).

59. Respondents were asked to identify the geographical unity they considered to be their region. They were then asked to rate their degree of attachment to their town or village, their region, their nation, the European Union and Europe as a whole. Our measure of regionalism captures attachment to the region relative to that of the nation by subtracting national attachment from regional attachment.

60. Interviews with the authors.

61. See Alberta Sbragia (1993) for a discussion of the role of territory in structuring EU political institutions.

62. See Acknowledgements.

63. On this see in particular the work of Fritz Scharpf.

64. While the democratic defence of nationalism explains the absence of democratic political institutions at European level by the absence of a common 'European identity', one might ask whether to the contrary the development of collective identities and solidarities does not depend on the availability of institutional opportunities for successful collective action in pursuit of collective benefits. In this case, it would not be nationalism that would explain the persistence of the (democratic) nation-state, but, vice versa, the nation-state, in particular its control over the articulation of border-crossing collective interests and its institutional monopoly on democratic participation, would account for the persistence of nationalism.

65. To the extent that such rules cannot be simple, and creating them requires institutional innovation, under fragmented sovereignty the latter is typically about how to ensure cross-national tradability of goods and services while interfering as little as possible with the sovereignty of participating nation-states, and especially about avoiding needs for state-like governance at supranational level.

66. It is in this context that the, on the surface, severest curtailment of national sovereignty within the European integration project must be seen, the intended creation under the Maastricht Treaty of a common currency and a European central bank, or 'Eurofed'. In my view, the way monetary union has been designed by the member states, it perfectly fits the logic of the alliance of nationalism and neo-liberalism, and cannot be claimed as evidence of a commitment of member states to supranational restoration of domestic political sovereignty. Most European countries have long effectively lost control over their monetary policies, as they have had for about two decades now to follow the lead of the *Deutsche Bundesbank*. Moreover, the *Bundesbank* became the *de facto* European central bank, not just because of the size of the German economy, but because of the bank's independence from the German government and its insulation from political pressure that made it uniquely capable of behaving in conformity with the pressures of internationalized capital markets. It is on this model that the Eurofed, if at all, will be built.

In agreeing to monetary union, European states will formally give up something that they effectively no longer have. This holds also for Germany, which, among other things precisely because of the special status of its central bank, has been aptly characterized by Peter Katzenstein (1987) as a 'semi-sovereign state'. Moreover, under monetary union European monetary policy will be handed over to an institution that is carefully crafted, in the image of the *Bundesbank*, not to require or encourage the growth of a supranational state. Instead the Eurofed will operate like an independent regulatory agency, reflecting and responding to 'market forces', rather than to a political will to 'correct' or, for that matter, 'distort' markets; protecting the common currency from being put at the service of political purposes like full employment; and accommodating not political pressure, but an international capital market that has long outgrown national borders and national control.

67. The reasons why majority voting, even of the 'qualified' kind, is rarely used in intergovernmental relations have been pointed out, among others, by Scharpf (1988).

68. On interest groups in the European Community, see Streeck and Schmitter (1991).

69. An equally frequently used but less appropriate term is 'Europe of different speeds' – a concept that assumes that ultimately all member countries will arrive at an identical destination, where they will be subject to one and the same system of supranational authority.

70. On the conceptual distinctions, see Marshall (1964).

71. It was to this developing core of a minimalist, market-making European social policy that the European Court of Justice later attached its own project, by reading individual and personal rights to equal treatment into the obligation of member states not to obstruct the free movement of labour, and trying to work from there towards a judicially based, non-statist construction of common European citizenship. Rather than introducing collective rights and substantive entitlements in a civil law system of contractual labour market relations – as traditionally social policy had done – the European Court, to the contrary tried to use rights to equal participation in labour markets to construct rights to equal treatment under the law in areas far removed from the labour market, and the farther removed the better. Also, regardless of their civil rights rhetoric, in their core the rulings of the Court always had to refer back as their legal base to intergovernmental commitments to market-making, enshrined in agreements among sovereign states that left their sovereignty intact and grounded the rights of non-nationals in participating countries on commitments in international law, not to common citizenship, but to a 'common market'.

72. Not necessarily the stability of the social policy regimes themselves. While these may have to be adjusted in response to market pressures or changing political fashions, the problem for the preservation of the nation-state is to protect the ability of governments to preside over such changes and maintain the appearance that they take place, or at least could take place, under political control, i.e. as a result of national political choices. 'Saving face' in this sense is not the least important part of the defence of national sovereignty under international interdependence.

73. It was at this time that European social policy first began to become involved in industrial relations, something that after the European-wide worker unrest of 1968 and 1969 seems to have been non-controversial. Legally the move could be justified by a broad reading of the Treaty's commitment to 'dialogue between management and labor'.

74. Just as state formation can be instrumental to social policy, the latter, as Bismarck, among others, knew, may be instrumental to state formation. In Western Europe today, unions and social democrats tend to be federalist in their pursuit of political resources for market intervention, while the federalists in the Commission pursue social policy as a means for building legitimacy for a European supranational state. The coalition between the two reflects the fact that each side can regard the other's ends as means to its own ends, and the other's success as contributing to its own success.

75. Apart from several directives on equality of pay for women and on workplace health and safety (see below), all that was accomplished were three directives on employment protection (passed in 1975, 1977 and 1980), which, with minor exceptions, did not require changes in national practice (Addison and Siebert 1991: 601). All other initiatives, most prominently the so-called 'Vredeling proposal', were defeated by an increasingly well-entrenched, British-led coalition between neo-liberal advocates of labour market 'flexibility' and nationalist resistance to 'harmonization'.

76. Symbolism is far from unimportant in European policy-making. In fact, in response to pressures from a Parliament that has not much else to do, and to satisfy European-minded segments of the population, a major share of European policy is devoted to building supra-national façades for the Union's intergovernmental structure. An example is the 'common European passport', which on closer inspection reduces to national passports issued by national governments with covers of identical colour and in all Union working languages. Typically such cosmetic exercises are defended by suggestions that in the future they may somehow assume a life of their own, with the façade 'in the long run' somehow modifying the structure.

77. The intention of the Treaty seems to have had little to do with feminism, and certainly not with the emergent feminism of the 1970s. While French legislation going back to the Popular Front prescribed equal wages for women, no such legislation existed in other countries, raising fears among the French government that these might cut their costs and become more competitive by increasing female employment at lower wages. To the extent that legally enforced wage equality helps keep female labour market participation low, the Treaty

would have had the, perhaps not entirely unintended, effect of preserving traditional family structures.

78. Note in addition that health and safety policy as such is not market-correcting but what Peter Lange (1992) has aptly called 'market-braking' – designed to prevent an 'overheating' of markets that would result in destruction of productive resources – correcting not market outcomes, but market failure (Majone 1993, 1994c). This has little to do with promoting social citizenship (Kenis 1991). Indeed public intervention to protect the physical integrity of workers was compatible even with nineteenth-century Victorian liberalism. As the British example shows, early development of a health and safety regime at work does not foreshadow an early and stable transition to redistributive social policy. While it is probably true that even the Thatcher government did not want to be seen by its voters as improving the competitiveness of the British economy at the expense of workers' health and safety, in all other areas of social policy it had no such compunctions at all.

79. Technically, all twelve member states signed a 'Protocol on Social Policy' allowing the eleven countries that 'wish[ed] to continue along the path laid down in the Social Charter of 1989' to use the institutions of the Community for making 'the necessary decisions'. The Protocol makes clear that such decisions will be of no consequence for the United Kingdom.

80. Like American firms, firms with headquarters in Britain that would not want to have a multinational works council or to comply with information and consultation obligations could refuse to obey 'foreign' law and ask their government to protect them, and itself, from intrusion by a foreign state. To avoid writing unenforceable, and technically illegal, law for 'foreign' citizens acting in a 'foreign' country – i.e. for multinationals based and incorporated in Britain – the Eleven would have to designate, just as successive drafts of the Works Council directive envisaged for non-European firms, the largest subsidiary of a British multinational in the Eleven countries as its 'headquarters' liable under 'Eleven' law.

81. In the summer of 1994, two-and-a-half years after Maastricht, not a single piece of legislation had been passed by the Eleven under the Agreement. The first subject for which the Agreement was invoked was the draft European Works Councils directive.

82. In discussing subsidiarity, Goetschy notes 'the striking fact . . . that the social and political actors [at the European level during the 'social dimension' campaign] have been very careful not to jeopardize the national dynamics or national coherences at work', which she attributes to the 'prudence' of European decision-makers rather than their impotence (1991: 270). Goetschy correctly notes that subsidiarity, as understood by the Community, 'took its full meaning [only] when the harmonization principle was supplemented by the mutual recognition principle' (1991: 269), i.e. by an explicit or implicit assumption of functional equivalence of member countries' national social policy regimes.

83. Application of subsidiarity to subnational levels of government, like regions or *Länder*, is largely rhetorical, except perhaps where, like in Germany, subnational units have strong constitutional standing in national law.

84. For a detailed analysis of the co-decision procedure see Streeck (1993: esp. 151–152 and 168–171).

85. It may have been precisely because the concept of subsidiarity, taken out of its original context, invites not only nationalist but also neo-liberal – or Protestant, Thatcherite and 'British' – misunderstandings that it was introduced as a tactical peace formula by promoters of supranational state-building.

86. Hauser (1991) believes that – with the Union having neither taxing powers nor control over transfer payments and social services – diffusion of best practice, promoted among other things by Community sponsoring of comparative research and of policy 'observatories', will be the most important force against what he calls the 'immobility scenario' in European social policy. Similarly Mitchell and Rojot, who believe that 'growing awareness of differences in approach to benefits across countries could have important long-term effects on benefits and social insurance within Europe. The fact that there are alternative routes to retirement income and health care is becoming more and more evident' (1993: 164). See also Collins (1985: 184), who argues that the main role of the European Social Fund in vocational training lies in its funding of pilot projects that spread information on innovative or superior methods.

87. The reason for this was British resistance. In return for the Charter remaining non-binding, the British government allowed the eleven other members to pass it, with Britain not participating in spite of several British objections having been taken into account. The procedure prefigured the Maastricht 'Social Protocol'.

88. It is true, however, that had the Charter become law, it would have meant a major change in one Community country, the United Kingdom – which is why it ultimately *had* to remain non-binding. In Britain the notion of constitutionally guaranteed basic rights for workers and trade unions is unknown. While the Parliament is free to legislate such rights as it sees fit, a new Parliament with a different majority is free to revoke them. Legal rights were therefore never high on British unions' political agenda, and, unlike other countries, could never become an important commodity for political exchange. However, the Thatcher experience in the 1980s taught British unions that their capacity to resist a hostile government through industrial and political as distinguished from legal action had sharply declined. Not being able to get legal protection from their national state, British unions began in the late 1980s to place their hopes on Brussels, whose proposed Charter of Fundamental Rights of Workers, largely trivial for unions elsewhere in Europe, came to be increasingly seen as a potential substitute for a constitutionalized floor of legal protection that would be enforceable even on a Conservative parliamentary majority. It is very likely that this goes a long way to explain the change in British unions' attitudes towards the European Community, as well as Thatcher's vigorous defence of the 'sovereignty' of the British Parliament.

89. Information and consultation may in principle be made obligatory by a European directive, which could be enacted by qualified-majority vote among the eleven members of the Maastricht 'Social Policy Community'. To avoid legislating, the Community has long promoted voluntary arrangements for information and consultation, called 'European Works Councils'. See Streeck and Vitols (1995).

90. This too may be defended as required for the preservation of national diversity: 'To make sure that the various traditions and susceptibilities in this Community of ours are respected, the Commission has proposed a choice between three forms of worker participation as a preliminary to drawing up the European Company Statute' (Delors 1989: 7).

91. The version of the European Works Council directive that was finally passed admits any information and consultation arrangement that is agreed between management and labour, as long as it satisfies a set of minimum requirements.

92. While observing that 'neither the Charter nor the action programme put important new constraints on labour markets or on national employment policies', Teague and Grahl (1991: 209) hope that they will 'increase the weight of Community comparisons and comparators both in the formation of public policy at national level and, ultimately, in employment bargaining itself'. This, of course, is hardly borne out by the British experience; namely the re-election of the Major government in 1992 in spite of its opt-out, only a few months previously, of European social policy.

93. Many British observers believe that multinational firms operating in Britain will for this reason have to include their British workforces in the European Works Council they may under future European legislation be forced to have for their operations in member countries covered by the Social Protocol. In this way, regime diffusion is expected to bring potentially fundamental change to British industrial relations.

94. Majone puts the same matter more affirmatively when he observes that 'in the Community, but increasingly also in the member states, social-policy measures will be accepted only if they can be shown to be consistent with the values of a liberal economic order' (1992: 4). Majone's notion of a 'regulatory' social policy shares with the concept of neo-voluntarism a strict rejection of functionalist expectations of social policy expansion: 'The historical development of the Community has shown again and again the limits of such functionalist logic' (1992: 9). It also discards the prospect of a nation-state-like social policy at European level: 'We may conclude that no such policy will be adopted, now or in the foreseeable future' (1992: 11). According to Majone, 'social regulation' as an alternative form of social policy is not adequately described in Marshallian terms; it is, however, compatible with the limited resources controlled by the Community, as well as with 'subsidiarity' and the preservation of

national 'diversity'. Being free from traditional concerns with redistribution, social regulation 'addresses primarily quality-of-life issues, and reflects the political culture of post-industrial society' (1992: 7), whatever that may be.

95. These observations are based on interviews with German union officials.

96. In effect, this amounts to the passage of a 'balanced budget amendment' by way of an international treaty.

97. It is true that the European Trade Union Confederation has no real negotiating competence either. The difference is, however, that the weakness of its peak association weakens the class-political capacities of labour, with the failure of organizational centralization amounting to political failure. For capital, to the contrary, non-centralization is an interest-conscious strategic move.

98. Employers can live with this, even in systems that they find in principle uncomfortable. This is because international competitive pressure reinforces the position of capital inside national systems regardless of whether the formal rules remain unchanged. Changes in such rules can in any case later be sought in the course of 'cooperative' efforts to increase competitiveness and secure employment.

99. See Acknowledgements.

100. For simplicity we use the term 'European Union' to apply to the various institutions – the European Economic Community, the European Community – that are the precursors of the current Union.

101. See Chapter 3 above for details of the regional representation in Brussels.

102. This point was forcefully made to the first author in interviews with directors of regional offices in Brussels. On the limits placed by existing member states on the development of a Europe of the Regions, see Anderson (1991).

103. The MAT was also preceded very closely by an agreement with the EFTA countries – Austria, Finland, Iceland, Liechtenstein, Norway, Sweden and Switzerland – to establish the European Economic Area (EEA). Originally conceived as a way of postponing the issue of enlargement, it would extend most of the provisions of the SEA (and, hence, most EC rules) to all nineteen members, while leaving some especially sensitive issues such as agriculture, fishing, energy and industrial subsidies pending. Although widely hailed as a success after protracted negotiations, it does not seem to have had the intended effect of putting off the issue of full membership until further progress has been made on monetary and political union. Switzerland's citizenry subsequently rejected the opportunity to join.

104. Reading it, one sympathizes with de Gaulle's disdainful reference to supranationality for leading to the creation of a new European language: '*Volapuk intégré*'.

105. Stephen Krasner (1991) has subjected the Treaty (or, better, Treaties) of Westphalia to detailed scrutiny. He demonstrates quite convincingly how difficult it would have been for an observer at the time to discern their significance. In retrospect, they have come to be regarded as a watershed in the historical development of the European state system. Reading the texts themselves, Krasner finds – in addition to the (few) clauses that consecrate the state as a uniquely endowed type of political actor – many that explicitly protected the status of a considerable variety of non-state entities (bishoprics, imperial cities, the Holy Roman Empire itself) and sanctioned a level of interference in domestic affairs that manifestly contradicted the notion of national sovereignty. I suspect that should the Maastricht Treaty in retrospect be credited with marking an analogous watershed in the development of the 'post-state', future political archaeologists will scrutinize its clauses and wonder how that could have been possible.

106. It also 'warns' the member states that three other policy fields will shortly be added to the current listing: civil protection, energy and tourism (Annex II, Protocol 2).

107. In his 'speculative' effort to explain how countries put themselves in this unprecedented situation, Weiler (1991: 2443–2447) stresses two factors: (1) that in situations of complex interdependence, national actors may prefer to forgo their own unitary veto power in order to be able to force a recalcitrant member to conform; (2) that member states may have unwittingly fallen into the 'trap' of Community discipline when the immediate stakes were high and when they were not fully cognizant of the longer-term consequences of what

they were agreeing to. Both of these are eminently respectable reasons from a neo-functionalist perspective.

108. The reference to 'peoples' rather than 'states' is unusual – and significant since it opens up novel possibilities for an eventual shift to constituencies other than those defined at the national level by existing states. Needless to say, none of the founding treaties or their amendments make an effort to define what 'Europe' is.

109. Which is (more or less) defined elsewhere (Art. 3b) as follows: 'In areas which do not fall in its exclusive jurisdiction, the Community shall take action, in accordance with the principle of subsidiarity, only if and insofar as the objectives of the proposed action cannot be sufficiently achieved by the Member State and can, therefore, by reason of the scale or effects of proposed action be better achieved by the Community.' Who should determine what 'sufficiently' means and what criteria would be applied to estimate the economies of scale or the extent of externalities is presumably left to an unspecified political process. For a particularly stimulating discussion of the ambiguities of subsidiarity, see Gretschmann (1991).

110. The *acquis communautaire* is one of the most sacred of EC, now EU, concepts. It refers to the sum total of obligations that have accumulated since the founding of the ECSC and are imbedded in innumerable treaties and protocols. So far, any state which applies to the EC/EU is expected to accept as a matter of principle the responsibility for fulfilling all these obligations, although in the actual negotiations for entry it is possible to delay the application of some of them. It is expressly designed to prevent any prospective member from 'shopping around' for its own mix of obligations.

111. There is another peculiar item of 'corporatist-type subsidiarity' in the Declaration on Co-operation with Charitable Associations (Annex II, Protocol 22), in which the signatories stress the importance of working through these intermediaries when dealing with social policy.

112. For an almost caricatural example of unrequited neo-realism, see Mearsheimer (1990). For a discussion of the prospects for German hegemony, see Saña (1990).

113. Since writing this, I have chanced upon Quermonne (1992), in which the treaty is given a similarly ambiguous, 'tripartite' reading.

114. For a particularly eloquent defence of its 'limited but real powers', see Hoffmann (1982). Also Puchala, where it is found, even after the signing of the SEA, that 'the weight of evidence tends to lie on the side of (European integration's having) strengthened states' (1988: 461).

115. Perhaps it is also significant that many of the new items of Euro-speak seem to be emerging in English, rather than French, which was the language initially dominant within the Eurocracy.

The Economist (14 December 1991: 54) asked its readers: 'Sprechen Sie Maastricht?' To the concepts of cohesion, convergence, competence, opting out, subsidiarity and unanimity, they added: 'in every nook and cranny', which they defined as 'a quaint English phrase to describe where Brussels bureaucrats would be if there were no subsidiarity'. An industrious Frenchman, François Gondrand (1991), has compiled a glossary of Euro-speak with 1,000 entries!

116. From this perspective, the British allergy to the 'F-word', which seems so ridiculous to a North American or German, is well founded. What they are objecting to is the possible emergence of a supranational *stato*, i.e. any political form – however decentralized or decon-centrated – that accumulates sovereign powers within a single set of institutions at the European level. Cf. the discussion between Ian Davidson (1991) and Martin Wolf (1991) in the *Financial Times*. Samuel Brittan (1991) has attempted to clarify the terms of discussion for the British and concludes that 'the true dividing lines are between different ideas on the role of the state rather than between countries or between federalists and nationalists'.

117. For a brief account of the failure of Euro-corporatism, see Schmitter and Streeck (1991).

118. Alberta Sbragia (1992) pays special attention to the Swiss and German versions of federalism because they accord a prominent and guaranteed role to subnational political units in their respective upper houses of parliament. Fritz Scharpf (1988) has explicitly explored the parallels between the German federal system and the EC. For the historical lessons Switzerland has to offer, see Muret (1966) and Böckenförde (1991).

119. Although Ernst B. Haas was careful to avoid this assumption in his *Beyond the Nation-State*, in which he defined as his dependent variable 'the process of increasing the interaction and the mingling so as to obscure the boundaries between the system of international organizations and the environment provided by their nation-state members' (1964: 29). In their *Europe's Would-be Polity*, Leon Lindberg and Stuart Scheingold admit candidly that 'we have no concept of a termination state for the Community' (1970: 138).

120. In all fairness, I should note Donald Puchala's (1972) effort to delineate a 'concordance system' which resembles something approaching my *confederatio* type; Leon Lindberg and Stuart Scheingold's (1970) discussion of a 'sector-integrated supranational system' which is close to the *consortio* type; and Ernst B. Haas's (1971) musings on 'regional communes' (also a *consortio*) and 'asymmetrical regional overlap' (perhaps something like my *condominio*).

121. There is one very important exception to this generalization. From very early on, the German *Länder* insisted that they be informed and participate at least indirectly in the deliberations of the Council of Ministers on issues assigned exclusively to them by the constitution of the Federal Republic. See Hrbek and Thaysen (1986).

122. For some appropriately critical remarks on the likelihood of the emergence of a '*Europe des Régions*' rather than a '*Europe des États*', see Marks (1992) and Anderson (1991). One of the most obvious impediments is the very asymmetric fashion in which regional governance is distributed across national polities in Europe. Great Britain, for example, completely lacks this intermediate layer (although the issue of devolution of authority to Scotland did emerge during the 1992 elections). Portugal and Greece have only recently begun to experiment with regionalization in order to attract more EC funds. Unfortunately for the issue of economic and social cohesion, it is invariably the most developed internal regions that are the best equipped and most eager to exploit the Brussels connection.

123. For the notion of an 'implementation deficit', see Schaefer (1991).

124. The deliberations of both the European Council and the Council of Ministers are secret. Neither publicizes the voting behaviour of its members or the positions taken by them on a given issue. The only way of learning what governments have proposed or how they have voted is to rely on leaks to the press and the efforts of journalists to reconstruct what happened. This lack of transparence contributes, along with the modest powers of the European Parliament, to the so-called 'democracy deficit' and to the generally low level of public attention to Community issues.

125. The Treaty of Rome only specifies that 'Any European State may apply to become a member of the Community' (Art. 237), although later Council decisions made it explicit that their national political institutions had to be democratic (without defining what this meant). The cultural boundaries of European-ness remain ambiguous, and are currently being tested by Turkey's (so far, frustrated) application for full membership.

There are no explicit treaty provisions for exiting from the EC/EU, although this is presumably a right for all member states. In 1985, some twelve years after Denmark's accession, Greenland subsequently chose to withdraw and was allowed to do so peacefully. In any case, the Community lacks the military-coercive capacity to prevent any such defection.

For a general discussion of the enlargement issue (without any theoretical guidance), see Church (1990). For a more recent treatment that goes a long way to placing the issue in its broader theoretical context, see Michalski and Wallace (1992).

126. Under the new rules, the European Parliament possesses the right to veto both the initial discussion and the eventual admission of new members. The threat to do either could give it a considerably enhanced, direct influence over the eventual design of EC/EU institutions. All the Euro-deputies would have to say is 'no new members until the democracy deficit is filled'! In the past, they have shown a strong desire to increase not just their own powers, but also the federalist properties of the system as a whole. For evidence that the MEPs are prepared to use this capacity for blackmail to extort changes from the Commission or the Council of Ministers, see Lange (1992: 247).

127. It should be noted in passing how very important (and fortuitous) it was that the signing of the SEA and, hence, deepening of member commitment to the EC preceded the

transformative events in the East. How different the outcome might have been if Western European integration had not accelerated *prior* to the disintegration of Eastern Europe!

128. It is not clear whether the loose arrangements surrounding the WEU 'defense pillar' in the MAT are going to be considered part of the *acquis communautaire* and, hence, whether new applicants will be required to join it as a condition for full membership. This could cause additional difficulty since most of those likely to be in the first round are neutrals which might prefer to be absolved of such a collective responsibility – if only to facilitate the passage of eventual national referenda. Countries in the second round, such as the Czech Republic, Hungary and Poland, presumably would jump at the chance to be brought under the WEU umbrella.

129. As he has done often in the past, Stanley Hoffmann put the matter most dramatically: 'Goods can be "integrated" and maximized, so to speak, anonymously; the integration of foreign and military policies, in a world in which security and leadership are the *scarcest of values*, means *what it has always meant*: the acceptance by some of the predominance of others' (1964: 1275). The present issues in Europe are (a) whether security is still the same scarce commodity and (b) whether the amount needed can be produced collectively without the hegemony of a single national state.

130. Hence, the notion that the EC is on its way to becoming the world's first 'great civilian power', i.e. capable of acting as a unit in a variety of arenas of international politics, but not of backing up its actions with armed force. See Pinder (1991: 169–198), although the originator of this notion seems to have been Duchêne (1972: 43). For the contrary view that the EC is likely to develop into an aggressive superpower imposing *Pax Bruxellana* on the world, see Galtung (1973).

Since 1970, regular meetings of foreign ministers and senior civil servants have sought to elaborate a common foreign policy through a procedure known as European Political Cooperation (EPC). This has resulted in a steadily increased flow of information across member states and some successful collective efforts, e.g. in the Conference on Security and Cooperation in Europe (CSCE), in the peace process in Central America and in negotiations with other economic blocs such as the Association of South-East Asian Nations (ASEAN). It has also produced some notable failures to come up with common positions, e.g. with regard to South Africa and the Middle East. For a useful overview, see Pijpers et al. (1988) and Ginsberg (1989).

131. The *locus classicus* for an analysis of this interaction between war-making and state-building is Charles Tilly (1975), especially the introductory 'Reflections' by Tilly and the chapters by Samuel Finer and Gabriel Ardant. See also Tilly (1985). I am also indebted to a seminar conducted at the Center for Advanced Study in the Behavioral Sciences by Charles Tilly for the benefit of the Consortium for 1992 on 16 January 1992, at which these issues were discussed extensively in relation to the emerging structures of the EC.

132. For a provocative discussion of 'alternative security policies for Europe', see Galtung (1989: 118–136).

133. It is tempting to interpret this outcome in terms of a race between two competing sources of differentiation for the politicization of their respective publics: *regionalization*, which would aggregate interests along lines of historical–cultural discrimination and/or around locationally specialized systems of production, vs *sectoralization*, which would bring together actors according to product lines or policy arenas that transcend national boundaries. The basic administrative structure of the Commission with its twenty-three sectorally defined Directorates-General favours the latter, although there is growing evidence of experimentation with the former.

134. I leave aside the early stages of the integration process in which the French administrative style was clearly hegemonic – for both reasons. Not only has the prestige of the statist, *grandes écoles* approach declined (along with French administrative performance), but enlargement has greatly augmented the variety of available policy styles. Also, to the extent that the outcome of integration becomes less 'concentric', i.e. less coordinated by the Commission in Brussels, the EC/EU institutions dispersed throughout Europe should be

expected to acquire at least some of the administrative traits of the sites where they will be located.

135. For a discussion that argues that the shift in scale is one of several factors that have affected the emerging system of European interest representation and that is driving it in the direction of a more pluralist, American-style outcome than is presently characteristic of any of the member states of the EC/EU, see Streeck and Schmitter (1991).

136. The literature on Euro-federalism is considerable, but unsatisfactory on the key issue of agency. It is much better at asserting why 'the federal method' would be a rational solution to a multitude of European problems, than at explaining who might bring it off. Federalists take great comfort in *Euro-Barometer* data that show 76 per cent of a sample of the European public saying that they are in favour of the EC's developing into the USE (United States of Europe), but that does not offer a convincing answer to the question of how to get these people sufficiently concerned so that they will actively promote such an outcome. For a history of federalist efforts, see Burgess (1989). For more recent advocacy of federalist solutions, see Wistrich (1989) and Pinder (1991).

137. William Wallace has suggested drawing a distinction between two parallel integration processes: 'Informal integration consists of those intense patterns of interaction which develop without the impetus of deliberate political decisions, following the dynamics of markets, technology, communications networks, and social change. Formal integration consists of those changes in the framework of rules and regulations which encourage – or inhibit, or redirect – informal flows. Informal integration is a continuous process, a flow: it creeps unawares out of the myriad transactions of private individuals pursuing private interests. Formal integration is discontinuous: it proceeds decision by decision, bargain by bargain, treaty by treaty' (1990: 9). Coming from one of the leading spokesmen for 'intergovernmentalism', this recognition of the importance of functional interdependencies and influence processes is a bit surprising, but most welcome. The book in which these remarks appeared, however, is devoted almost exclusively to bargaining among national states and the operations of international organizations.

138. One very salient example is the increased self-assertion of the German *Länder* with regard to the ratification of the MAT by the *Bundesrat*. See the feature article in *Der Spiegel* (23 March 1992). During the 1992 British elections, increased autonomy for Scotland became such a major issue that the then Conservative Foreign Secretary, Douglas Hurd, felt compelled to remind the Scots that it might not be so easy: 'Scotland could not slide out of the United Kingdom on Monday and slide into the Community as the thirteenth member on Tuesday. . . . The lawyers would have a series of field days. There would be many months or years of disputes and uncertainty. . . . Many European countries could put obstacles in Scotland's path as they would be reluctant to set a precedent for their own potential breakaway regions.' *Financial Times* (21–22 March 1992).

References

Addison, J.T. and Siebert, W.S. (1991) 'The Social Charter of the European Community: Evolution and Controversies', *Industrial and Labor Relations Review* 44: 597–625.

Adler, E. and Haas, P.M. (1992) 'Conclusion: Epistemic Communities, World Order, and the Creation of a Reflective Research Program', *International Organization* 46: 367–390.

Alber, Jens and Bernardi-Schenkluhn, Brigitte (1992) *Westeuropäische Gesundheitssysteme im Vergleich: Bundesrepublik Deutschland, Schweiz, Frankreich, Italien, Großbritannien.* Frankfurt/M.: Campus.

Alter, Karen J. and Meunier-Aitsahalia, Sophie (1994) 'Judicial Politics in the European Community: European Integration and the Pathbreaking *Cassis de Dijon* Decision', *Comparative Political Studies* 26: 535–561.

Anderson, Jeffrey J. (1991) 'Skeptical Reflections on a "Europe of Regions": Britain, Germany, and the European Regional Development Fund', *Journal of Public Policy* 10: 417–447.

Axelrod, Robert (1984) *The Evolution of Cooperation.* New York: Basic Books.

Azzi, C. (1985) *L'application du droit communautaire par les états membres.* Maastricht: European Institute of Public Administration.

Bache, Ian, George, Stephen and Rhodes, R.A.W. (1996) 'Cohesion Policy and Subnational Authorities in the United Kingdom', in Liesbet Hooghe (ed.) *European Integration and Cohesion Policy. Building Multi-Level Governance.* Oxford: Oxford University Press.

Behrens, Peter (1994) 'Die Wirtschaftsverfassung der Europäischen Gemeinschaft', pp. 73–90 in Gert Brüggemeier (ed.) *Verfassungen für ein ziviles Europa.* Baden-Baden: Nomos.

Böckenförde, Ernst-Wolfgang (1991) 'Die Schweiz – Vorbild für Europa?', *Neue Zürcher Zeitung*, 14–15 December 1991.

Brand, Karl-Werner (1990) 'Cyclical Aspects of New Waves of Social Cultural Criticism and Mobilization Cycles of New Middle-Class Radicalism', pp. 23–42 in R. Dalton and M. Kuechler (eds) *Challenging the Political Order.* Oxford: Oxford University Press.

Brittan, Samuel (1991) 'Let Fools Contend about the Forms', *Financial Times*, 21 November, p. 21.

Bull, Hedley (1977) *The Anarchical Society: A Study of Order in World Politics.* London: Macmillan.

Burgess, Michael (1989) *Federalism and European Union: Political Ideas, Influences and Strategies in the European Community, 1972–1987.* London: Routledge.

Burley, Anne-Marie and Mattli, Walter (1993) 'Europe Before the Court: A Political Theory of Legal Integration', *International Organization* 47: 41–76.

Calhoun, Craig (1992) 'New Social Movements of the Early Nineteenth Century', unpublished ms.

Calhoun, Craig (1993) 'Nationalism and Civil Society: Democracy, Diversity and Self-Determination', *International Sociology* 8: 387–412.

Caporaso, J.A. and Keeler, John (1993) 'The European Community and Regional Integration Theory', paper presented at the Conference of the European Community Studies Association, Washington, DC, 27–29 May.

Christiansen, Thomas (1994) 'Territorial Politics and Multilevel Governance in the European Union: The Case of Wales', unpublished ms, European University Institute, Florence, Italy.

Church, Clive H. (1990) *Widening the Community Circle?* London: University Association for Contemporary European Studies, UACES Occasional Paper No. 6.

Collins, D. (1985) 'The New Role of the European Social Fund', in Jacques Vandamme (ed.) *New Dimensions in European Social Policy*. London: Croom Helm.

Commission of the European Communities (1990) *Annual Report on the Implementation of the Reform of the Structural Funds, 1989*. Luxemburg: Office for Official Publications of the European Community.

Commission of the European Communities (1992a) *Second Annual Report on the Implementation of the Reform of Structural Funds*. Brussels/Luxemburg: Commission of the European Communities.

Commission of the European Communities (1992b) *Treaty on European Unity*. Brussels/Luxemburg: Commission of the European Communities.

Constanelos, J. (1994) 'Multi-level Lobbying in the European Union: Regional Interest Group Strategies in France and Italy', paper presented at the American Political Science Association Meeting, New York.

Crouch, Colin (1993) *Industrial Relations and European State Traditions*. Oxford: Clarendon Press.

Dahl, Robert A. (1994) 'A Democratic Dilemma: System Effectiveness versus Citizen Participation', *Political Science Quarterly* 109: 23–34.

Dalton, R., Kuechler M. and Burklin W. (1990) 'The Challenge of New Movements', pp. 3–20 in R.J. Dalton and M. Kuechler (eds) *Challenging the Political Order*. Oxford: Oxford University Press.

Davidson, Ian (1991) 'New era for EC family', *Financial Times*, 3 December, p. 21.

Dehousse, Renaud (1993) 'Does Subsidiarity Really Matter?', Florence: EUI Working Paper Law No. 92/32.

Dehousse, Renaud (1995) 'Institutional Reform in the European Community. Are there Alternatives to the Majoritarian Avenue?', Florence: EUI Working Paper RSC No. 95/4.

Dehousse, Renaud and Weiler, Joseph H.H. (1990) 'The Legal Dimension', pp. 242–260 in William Wallace (ed.) *The Dynamics of European Integration*. London: Pinter.

della Porta, Donatella and Rucht, Dieter R. (1991) 'Left-Libertarian Movements in Context: A Comparison of Italy and West Germany, 1965–1990'. Discussion paper FS III, Wissenschaftszentrum Berlin.

Delors, Jacques (1989) 'Statement on the Broad Lines of Community Policy, presented by Jacques Delors, President of the Commission, to the European Parliament and reply to the ensuing Parliamentary debate', Strasburg, 17–18 January, *Bulletin of the European Communities*, Supplement 1/89, Luxemburg: Office for Official Publications of the European Communities.

Delors, Jacques (1992) *Le nouveau concert européen*. Paris: Éditions Odile Jacob.

Deutsch, Karl (1953) *Nationalism and Social Communication: An Inquiry into the Foundations of Nationality*. Cambridge, MA: MIT Press.

Deutsch, Karl et al. (1957) *Political Community and the North Atlantic Area*. Princeton, NJ: Princeton University Press.

Deutsch, Karl et al. (1964) *The Integration of Political Communities*. Philadelphia: Lippincott.

DeVos, T. (1989) *Multinational Corporations on Democratic Host Countries: US Multinationals and the Vredeling Proposal*. Dartmouth: Aldershot.

Dosser, D., Gowland, D. and Hartley, K. (1982) *The Collaboration of Nations: A Study of European Economic Policy*. Oxford: Martin Robertson.

Duchêne, F. (1972) 'Europe's Role in World Peace', in R. Mayne (ed.) *Europe Tomorrow*. London: Fontana/Collins.

Eco, Umberto (1986) 'Living in the New Middle Ages', pp. 73–86 in *Travels in Hyperreality*. San Diego: Harcourt Brace Jovanovich.

Eichener, Volker (1993) 'Soziales Dumping oder innovative Regulation? Interessenkonfigurationen und Einflußchancen im Prozeß der Harmonisierung des technischen Arbeitsschutzes', pp. 207–235 in Werner Süß and Gerhard Becher (eds) *Technologieentwicklung und europäische Integration*. Berlin: Duncker und Humblot.

Eisinger, Peter (1973) 'The Conditions of Protest Behavior in American Cities', *American Political Science Review* 67: 11–28.

Engel, Christian (1993) *Regionen in der EG: Rechtliche Vielfalt und integrationspolitische Rollensuche*. Bonn: Europa Union Verlag.

Esping-Andersen, Gøsta (1990) *The Three Worlds of Welfare Capitalism*. Cambridge: Polity Press.

Fastenrath, Ulrich (1990) 'Länderbüros in Brüssel', *Zeitschrift für Öffentliches Recht und Verwaltungswissenschaft* 4: 125–136.

Featherstone, Kevin (1994) 'Jean Monnet and the "Democratic Deficit" in the European Union', *Journal of Common Market Studies* 32: 149–170.

Fechtner, Detleft (1992) 'Die Länderbüros in Brüssel', *Verwaltungsrundschau* 38: 157–159.

Fligstein, Neil and Mara-drita, Iona (1993) 'How to Make a Market: Reflections on the Attempt to Make a Single Unitary Market in Western Europe', paper presented at the European Community Studies Association Meeting, Washington, DC, May.

Fröhlich, Thomas (1992) 'Reif für die Mülltonne: Die EG-Verpackungspläne beweisen, daß der Umweltschutz dem Binnenmarkt geopfert werden soll', *Süddeutsche Zeitung* 25–26.7, p. 33.

Galtung, Johan (1973) *The European Community: A Superpower in the Making*. Oslo: Universitetsforlaget.

Galtung, Johan (1989) *Europe in the Making*. New York: Crane Russak.

Gamson, William (1990) *The Strategy of Social Protest*. 2nd edn. Belmont, CA: Wadsworth.

Ganslandt, Herbert (1993) 'Das System der sozialen Sicherung in Griechenland', pp. 185–203 in Günther Lottes (ed.) *Soziale Sicherheit in Europa. Renten- und Sozialversicherungssysteme im Vergleich*. Heidelberg: Physica.

Garrett, Geoffrey (1992) 'International Cooperation and Institutional Choice: The European Community's Internal Market', *International Organization* 46: 533–560.

Garrett, Geoffrey (1995) 'The Politics of Legal Integration in the European Union', *International Organization* 49: 171–181.

Garrett, Geoffrey and Weingast, Barry (1992) 'Norms, Institutions and European Integration: The Role of Law in the Internal Market', unpublished ms, Department of Political Science, Stanford University.

Gerhards, Jürgen (1993) 'Westeuropäische Integration und die Schwierigkeiten der Entstehung einer europäischen Öffentlichkeit', *Zeitschrift für Soziologie* 22: 96–110.

Ginsberg, Roy H. (1989) *Foreign Policy Actions of the European Community: The Politics of Scale*. Boulder, CO: Lynne Reiner.

Ginsberg, Roy H. (1991) 'European Community Foreign Policy Actions in the 1980s', paper presented to the Second Biennial International Conference of the European Community Studies Association, George Mason University.

Goetschy, J. (1991) '1992 and the Social Dimension: Normative Frames, Social Actors and Content', *Economic and Industrial Democracy* 19: 259–275.

Gondrand, François (1991) *Parlez-vous Eurocrate?* Paris: Édition d'Organisation.

Graebner, William (1977) 'Federalism in the Progressive Era: A Structural Interpretation of Reform', *Journal of American History* 64: 331–357.

Gretschmann, Klaus (1991) 'The Subsidiarity Principle: Who is to do What in an Integrated Europe?', pp. 45–61 in *Subsidiarity: The Challenge of Change*, Proceedings of the Jacques Delors Colloquium, Maastricht: European Institute of Public Administration.

Grimm, Dieter (1992) 'Der Mangel an europäischer Demokratie', *Der Spiegel*, 19.10, pp. 57–59.

Grodzins, Morton (1967) 'American Political Parties and the American System', pp. 127–146 in Aaron Wildavsky (ed.) *American Federalism in Perspective*. Boston: Little Brown.

Groeben, Hans von der (1992) 'Probleme einer europäischen Wirtschaftsordnung', pp. 99–123 in Jürgen F. Baur, Peter-Christian Müller-Graff and Manfred Zuleeg (eds) *Europarecht, Energierecht, Wirtschaftsrecht: Festschrift für Bodo Börner*. Cologne: Carl Heymanns.

Haas, Ernst B. (1964) *Beyond the Nation-State: Functionalism and International Organization*. Stanford: Stanford University Press.

Haas, Ernst (1971) 'The Study of Regional Integration: Reflections on the Joy and Anguish of

Pretheorizing', in Leon N. Lindberg and Stuart A. Scheingold (eds), *Regional Integration: Theory and Research*. Cambridge: Harvard University Press.

Haas, Ernst B. (1976) 'Turbulent Fields and the Theory of Regional Integration', *International Organization* 30: 173–212.

Haas, Peter M. (1992) 'Introduction: Epistemic Communities and International Policy Coordination', *International Organization* 46: 1–37, 367–390.

Hank, Rainer (1994) 'Die Eisenacher und die Rüsselsheimer: Im Opel-Werk an der Wartburg hat die Zukunft schon begonnen', *Frankfurter Allgemeine Zeitung* 6.8, p. 11.

Hauser, R. (1991) 'A Common European Poverty Regime? Possible Futures for Social Europe', paper presented at a Workshop on 'Prospects for Social Europe', Center for European Studies, Harvard University, November.

Heckathorn, Douglas D. and Maser, Steven M. (1987) 'Bargaining and Constitutional Contracts', *American Journal of Political Science* 31: 142–168.

Heisbourg, F. (1992) 'From a Common European Home to a European Security System', pp.35–38 in G.F. Treverton (ed.) *The Shape of the New Europe*. New York: Council on Foreign Relations Press.

Henningsen, B. (1989) 'Europäisierung Europas durch eine europäische Sozialpolitik?', pp. 55–80 in Peter Haungs (ed.) *Europäisierung Europas?*, Vol. 6. Baden-Baden: Nomos.

Héritier, Adrienne, Mingers, Susanne, Knill, Christoph and Becka, Martina (1994) *Die Veränderung von Staatlichkeit in Europa. Ein regulativer Wettbewerb: Deutschland, Großbritannien und Frankreich in der Europäischen Union*. Opladen: Leske und Budrich.

Hoffmann, Stanley (1964) 'Europe's Identity Crises: Between Past and America', *Daedalus* 93: 1244–1297.

Hoffmann, Stanley (1966) 'Obstinate or Obsolete? The Fate of the Nation-State and the Case of Western Europe', *Daedalus* Summer: 862–915.

Hoffmann, Stanley (1982) 'Reflections on the Nation-State in Western Europe Today', *Journal of Common Market Studies* 21: 21–38.

Hooghe, Liesbet (ed.) (1996) *Cohesion Policy, the European Community and Subnational Government*. Oxford: Oxford University Press.

Hooghe, Liesbet and Keating, Michael (1994) 'The Politics of EC Regional Policy', *Journal of European Public Policy* 1: 367–393.

Hooghe, Liesbet and Marks, Gary (forthcoming) '"Europe with the Regions": Channels of Regional Representation in the European Union', *Publius*.

Hrbek, R. and Thaysen, U. (1986) *Die Deutschen Länder und die Europäische Gemeinschaften*. Baden-Baden: Nomos.

Inglehart, Ronald (1977) *The Silent Revolution: Changing Values and Political Styles Among Western Publics*. Princeton, NJ: Princeton University Press.

Inglehart, Ronald (1990) *Culture Shift in Advanced Industrial Society*. Princeton, NJ: Princeton University Press.

International Monetary Fund (1993) *Government Finance Statistics Yearbook*, Vol. 17. Washington, DC: IMF.

Jeffery, Charlie (1995) 'Regional Information Offices and the Politics of "Third Level" Lobbying in Brussels', paper presented to the UACES Conference, Leicester University.

Joerges, Christian (1991) 'Markt ohne Staat? Die Wirtschaftsverfassung der Gemeinschaft und die regulative Politik', pp. 225–268 in Rudolf Wildenmann (ed.) *Staatswerdung Europas? Optionen für eine Europäische Union*. Baden-Baden: Nomos.

Joerges, Christian (1994a) 'Legitimationsprobleme des europäischen Wirtschaftsrechts und der Vertrag von Maastricht', pp. 91–130 in Gert Brüggemeier (ed.) *Verfassungen für ein ziviles Europa*. Baden-Baden: Nomos.

Joerges, Christian (1994b) 'Rationalisierungsprozesse im Vertragsrecht und im Recht der Produktsicherheit: Beobachtungen zu den Folgen der Europäischen Integration für das Privatrecht', Florence: EUI Working Paper Law No. 94/5.

Jopp, M., Rummel R. and Schmidt P. (1991) *Integration and Security in Western Europe: Inside the European Pillar*. Boulder, CO: Westview Press.

Kapteyn, Paul (1991) '"Civilization under Negotiation": National Civilizations and European Integration: The Treaty of Schengen', *Archives Européennes de Sociologie* 32: 363–380.

Katzenstein, P.J. (1987) *Policy and Politics in West Germany: The Growth of a Semisovereign State*. Philadelphia: Temple University Press.

Keating, Michael (1988) *State and Regional Nationalism: Territorial Politics and the European State*. Brighton: Harvester Wheatsheaf.

Keating, Michael and Jones, Barry (eds) (1995) *Regions in the European Community*. Oxford: Oxford University Press.

Kenis, P. (1991) 'Social Europe in the 1990s: Beyond an Adjunct to Achieving a Common Market?', *Futures* 23: 724–738.

Keohane Robert O. (1986) *Neo-Realism and Its Critics*. New York:

Keohane, Robert O. and Hoffmann, Stanley (1991) *The New European Community: Decisionmaking and Institutional Change*. Boulder, CO: Westview Press.

Kielmansegg, Peter Graf (1992) 'Ein Maß für die Größe des Staates. Was wird aus Europa? Europa fehlt die Zustimmung seiner Bürger', *Frankfurter Allgemeine Zeitung* 2.12, p. 35.

Klausen, Jytte (1992) 'Social Democracy and the New Europe: The Domestic Politics of Economic Interdependence', paper presented at the American Political Science Association Meeting, 30 Aug.–2 Sept., Chicago.

Kosonen, Pekka (1994) 'The Impact of Economic Integration on National Welfare States in Europe', unpublished ms, Department of Sociology, University of Helsinki.

Krasner, Stephen (1988) 'Sovereignty: An Institutional Perspective', *Comparative Political Studies* 21: 66–94.

Krasner, Stephen (1991) 'Westphalia', unpublished ms, Department of Political Science, Stanford University.

Kriesi, H. and van Praag, P. Jr. (1987) 'Old and New Politics: The Dutch Peace Movement and the Traditional Political Organizations', *European Journal of Political Science* 15: 319–346.

Lane, Jan-Erik and Ersson, Svante (1991) *Politics and Society in Western Europe*. 2nd edn. London: Sage.

Lange, Peter (1992) 'The Politics of the Social Dimension', pp. 225–257 in Alberta Sbragia (ed.) *The Political Consequences of 1992 for the European Community*. Washington, DC: Brookings Institution.

Lange, Peter (1993) 'Maastricht and the Social Protocol: Why Did They Do It?', *Politics & Society* 21: 5–36.

Langeheine, Bernd and Weinstock, Ulrich (1984) 'Graduated Integration: A Modest Path Towards Progress', *Journal of Common Market Studies* 23: 185–197.

Lapham, Lewis (1988) 'Leviathan in Trouble', *Harper's*, September: 8–9.

Leibfried, Stephan and Pierson, Paul (1992) 'Prospects for Social Europe', *Politics & Society* 20: 333–366.

Leibfried, Stephan and Pierson, Paul (1995) 'Semi-Sovereign Welfare States: Social Policy in a Multi-Tiered Europe', in Stephan Leibfried and Paul Pierson (eds) *Fragmented Social Policy: The European Union's Social Dimension in Comparative Perspective*. Washington: Brookings Institution.

Lindberg, L. and Scheingold, S. (1970) *Europe's Would-be Polity*. Englewoood Cliffs, NJ: Prentice-Hall.

Lodge, Juliet (1989a) 'Social Europe: Fostering a People's Europe?', in J. Lodge (ed.) *The European Community and the Challenge of the Future*. London: Pinter.

Lodge, Juliet (1989b) 'The Political Implications of 1992', *Politics* 9: 2.

Lowery, David and Gray, Virginia (1995) 'The Population Economy of Gucci Gulch, or the Natural Regulation of Interest Group Numbers in the American States', *American Journal of Political Science* 39: 1–29.

McAdam, Doug (1982) *Political Process and the Development of Black Insurgency, 1930–1970*. Chicago: University of Chicago Press.

McCarthy, John D. and Zald, Mayer N. (1973) *The Trend of Social Movements in America: Professionalization and Resource Mobilization*. Morristown, NJ: General Learning Press.

McCarthy, John D. and Zald, Mayer N. (1977) 'Resource Mobilization and Social Movements: A Partial Theory', *American Journal of Sociology* 82: 1212–1241.

Majone, Giandemonico (1992) *The European Community between Social Policy and Social Regulation*. Florence: European University Institute.

Majone, Giandomenico (1993) 'The European Community between Social Policy and Social Regulation', *Journal of Common Market Studies* 31: 153–170.

Majone, Giandomenico (1994a) 'The European Community: An "Independent Fourth Branch of Government"?', pp. 23–43 in Gert Brüggemeier (ed.) *Verfassungen für ein ziviles Europa*. Baden-Baden: Nomos.

Majone, Giandomenico (1994b) 'Independence vs Accountability? Non-Majoritarian Institutions and Democratic Government in Europe', Florence: EUI Working Paper SPS No. 94/3.

Majone, Giandomenico (1994c) 'The Rise of the Regulatory State in Europe', *West European Politics*.

Majone, Giandomenico (1994d) 'The Development of Social Regulation in the European Community: Policy Externalities, Transaction Costs, Motivational Factors', unpublished ms. Department of Political and Social Sciences, European University Institute, Florence, Italy.

Marks, Gary (1989) *Unions in Politics: Britain, Germany, and the United States in the Nineteenth and Early Twentieth Centuries*. Princeton, NJ: Princeton University Press.

Marks, Gary (1992) 'Structural Policy and 1992', pp. 191–224 in Alberta Sbragia (ed.) *Europolitics: Institutions and Policy Making in the 'New' European Community*. Washington, DC: Brookings Institution.

Marks, Gary (1993) 'Structural Policy and Multilevel Governance in the European Community', pp. 391–410 in A. Cafruny and G. Rosenthal (eds) *The State of the European Community*. New York: Lynne Rienner.

Marks, Gary (1996) 'Exploring and Explaining Variation in Cohesion Policy', in Liesbet Hooghe (ed.) *Cohesion Policy, the European Community and Subnational Government*. Oxford: Oxford University Press.

Marks, Gary (forthcoming) 'The Third Lens: European Integration and State Building Compared', University of North Carolina at Chapel Hill, mimeo.

Marks, Gary, Hooghe, Liesbet and Blank, Kermit (forthcoming) 'European Integration Since the 1980s: State–Centric Versus Multi-Level Governance', *Journal of Common Market Studies*.

Marsh, David (1991) 'A Bumpy Ride on the Roller-Coaster', *Financial Times* 18 December, Section III, p. 1.

Marshall, T.H. (1964) *Class, Citizenship and Social Development*, Garden City, NY: Doubleday.

Mattli, Walter and Slaughter, Anne-Marie (1995) 'Law and Politics in the European Union: A Reply to Garrett', *International Organization* 49: 190–193.

Mayntz, Renate and Scharpf, Fritz W. (eds) (1995) *Steuerung und Selbstorganisation in staatsnahen Sektoren*. Frankfurt: Campus.

Mazey, Sonia and Mitchell, James (1993) 'Europe of the Regions? Territorial Interests and European Integration: The Scottish Experience', in Sonia Mazey and Jeremy Richardson (eds) *Lobbying in the European Community*. Oxford: Oxford University Press.

Mazey, Sonia and Richardson, Jeremy (eds) (1993) *Lobbying in the European Community*. Oxford: Oxford University Press.

Mearsheimer, John (1990) 'Back to the Future: Instability in Europe after the Cold War', *International Security* 15: 5–56.

Melucci, Alberto (1980) 'The New Social Movements: A Theoretical Approach', *Social Science Information* 19: 199–226.

Mény, Yves (1982) *Dix ans de régionalisation en Europe: Bilan et perspectives (1970–1980)*. Paris: Éditions Cujas.

Merkel, Wolfgang (1993) *Ende der Sozialdemokratie? Machtressourcen und Regierungspolitik im westeuropäischen Vergleich*. Frankfurt/M.: Campus.

Mestmäcker, Ernst-Joachim (1992) 'Widersprüchlich, verwirrend und gefährlich. Wettbewerbsregeln oder Industriepolitik: Nicht nur in diesem Punkt verstößt der Vertrag von Maastricht gegen bewährte Grundsätze des Vertrages von Rom', *Frankfurter Allgemeine Zeitung* 10.10, p.15.

Mestmäcker, Ernst-Joachim (1994) 'Zur Wirtschaftsverfassung in der Europäischen Union', pp. 263–292 in Rolf H. Hasse, Josef Molsberger and Christian Watrin (eds) *Ordnung in Freiheit: Festgabe für Hans Willgerodt zum 70. Geburtstag*. Stuttgart: Fischer.

Michalski, A. and Wallace, H. (1992) *The European Community: The Challenge of Enlargement*. London: Royal Institute of International Affairs.

Mitchell, D.J.B. and Rojot, J. (1993) 'Employee Benefits in the Single Market', pp. 128–166 in L. Ulman, B. Eichengreen and W. T. Dickens (eds) *Labor and an Integrated Europe*, Washington, DC: Brookings Institution.

Mitchell, William C. and Munger, Michael C. (1991) 'Economic Models of Interest Groups', *American Political Science Review* 35: 512–546.

Mitrany, David (1966) *A Working Peace System*. Chicago: Quadrangle Books (originally published in 1943).

Moravcsik, Andrew (1991) 'Negotiating the Single European Act', pp.41–84 in Robert O. Keohane and Stanley Hoffmann (eds) *The New European Community*. Boulder, CO: Westview Press.

Moravcsik, Andrew (1993) 'Preferences and Power in the European Community: A Liberal Intergovernmental Approach', *Journal of Common Market Studies* 31: 473–524.

Mueller, Dennis G. and Murrell, Peter (1986) 'Interest Groups and the Size of Government', *Public Choice* 48: 125–145.

Müller-Armack, Alfred (1956) 'Soziale Marktwirtschaft', pp. 243–249 in *Wirtschaftsordnung und Wirtschaftspolitik: Studien und Konzepte zur sozialen Marktwirtschaft und zur europäischen Integration*. Freiburg i. B.: Rombach.

Münster, Winfried (1993) 'Vater Staat schafft es nicht mehr. Die EG im Kampf gegen die Arbeitslosigkeit. Nur neue Märkte können verlorne Arbeitsplätze ersetzen', *Süddeutsche Zeitung* 23.10, p. 31.

Muret, Charlotte (1966) 'The Swiss Pattern for a Federated Europe', pp. 149–174 in *International Political Communities*. Garden City, NJ: Anchor Books.

Mutimer, David (1989) '1992 and the Political Integration of Europe: Neofunctionalism Reconsidered', *Revue d'Intégration Européenne* 13: 75–101.

Nathan, Richard (1991) 'Implications for Federalism of European Integration', in Norman Ornstein and Mark Perlman (eds) *Political Power and Social Change: A United States Faces a United Europe*. Washington, DC: AEI Press.

Nicoll, William (1984) 'Paths to European Unity', *Journal of Common Market Studies* 23: 199–206.

Nugent, Neill (1995) *The Government and Politics of the European Community*. 3rd edn. Durham, NC: Duke University Press.

Nye, Joseph (1965) 'Patterns and Catalysts in Regional Integration', *International Organization* 19: 882–884.

O'Cleireacain, S. (1989) 'The Emerging Social Dimension of Europe 1992', *Occasional Papers* 4, City University of New York, Center for Labor Management Policy Studies.

Offe, Claus (1985) 'New Social Movements: Changing Boundaries of the Political', *Social Research* 52: 817–868.

Pelkmans, J. (1985) 'The Institutional Economics of European Integration', pp. 318–396 in M. Cappelletti, M. Secombe and J. Weiler (eds) *Integration Through Law*, Vol. 1, *Methods, Tools and Institutions*, Book 1, *A Political, Legal and Economic Overview*. Berlin and New York: de Gruyter.

Peters, B. Guy (1992) 'Bureaucratic Politics and the Institutions of the European Community', pp. 75–122 in Alberta Sbragia (ed.) *Euro-politics: Institutions and Policy Making in the 'New' European Community*. Washington, DC: Brookings Institution.

Pierson, Paul (1995) 'The Path to European Integration: An Historical Institutionalist Perspective', unpublished ms, Harvard University.

Pijpers, A., Regeklsberger, G. and Wessels, W. (1988) *European Political Cooperation in the 1980s: Towards a Foreign Policy for Western Europe*. The Hague: Nijhoff.

Pinder, John (1991) *European Community: The Building of a Union*. Oxford: Oxford University Press.

Pineau, C. and Rimbaud, C. (1991) *Le grand pari: L'aventure du Traité de Rome*. Paris: Fayard.

Polanyi, Karl (1957) *The Great Transformation: The Political and Economic Origins of Our Time*. Boston: Beacon.

Pollack, Mark A. (1995) 'Regional Actors in an Intergovernmental Play: The Making and Implementation of EC Structural Policy', in S. Mazey and C. Rhodes (eds) *The State of the European Union*, Vol. III. Boston: Lynne Rienner.

Puchala, Donald (1972) 'Of Blind Men, Elephants and International Integration', *Journal of Common Market Studies* 10: 267–285.

Puchala, Donald (1981) 'Integration Theory and International Relations', pp. 145–164 in R.L. Merritt and B.M. Russett (eds) *From National Development to Global Community*. London: George Allen & Unwin.

Puchala, Donald (1988) 'The European Common Market and the Resilience of the National State', *Il Politico* 53: 447–466.

Putnam, Robert (1993) *Making Demcoracy Work: Civic Traditions in Modern Italy*. Princeton, NJ: Princeton University Press.

Putnam, Robert (1995) 'Bowling Alone: America's Declining Social Capital', *Journal of Democracy* 6: 65–78.

Quermonne, Jean-Louis (1992) 'Trois lectures du Traité de Maastricht', *Revue Française de Science Politique* 42: 802–818.

Rehbinder, Eckard and Stewart, Richard (1984) *Environmental Protection Policy; Integration Through Law. Europe and the American Federal Experience*, Vol. 2. Berlin: de Gruyter.

Rhodes, Martin (1992) 'The Future of the "Social Dimension": Labour Market Regulation in Post-1992 Europe', *Journal of Common Market Studies* 30: 23–51.

Rhodes, Martin (1995) 'A Regulatory Conundrum: Industrial Relations and the "Social Dimension"', in Stephan Leibfried and Paul Pierson (eds) *Fragmented Social Policy: The European Union's Social Dimension in Comparative Perspective*. Washington: Brookings Institution.

Rochon, Thomas (1990) 'The West European Peace Movement and the Theory of New Social Movements', pp. 105–121 in R.J. Dalton and M. Kuechler (eds) *Challenging the Political Order*. Oxford: Oxford University Press.

Ross, George (1992) 'Russian Dolls and Resource Mobilization: Thoughts on Supranational Strategies, Interstate Systems and the European Community after Maastricht', paper prepared for the Council of European Studies, Eighth International Conference of Europeanists, 11–13 March, Chicago.

Rucht, Dieter (forthcoming) 'Environmental Policy for the European Community: Problems of Mobilizing Influence in Brussels', in Charles Chatfield, Ron Pagnucco and Jackie Smith (eds) *Solidarity Beyond the State: The Dynamics of Transnational Social Movements*. Syracuse: Syracuse University Press

Ruggie, John Gerard (1995) 'At Home Abroad, Abroad at Home: International Liberalization and Domestic Stability in the New World Order', Jean Monnet Chair Papers 20, Florence: European University Institute.

Salisbury, Robert H. (1984) 'Interest Representation: The Dominance of Institutions', *American Political Science Review* 78: 64–76.

Salk, Jane E. (1993) 'Direct Expression of Regional Identity and Collective Interests in Brussels: Regional Information Offices as a Vehicle for Collective Action', paper presented at the American Sociological Association Meeting, Miami.

Salk, Jane, Nielsen, François and Marks, Gary (1995) 'Ecology of Collective Action and Regional Representation in the European Union', unpublished ms., Duke University and University of North Carolina.

Saña, Heleno (1990) *Das Vierte Reich*. Hamburg: Rascher & Röhring.

Sandholtz, W. and Zysman, J. (1989) '1992: Recasting the European Bargain', *World Politics* 42: 1–30.

Sauter, Wolf (1995) 'The Telecommunications Law of the European Community', *European Law Journal* 1: 92–111.

Sbragia, Alberta (1992) 'Thinking about the European Future: The Uses of Comparison', pp. 257–290 in Alberta Sbragia (ed.) *Euro-Politics*. Washington, DC: Brookings Institution.

Sbragia, Alberta (1993) 'The European Community: A Balancing Act', *Publius* 23: 23–38.

Schaefer, Guenther F. (1991) 'The Rise and Fall of Subsidiarity', *Futures* 23: 7 (September), 685–6.

Scharpf, Fritz W. (1970) *Demokratietheorie zwischen Utopie und Anpassung*. Konstanz: Universitätsverlag.

Scharpf, Fritz W. (1988) 'The Joint-Decision Trap: Lessons from German Federalism and European Integration', *Public Administration* 66: 239–278.

Scharpf, Fritz W. (1991a) *Crisis and Choice in European Social Democracy*. Ithaca: Cornell University Press.

Scharpf, Fritz W. (1991b) 'Kann es in Europa eine stabile föderale Balance geben? (Thesen)', pp. 415–428 in Rudolf Wildenmann (ed.) *Staatswerdung Europas? Optionen für eine Europäische Union*. Baden-Baden: Nomos.

Scharpf, Fritz W. (1992a) 'Europäisches Demokratiedefizit und deutscher Föderalismus', *Staatswissenschaften und Staatspraxis* 3: 293–306.

Scharpf, Fritz W. (1992b) 'Koordination durch Verhandlungssysteme: Analytische Konzepte und institutionelle Lösungen', pp. 51–96 in Arthur Benz, Fritz W. Scharpf and Reinhard Zintl, *Horizontale Politikverflechtung: Zur Theorie von Verhandlungssystemen*. Frankfurt/ M.: Campus.

Scharpf, Fritz W. (1993) 'Autonomieschonend und gemeinschaftsverträglich: Zur Logik der europäischen Mehrebenenpolitik', *Discussion Paper* 93/9, Cologne: Max-Planck-Institut für Gesellschaftsforschung.

Scharpf, Fritz W. (1994) 'Community and Autonomy: Multilevel Policy-Making in the European Union', *Journal of European Public Policy* 1: 219–242.

Schmidt, Susanne K. (1995) 'The Integration of the European Telecommunications and Electricity Sectors in the Light of International Relations Theories and Comparative Politics', unpublished ms., Cologne: Max-Planck-Institut für Gesellschaftsforschung.

Schmitter, Philippe C. (1969) 'La dinámica de contradicciones y la conducción de crísis en la integración centroamericana', *Revista de la Integración* (Buenos Aires) 5: 87–151.

Schmitter, Philippe C. (1970) 'A Revised Theory of Regional Integration', pp. 232–264 in Leon Lindberg and Stuart Scheingold (eds) *Regional Integration: Theory and Research*. Cambridge, MA: Harvard University Press.

Schmitter, Philippe C. and Streeck, Wolfgang (1991) 'Organized Interests and the Europe of 1992', pp. 46–67 in N.J. Ornstein and M. Perlman (eds) *Political Power and Social Change*. Washington, DC: AEI Press.

Schneider, Volker (1995) 'Institutionelle Evolution als politischer Prozeß: Die Entwicklung der Telekommunikation im historischen und internationalen Vergleich', unpublished ms, Cologne: Max-Planck-Institut für Gesellschaftsforschung.

Schwartz, Bernard (1957) *The Supreme Court: Constitutional Revolution in Retrospect*. New York: Ronald Press.

Seidentopf, H. and Ziller, J. (1988) *Making European Policies Work: The Implementation of Community Legislation in the Member States*. London: Sage.

Sewell, William (1990) 'Collective Violence and Collective Loyalties in France: Why the French Revolution Made a Difference', *Politics & Society* 18: 527–552.

Sharpe, L.J. (1989) 'Fragmentation and Territoriality in the European State System', *International Political Science Review* 10: 223–238.

Sieber, Wolfgang (1993) 'Die soziale Sicherung in Portugal vor dem Hintergrund von EG-Integration und beschleunigtem wirtschaftlich–sozialem Strukturwandel', pp. 171–185 in Günther Lottes (ed.) *Soziale Sicherheit in Europa: Renten- und Sozialversicherungssysteme im Vergleich*. Heidelberg: Physica.

Sinn, Hans-Werner (1994) 'Wieviel Brüssel braucht Europa? Subsidiarität, Zentralisierung und Fiskalwettbewerb im Lichte der ökonomischen Theorie', *Staatswissenschaften und Staatspraxis* 5: 155–186.

Sinn, Stefan (1993) 'The Taming of Leviathan: Competition among Governments', *Constitutional Political Economy* 3: 177–221.

Smelser, Neil (1963) *Theory of Collective Behavior*. New York: Free Press.

Streeck, Wolfgang (1993) 'European Social Policy after Maastricht: The "Social Dialogue" and "Subsidiarity"', *Economic and Industrial Democracy* 15: 151–177.

Streeck, Wolfgang (1995) 'From Market-Making to State-Building? Reflections on the Political Economy of European Social Policy', in S. Leibfried and P. Pierson (eds) *Prospects for Social Europe: The European Community's Social Dimension in Comparative Perspective*. Washington, DC: Brookings Institution.

Streeck, Wolfgang and Schmitter, Philippe C. (1991) 'From National Corporatism to Transnational Pluralism: Organized Interests in the Single European Market', *Politics & Society* 19: 133–64. Also in W. Streeck (1992) *Social Institutions and Economic Performance: Studies of Industrial Relations in Advanced Capitalist Economies*. London and Beverley Hills: Sage.

Streeck, Wolfgang and Vitols, Sig (1995) 'The European Community: Between Mandatory Consultation and Voluntary Information', in J. Rogers and W. Streeck (eds) *Works Councils: Consultation, Representation, and Cooperation in Industrial Relations*, Boston: National Bureau for Economic Research; Chicago: Chicago University Press.

Streit, Manfred E. and Mussler, Werner (1995) 'The Economic Constitution of the European Community: From "Rome" to "Maastricht"', *European Law Journal* 1: 5–30.

Tarrow, Sidney (1994) *Power in Movement: Social Movements, Collective Action and Mass Politics in the Modern State*. Cambridge: Cambridge University Press.

Tarrow, S., Katzenstein P. and Graziano L. (1978) *Territorial Politics in Industrial Nations*. New York: Praeger.

Taylor, Paul (1991) 'The European Community and the State: Assumptions, Theories and Propositions', *Review of International Studies* 17: 109–125.

Teague, P. and Grahl, J. (1991) 'The European Community Social Charter and Labour Market Regulation', *Journal of Public Policy* 11: 207–232.

Tilly, Charles (ed.) (1975) *The Formation of National States in Western Europe*. Princeton, NJ: Princeton University Press.

Tilly, Charles (1978) *From Mobilization to Revolution*. Reading, MA: Addison-Wesley.

Tilly, Charles (1982) 'Britain Creates the Social Movement', pp. 21–51 in J. Cronin and J. Schneer (eds) *Social Conflict and the Political Order in Britain*. New Brunswick, NJ: Rutgers University Press.

Tilly, Charles (1985) 'War-Making and State-Making as Organized Crime', in Peter B. Evans. Dietrich Rueschemeyer and Theda Skocpol (eds) *Bringing the State Back In*. Cambridge Cambridge University Press.

Tilly, Charles, Tilly, Louise and Tilly, Richard (1975) *The Rebellious Century, 1830–1930*. Cambridge, MA: Harvard University Press.

Tinbergen, Jan (1965) *International Economic Integration*. 2nd edition. Amsterdam: Elsevier.

Tocqueville, Alexis de (1954) *Democracy in America*. New York: Vintage Books (originally published in 1835).

Touraine, Alain (1981) *The Voice and the Eye: An Analysis of Social Movements*. Cambridge: Cambridge University Press.

Tsebelis, George (1995) 'Decisionmaking in Political Systems: Veto Players in Presidentialism, Parliamentarism, Multicameralism, and Multipartism', *British Journal of Political Science* 25: 289–326.

Tucker, K.H. (1991) 'How New are the New Social Movements?', *Theory, Culture & Society* 8: 75–98.

Van Wagenen, Richard W. (1952) 'Research in the International Organization Field: Some Notes on a Possible Focus', Princeton, NJ, Center for Research on World Political Institutions, Princeton University, Publication No. 1.

VerLoren van Themaat, Pieter (1987) 'Die Aufgabenverteilung zwischen dem Gesetzgeber und dem Europäischen Gerichtshof bei der Gestaltung der Wirtschaftsverfassung der Europäischen Gemeinschaften', pp. 425–443 in Ernst-Joachim Mestmäcker, Hans Möller and Hans-Peter Schwarz (eds) *Eine Ordnungspolitik für Europa: Festschrift für Hans von der Groeben.* Baden-Baden: Nomos.

Visser, Jelle and Ebbinghaus, Bernhard (1992) 'Making the Most of Diversity? European Integration and Transnational Organization of Labour', pp. 206–238 in J. Greenwood, J. Grote and K. Ronit (eds) *Organized Interest and the European Community.* London: Sage.

Voelzkow, Helmut (1993) 'Staatseingriff und Verbandsfunktion: Das verbandliche System technischer Regelsetzung als Gegenstand staatlicher Politik', Discussion Paper 93/2, Cologne: MPI für Gesellschaftsforschung.

Wallace, William (1990) 'Introduction: The Dynamics of European Integration' in W. Wallace (ed.) *The Dynamics of European Integration.* London: Pinter.

Wallerstein, Michael (1990) 'Class Conflict as a Dynamic Game', pp. 189–212 in Roger Friedland and A.F. Robertson (eds) *Beyond the Marketplace: Rethinking Economy and Society.* New York: de Gruyter.

Weidenfeld, Werner (1995) *Europe '96. Reforming the European Union.* Gütersloh: Bertelsmann Foundation Publishers.

Weiler, Joseph H.H. (1981) 'The Community System. The Dual Character of Supranationalism', *Yearbook of European Law* 1: 257–306.

Weiler, Joseph H.H. (1991) 'The Transformation of Europe', *Yale Law Journal* 100: 2403–2483.

Weiler, Joseph H.H. (1994) 'A Quiet Revolution: The European Court of Justice and Its Interlocutors', *Comparative Political Studies* 26: 510–534.

Weizsäcker, Ernst-Ulrich von (1989) 'Internationale Harmonisierung im Umweltschutz durch ökonomische Instrumente - Gründe für eine europäische Umweltsteuer', *Jahrbuch zur Staats- und Verwaltungswissenschaft* 3: 203–216.

Wight, Martin (1991) *International Theory: Three Traditions.* London: Leicester University Press.

Williams, Shirley (1991) 'Sovereignty and Accountability in the European Community', pp. 155–176 in Robert O. Keohane and Stanley Hoffmann (eds) *The New European Community: Decision Making and Institutional Change.* Boulder, CO: Westview Press.

Wilson, Thomas M. and Smith, M. Estellie (eds) (1993) *Cultural Changes and the New Europe: Perspectives on the European Community.* Boulder, CO: Westview Press.

Wistrich, Ernest (1989) *After 1992: the United States of Europe.* London: Routledge.

Wistrich, Ernest (1992) 'Ja, aber: Blockieren die Bundesländer Kohls Pläne einer Politischen Union in Europa?', *Der Spiegel* 13: 68–73.

Wolf, Martin (1991) 'Federalism Before a Fall', *Financial Times* 3 December, p. 21.

Zumschlinge, Konrad von (1989) 'Die Informationsbüros der Bundesländer in Brüssel', *Die Verwaltung* 15: 215–236.

Index